BLACK MOVEMENTS

IN AMERICA

BLACK MOVEMENTS

IN AMERICA

*　　*　　*

CEDRIC J. ROBINSON

ROUTLEDGE
New York and London

Published in 1997 by

Routledge
29 West 35th Street
New York, NY 10001

64

Published in Great Britain in 1997 by

Routledge
11 New Fetter Lane
London EC4P 4EE

Copyright © 1997 by Routledge

Printed in the United States of America
Design: Jack Donner

Library of Congress Cataloging-in-Publication Data

Robinson, Cedric J.
   Black movements in america / Cedric J. Robinson.
       p.   cm.   —   (Revolutionary thought/radical movements)
   Includes bibliographical references.
   ISBN 0-415-91222-9 (pbk.). — ISBN 0-415-91223-7 (hardbound)
   1. Afro-Americans—History.   2. Civil rights movements—United States—History.
3. Afro-Americans—Civil rights.   I. Title.   II. Series.
E185.R68   1997
973'.0496073—dc20   96-21986
                                                                    CIP

*For Corrine, Cissy, Clara, Lillian, Wilma, and Margarite
(and at least one moment of sanity);
for Ruby, Rose, Barbara, Gwendolyn, and Fuzzy;
for Elizabeth and Najda.*

Contents

✳   ✳   ✳

CHAPTER ONE

The Coming to America

* * *

Virginians owned more than 40 percent of all the slaves in the new nation. . . . And Virginia furnished the country's most eloquent spokesmen for freedom and equality.

—Edmund S. Morgan, *American Slavery American Freedom*

The explicit moral paradox presented in Morgan's observations was intended to discomfort his late twentieth-century readers. On the eve of the celebration of two hundred years of American independence, one of the most respected historians of colonial and revolutionary America sought to ferret out what inevitably would be concealed in the official spectacles of national pride—the parades, exhibitions, newly minted histories, documentaries, and the like: America had been and is still a nation of freedom *and* injustice. Morgan reminded his readers that this enduring contradiction prevailed in the consciousness of those who led the country into rebellion against Britain in the late eighteenth century. In the same place, at the same time, and in the same minds, the utopian dreams of liberty and justice competed for right of place with the reality of slavery. By reconstructing the extreme passions of prerevolutionary America, Morgan instructed the nation's present citizenry to forgo hiding in the shadow of their patriotic rituals.

Blacks and Colonial English America

Colonial America was, of course, the historical crucible within which the paradox of slavery and freedom was stamped on the American Revolution

and the nation. These opposing desires were dramatized in 1619 at Jamestown just twelve years into the existence of that settlement. In that year,
the Virginia colony was the site of the first representative legislative assembly (the House of Burgesses) in English America and served as the disembarkation point of the first African bond laborers in the colony. Of course,
the enslavement for both Africans and Native Americans had already
begun in the New World; English colonists, merchants, pirates, and
financiers had been preceded by their Spanish, Portuguese, Dutch, and
French counterparts. The appearance of unfree labor at Jamestown, then,
was not exceptional, but it did historically alter the fate of the English
colonies. Subsidized by African labor, the economies of the English
colonies expanded from marginal to commercially productive through the
exporting of such commodities as tobacco. Economic independence fueled
a desire for political autonomy; in short, for the right to keep a larger share
of both the plunder and the well-gotten goods. In the seventeenth century—the first century of English immigration to North America—there
were already signs of this development, like Bacon's Rebellion in 1676. But
absolute self-governance would take another century to mature. Meanwhile, the very presence of slaves incited those who were not slaves to create a political order that would preserve their privileged status (just as was
done in ancient Athens). Alerted by their proximity to the enslaved, side-
by-side in those small communities, the colonists quickly resolved never to
taste the bitter brew of slavery themselves. To achieve this end, they had to
restrain their masters above as well as the classes and slaves below.

While the English colonial settlements in Virginia, Maryland, and New
England were of a modest size, and African slavery limited in importance,
no official attention was given to African slaves, Black servants, or free
Blacks. It was only a bare step above common sense, for example, when in
1639 that Virginia enacted a law forbidding slaves to possess or be given
firearms or other weapons. All this changed in the second half of the seventeenth century. After 1660, a number of laws were passed that provided
a window into the colony's troubling relationship with slavery and slaves.
In 1662, a law was passed preventing a child from inheriting the father's
status if the mother was a "negro woman"; in 1667, another law prevented
baptism from freeing "slaves by birth"; in 1680, a law was passed "for preventing Negroes Insurrections"; in 1692, another to aid "the more speedy
prosecution of slaves committing Capitall Crimes" established special
courts for slave trials.[1] Each of these laws, as well as those passed to regu-
late the civil rights of free Blacks (in 1668, a new law made free Black
women but not other women subject to poll tax; in 1670, another forbid
Christian Blacks from purchasing Christian servants; in 1691, another ban-

ished from the colony anyone involved in interracial marriage) marked a crossroads. Just as the laws targeting free Blacks reflected the bewilderment of colonial officials toward the ambiguity of "Black" and "free" (such as occasioned in 1656 by Elizabeth Key's suit for freedom since she was the child of an African slave woman and an English planter; or in 1667 by Fernando's suit for freedom since he was a Christian), the incremenetal construction of slave law mirrored reality: "Englishe" men were sexually consorting with African women; Africans were acculturating to colonial society; and slave workers were turning toward resistance. Since the latter is our particular concern here, it may be useful to reconstruct the social and political contexts of slave resistance during the colonial era.

The Blacks in English America were slaves, indentured servants, or freemen. In Virginia during the second half of the seventeenth century, the proportion of nonslaves among the Black population in counties like Northhampton rose as high as 29 percent (as in 1668, when 13 householders were freemen[2]). But as the import of African slaves increased dramatically in the 1670s, the proportion of free Blacks decreased rapidly and until the Civil War hovered between 4 and 10 percent. The overwhelming majority of imported Africans and creole Blacks were slaves or servants who worked in the towns, plantations, and farms. But here as well as elsewhere in these colonies, it is important to remember that these bondspeople and their few free representatives did not exist in a pristine complex of social binaries: masters and slaves, whites and Blacks.

The earliest English settlements, mirroring the great political and religious upheavals of seventeenth-century England, had radically different histories, rationales, and doctrinal characteristics. This was markedly so even in the southern colonies. Virginia was a commercial venture; Maryland, a retreat for Catholics; Carolina, a utopia spun from the imagination of a philosopher; and Georgia, a last chance for debtors. Eventually they all were dominated by a slave economy captained by aristocrats who had as little concern for their poorer countrymen as they did for their slaves. But the colonies' destiny of slaveowning was barely discernible from their origins. To be sure, in the absence of slavery these colonies might not have survived; but had they eschewed slavery it is certain that the history of America (and much of the Western world) would have been less dramatic.

The Virginia colony was begun for pure profit by a joint-stock concern, the Virginia Company of London. In political matters, the military stockholders of the Company appeared to have been given a free hand by their aristocratic and bourgeois partners. In any case, the adventurers established the form of the colony's governance. For the first seventeen years of the settlements, every man, woman, and child among the immigrants was given a military rank and subject to military discipline ("Laws Divine, Morall and Martial"). With an overrepresentation of gentlemen among the first colonists, the Company was compelled to augment its English-born artisans by recruiting craftsworkers and laborers from Italy, Holland, France, and Poland. And within the laboring classes, those immigrants incapable of paying passage contracted to work for the Company for seven or more years; such farm-tenants and servants constituted the European work force. They proved insufficient to meet the expanding colony's needs. The resulting pressure on Native American labor, land, and goods precipitated retaliations in 1622 (350 colonists were killed) and 1644 (500 were killed). Following the ravages of Indian wars, internal disputes, and epidemics, the company's charter was revoked in 1624 and it continued as a crown colony until the American Revolution. Meanwhile, substantial numbers of Africans were imported to augment colonial laborers. By the time of the revolution, the slave population numbered nearly 190,000.[3]

The second of the southern colonies, Maryland, was founded in 1632. It was granted to a single proprietor, George Calvert (Lord Baltimore), whose interests were both profit and religion. Baltimore's intention was to found a settlement as a refuge for Catholics, but Protestants soon outnumbered Catholics, although the latter were the dominant landholders. In part because of supplies from Virginia, the colonists achieved economic stability early on. When William and Mary acquired the English throne in 1689, they revoked the Calverts' charter. Proprietorship was returned to them only when the family renounced Catholicism in 1715. At the end of the seventeenth century, Maryland's slave population (in 1690 at 2,162) was second only to Virginia's (9,345), and throughout the eighteenth century, it remained one of the principle slaveowning colonies. By 1770, nearly 64,000 slaves resided in the colony, constituting almost a third of the total population (202,599).

North Carolina, founded in 1665 and South Carolina, founded in 1670, were largely based on secondary settlements, respectively, from Virginia and the West Indies, which were supported by the wealth of eight proprietors. The original grant for Carolina was made in 1629, but actual settlement did not begin until 1663. Even then the settlements did not reach substantial numbers until after 1718 due to the anticolonial resistance led by the Tuscarora and Yamasee. The original Carolina constitution of 1669 was coauthored by Anthony Ashley Cooper and John Locke, the philosopher. It was abandoned in 1693 to allow greater powers for the provincial assembly. The colony was officially separated into North and South in 1729, though by then provincial assemblies had long functioned as separate entities. With North Carolina largely characterized by small-scale farming, it was South Carolina with its production of indigo and rice for the European and West Indian markets that flourished with the import of African workers. Between 1700 and 1770, the slave population in South Carolina expanded from approximately 2,500 to 75,000—indeed, slaves made up more than half of the total population (which was 124,244 in 1770). In North Carolina, the number of slaves was nearly equal to South Carolina's, but the ratio of colonists to slaves was 3 to 1.

Georgia was founded in 1735 by a group of wealthy philanthropists led by James Oglethorpe, who was the owner of a slave plantation in South Carolina and a director of the Royal African Company. The profit for the investors in the scheme was to be had from silk production, a project never realized. Since their explicit purpose was to rehabilitate imprisoned debtors through labor, the original philanthropists prohibited slavery (as well as what were viewed as social vices among the poor: rum, self-governance, concentrations of property, and so on). "Experience hath Shewn," the trustees wrote in 1734, "that the manner of Settling Colonys and Plantations with Black Slaves or Negroes hath Obstructed the Increase of English and Christian Inhabitants . . . and hath Exposed the Colonys so settled to the Insurrections Tumults and Rebellions of such Slaves & Negroes."[4] But long before it was legalized, Georgians began importing Black and Indian slaves from South Carolina and Virginia. Thus began an enduring hostility with their international neighbors, the Creek nation and the Spanish in Florida. Fugitive slaves attempting to reach Spanish territory had to pass through Creek lands, and the Creeks were inconstant allies to the colonists in recapturing them. The Spanish were even less accommodating, not only harboring the fugitives but also disrupting British shipping and frustrating the crown's ambitions to control North America and the Caribbean. Eventually, the Georgians helped precipitate a war between Spain and Britain, ostensibly over the severing of Captain Robert Jenkins's ear, called the War of Jenkins' Ear (1739–42). By 1753, dissatisfaction among the colonists with the utopian restrictions against slavery was so intense that the crown revoked the charter and nullified the laws against slavery and the accumulation of property and capital. This was not enough to resolve the problem of maintaining the security of slave-holding in Georgia, however, an issue that would provoke important American wars in the next century. By the American Revolution, Georgia's slave population had grown to over 10,000, just short of half of the total population.

The northernmost colonies' role in slavery concerns us less for their accumulation of slave populations than for their transatlantic shipping of slaves—they provided the principal North American merchants and mariners in the slave trade. Regarding slave resistance, New Englanders were often quite literally caught in the middle; in midvoyage, their ships frequently became the loci of slave insurgency. Their foundings, however, are of interest because they at first seemed so remote from the circles of secular greed constituted by the English aristocracy and its upper-middle class. Among the New England colonies, religion was a principal motive for settlement. At Plymouth, founded in 1620, the colonists chartered by the Virginia Company were Pilgrims (Separatists or Congregationals) opposed to the clerical dictates of the Church of England. Despite their experience of aligned churches and states, they nevertheless founded the governance of their settlement on a theocratic model. Committed to a self-sufficient economy based on farming, fishing, and trade, the settlement largely avoided hostilities with nearby Indians (Wampanoag, Narragansett, and Pequot) until the Pequot War 1637. At Massachusetts Bay, founded in 1628, it was reform-minded Puritans rather than Pilgrims who controlled the colony.[5] Fueled by their disgust with the corruption of the Church of England, their colony was intended as a model of purity and orthodoxy. Their strict religious regimen, however, produced its own dissidence and new settlements based on even more radical extremism: in 1635, Reverend Thomas Hooker and some of his followers began the founding of Hartford, Windsor, and Wethersford; in 1638, Anne Hutchinson, who was branded a heretic, led her followers to found Portsmouth (then Pocasset); in 1636, the Calvinist Quaker Roger Williams was banished (or fled) and subsequently founded the Providence settlement; in 1639, William Coddington founded Newport; and in 1643, Samuel Gorton resettled at Warwick (then Shawomet). Meanwhile, Puritan loyalists founded New Haven in 1638. All were, of course, strongly theocratic in governance.

Slaves appeared in New England sometime between 1624 and 1638. The latter date is a certainty, for among the cargo of the *Desire*, which arrived in Boston on December 12, Captain William Pierce had brought Blacks for whom he had traded captive Pequots in the West Indies. In 1644, Boston merchants launched ships to Africa; and in 1676, frustrated by their inability to compete with the large European slavers on the Guinea Coast, they are reported to have innovated the scouring of East Africa and Madagascar for slaves. By the next century, the Puritan and Boston traders' pioneering had made the New England colonies, as Lorenzo Johnston Greene reports, "the greatest slave-trading section of America. There came into vogue the famous triangular slave trade with New England, Africa, and the West Indies as its focal points."[6] Notwithstanding New England merchants' central role in the slave trade, the number of slaves in permanent residence in New England was small; by the time of the American Revolution, slightly more than 16,000 slaves lived among the 659,000 New Englanders (which included New Hampshire, Vermont, Massachusetts, Rhode Island, and Connecticut). In this region, slave populations were maintained largely through natural increase rather than importation. For example, between 1750 and 1770, Massachusetts maintained its slave population at approximately 4,500. The largest of the slave-holding colonies of New England was Connecticut (in 1770 slaves numbered 5,698), followed by Massachusetts (4,500) and Rhode Island (3,761).

In the middle colonies of English America there was New Netherlands (founded in 1624). It was not colonized by the English but by Dutch merchants of the Dutch West Indies Company. In 1644, however, it was captured by the English and became the property of James, the Duke of York. The small number of Black servants and African slaves who arrived during the period of Dutch control inhabited an ambiguous legal domain, since slavery had no legal standing. One English captain taken prisoner during the war reported that Blacks "were very free and familiar . . . freely joining occasionally in conversation, as if they were one and all of the same household."[7] There were free Blacks (some even owning immigrant servants), intermarriage was legal, and many had been armed during the Indian war of 1641–44. But from 1644 on, the conditions of Blacks in the New Netherlands descended toward the hell existing in the southern colonies. Between 1682 and 1702 (when the Act for Regulating Slaves was passed), Blacks found themselves under a much more restrictive and harsh slave regime, indeed, "the most complete and the most severe of all the colonies north of Maryland," David Kobrin argues. In 1685, the duke became the King of England and what was then called New York became a royal colony. Whatever its formal designation, owing to the disgust of its Dutch merchant elites and colonists with monarchical abuses and doctrinal disputes, the colony was largely ungovernable from England or by James's agents. Further disturbances were caused in 1691 when a German trader, Jacob Leisler, led a successful revolt, inspired by Protestant zeal, in the names of William and Mary. By the mid-eighteenth century, as one of the most important depots for the slave trade, New York possessed the largest slave population north of Maryland. Slavers were concentrated in the down-counties of New York (18 percent of the population), Kings (34 percent), Queens (16 percent), and Richmond (19 percent), where the most affluent colonists resided. Slaves were employed in agriculture and as domestics, artisans, and manufacturing laborers. By 1770, 19,000 of the 163,000 residents of New York were slaves (8–9).

The Duke of York also owned New Jersey but in 1664 ceded it to two wealthy friends for their pleasure. John Berkeley sold his half (West Jersey) to the Quakers, later associated with the founding of the Pennsylvania

Colony in 1681. George Carteret maintained his proprietorship over East Jersey. Pressed by colonists dissatisfied with the conflicting administration of the settlements, the crown combined the two Jerseys into a royal province in 1702. (Slightly under 1,000 slaves then lived in New Jersey; their numbers would increase eightfold by the time of the revolution.) Meanwhile, high immigration from the Germanies and Ireland and the liberal policies of William Penn in advancing his "holy experiment" made Pennsylvania the site of the most diverse and dynamic of the "English" North American colonies. In the eighteenth century, as before, slavery remained at modest levels; by 1770, the slaves of Pennsylvania numbered only 5,761 of a total population of 240,000.

The European immigrants themselves were distinguishable then by nationality (in 1790, 60.9 percent were said to be English, 9.7 percent Irish, 8.7 percent German, 8.3 percent Scottish, 3.4 percent Dutch, 1.7 percent French, 0.7 percent Swedish, and 6.6 percent "unassigned"), culture, and religion. They were also separated by wealth and poverty. In the South, a few were merchants and planters, but more were middling farmers, soldier adventurers, or worse, and still more were servants; in the North, merchants, professionals, artisans, and farmers were more common.

Among the indigenous peoples, social order was no less complicated. Within the dominant in the Iroquois family, for instance, historical conflicts divided the triumphal tribes from their enemies and subordinates, who sometimes lived in near-feudal conditions. In the encounter with the colonial outposts of imperial England, some indigenous peoples (for instance, the Occaneechees, Pamunkeys, and Piscattaways in Virginia) were defeated but came to a reconciliation with the colonists, who perceived them as "tributary Indians." Other indigenous peoples (for example, the Susquehannahs in Virginia or the Narragansetts in the North) guarded their autonomy to the point of warfare. Finally, England had its competitor imperialists in the New World: French traders and soldier adventurers to the north, and Portuguese, French, and Spanish enterprises to the south. When Black resistance surfaced, its character insinuated itself into the unstable contradictions of an immigrant, slave, servant, and imperial social order.

The Early Black Movements of Resistance

Resistance among the slave and bonded laborers assumed various appearances: appeals to the courts, physical violence, flight, and rebelliousness. As the seventeenth century came to a close, the legal rights secured for the slaves had been suppressed emphatically: the comprehensive slave codes of South Carolina were codified in 1696, those of Virginia in 1705, New York's in 1702 and 1712, and Maryland's in 1663 and 1681 (slavery was legally prohibited in Georgia from its founding in 1735 until 1749). But before the codes achieved the racial division of servants from slaves, European servants and African slaves sometimes acted in tandem. In 1663, for an early documented instance, a plot against their masters by "white" servants and Black slaves was uncovered in Gloucester County, Virginia. Fourteen years later, in the turmoil of the Bacon Rebellion (spurred by Nathaniel Bacon's resolve to eradicate Native Americans in Virginia), one of the last rebel holdouts was a band of eighty slaves and twenty English servants.[8] This rebellion within a rebellion had nothing to do with the plunder that motivated Bacon and his freemen colleagues. Instead, this revolt rejected British and colonial masters alike, violating the 1639 Virginia ban on slaves bearing arms to achieve liberty from the bondage of indenture and slavery.

With the enactment of the slave codes, both Black and Native American slaves were denied allies in the Euro-American poor. They were now largely on their own in mounting resistance. But as the number of African and Black Creole slaves increased, so too did slave outbreaks and plots. Summarizing Joshua Coffin's findings, Harvey Wish reports that "the eastern counties of Virginia, where the Negroes were rapidly outnumbering the whites, suffered from repeated scares in 1687, 1709, 1710, 1722, 1723, and 1730." In South Carolina, slave rebels were even more daunting. On May 6, 1720, Black insurrectionists killed three whites. As Coffin discovered: "Forces were immediately raised, and sent after them: twenty-three of whom were taken, six convicted, three executed, and three escaped."[9] A plot to destroy Charleston was uncovered in 1730 and eight years later, in November 1738, a slave outbreak was documented. One year later, Coffin recorded multiple insurrections, including the Stono Uprising by Angolan Blacks:

> In 1739, there were three formidable insurrections of the slaves in South Carolina—one in St. Paul's Parish, one in St. Johns, and one in Charleston. In one of these, which occurred in September, they killed in one night twenty-five whites, and burned six houses. They were pursued, attacked, and fourteen killed. In two days, twenty more were killed and forty were taken, some of whom were shot, some hanged, and some *gibbeted alive!* This "more exemplary" punishment, as Gov. Gibbes called it, failed of its intended effect, for the next year there was another insurrection in South Carolina. There were then above 40,000 slaves, and about twenty persons were killed before it was quelled. (14)

Even the slaves purchased in other colonies and transferred to Georgia (Prince George County) were discovered plotting an insurrection in 1739.

Some slave rebels, Coffin observed, did not wait for their arrival on shore to express their rage: in 1731, Captain George Scott of Rhode Island escaped with his cabin boy when his crew was killed by his cargo; the next year, Captain John Major of Portsmouth, New Hampshire, "was murdered, with all his crew, and the schooner and cargo seized by the slaves"; in 1735, off the coast of Africa, the slaves carried by the *Dolphin*, "got into the powder room, and to be revenged, blew up themselves with the crew"; and in 1747, in the waters off the Cape Coast Castle of Ghana, only two of Captain Beers' Rhode Island crew survived when his cargo seized the ship. (14–15)

Among the northern colonies, similar affairs have come to light. On Sunday April 6, 1712, twenty-three slaves met at Mr. Cook's orchard near the center of the City of New York. Armed with guns, swords, hatchets, and knives, they lured colonists into an ambush by setting fire to one of Mr. Vantilburgh's outhouses. The insurrectionists killed nine colonists and seriously wounded five others. Reverend D. Humphreys provided some interesting details about the event: "In the year 1712, a considerable number of negroes of the Carmantee and Pappa Nations formed a plot to destroy all the English, in order to obtain their liberty; and kept their conspiracy so secret, that there was no suspicion of it till it came to the very execution." Twenty-seven slaves were tried and eighteen of these were executed by hanging or burning at the stake. The number of conspirators, however, must have been much larger, however, since Humphreys recorded of the plotters: "In their flight some of them shot themselves, others their wives, and then themselves; some absconded a few days, and then killed themselves for fear of being taken." (10–11)

Three decades later, in the midst of the War of Jenkins' Ear between Britain and Spain, a slave insurrection coincided with an anticipated attack on New York. During the months of February, March, and April 1741, arson struck nine buildings in the City of New York, including the Governor's House and Chapel. Two slaves, Caesar and Prince, and one colonist, John Hughson, were arrested, tried, and executed for the offense. The persecution precipitated by the slave conspiracy persisted for several months and into the next year, targeting far more than the original plotters. With slaves accounting for more than 14 percent of New York's total population of 60,000, and a large non-English population, there was no shortage of suspected conspirators. A Catholic priest was executed and

from May 11 to March 13, 1742, approximately one hundred and sixty slaves were accused and arraigned on charges of conspiracy against the City of New York . . . forty-one slaves were convicted of conspiracy, while seventy-seven confessed either at the stake or in court. Approximately thirteen slaves were burned alive at the stake, eighteen were hanged, and seventy-one were exported to islands in the Caribbean.[10]

Whether they were aboard slave ships, on the plantations, or in the urban areas, rebel slaves continued to be reported during the third quarter of the eighteenth century. In 1754, Black women in Charleston burned the buildings of C. Croft, a man who claimed to own them. Two of the women were punished by being burned alive. In 1755, two slaves from Cambridge, Massachusetts, were executed for poisoning their owner, John Codman, who had provided in his will for their manumission upon his death. Mark was hanged and Phillis was burned alive. In Charleston in August 1759, another plot was discovered and suppressed. In 1761, Captain Nichols of Boston saved his ship but lost forty slaves due to an insurrection.[11]

Beyond the rudimentary details of their trials—name, age, owner, time of commitment, disposition (e.g., burned, hanged, transported, imprisoned, or discharged)—we know so very little of these rebels. Colonial courts and magistrates of the seventeenth century were interested in guilt and exemplary punishment, not slave motives. We do know they were desperate; we guess that many, perhaps most, were courageous. In the cities, they anticipated that overwhelming force would be employed against them and that they would have to abandon familiar streets and buildings for the unknown. In the countryside, they faced unknown woods, forests, and rivers; hostile farmers and woodsmen; patrollers; and, if they were lucky to escape the settlements, the hostile or indifferent Indians. For those who had come from an African region, there were alien languages, cultures, psychologies, and skills to master. For those who were Creole or transferred from the West Indies, there was the oppressive realization that slavery was not a local monster, limited to some remote island in the Caribbean. And, finally, we know that the institution of slavery itself made them special. The scale of the slave trade was such that among the tens of thousands enslaved, most must have been ordinary, yet slavery forged the ordinary into the extraordinary. Slavery gave the lie to its own conceit: one could not create a perfect system of oppression and exploitation.

Marronage in North America

Less spectacular—at least at first—were the fugitives. For the early colonial years we have less information about them because of the absence of newspapers and the public notices that became so frequent in the eighteenth century. In the seventeenth century, there are only a few recorded instances of "runaways," as they were called, attempting to establish marronages (fugitive slave settlements). For generations historians believed that not even the most remarkable of the maroon settlements in North America (the Free Black town of Gracia Real de Santa Teresa de Mose [from 1738 to 1763] in Spanish Colonial Florida) was any rival to the achievement of seventeenth-century Palmares (from 1605 to 1695) in Brazil. But in a remarkable essay in 1939, "Maroons within the Present Limits of the United States," Herbert Aptheker attempted to correct the record. Aptheker opened his essay with an extraordinary claim:

> Evidence of the existence of at least fifty such communities in various places and at various times, from 1672 to 1864, has been found. The mountainous, forested, or swampy regions of South Carolina, North Carolina, Virginia, Louisiana, Florida, Georgia, Mississippi, and Alabama (in order of importance) appear to have been the favorite haunts for these black Robin Hoods. At times a settled life, rather than a pugnacious and migratory one, was aimed at, as is evidenced by the fact that these maroons built homes, maintained families, raised cattle, and pursued agriculture, but this all but settled life appears to have been exceptional.[12]

His account was documented by official records and correspondence and newspaper stories. Before Aptheker, serious attention to the Black maroons had been largely confined to Joshua R. Giddings's *The Exiles of Florida* (published in 1858), Frederick Olmstead's *Journey in the Back Country* (1860), and Harriet Beecher Stowe's novel, *Dred, A Tale of the Dismal Swamp* (1856). Aptheker was thus providing some facts to fill American historiography's own "dismal swamp."

Marronage was almost as embarrassing to historians in 1939 as it was a threat to colonial and American communities in the seventeenth, eighteenth, and nineteenth centuries. After all, in 1939 David Selznick's cinematic production of *Gone With the Wind* had been an enormous success, surpassing the impact on the popular imagination of even D. W. Griffith's *Birth of a Nation* twenty-four years earlier. And if one includes the lesser filmic productions set in the Old South, for nearly forty years American audiences had been exposed to a representation of slavery that portrayed it as a natural, necessary, and generally benevolent institution (more than seventy-five feature films depicted the Old South between 1929 and 1941).[13] But in their reality, the maroons provided a radically alternative picture of slavery, Blacks, class, and American history. For in the maroon communities of the previous three centuries, and the responses they provoked (from both amnesiac historians and frightened neighbors), one could discern the essential American contradictions. A report on Virginia maroons printed in Boston's *The Liberator* on March 19, 1831, displays one such contradiction: "There has been much shooting of negroes in this neighborhood recently, in consequence of symptoms of liberty having been discovered among them."[14] It was only a matter of time before someone would recognize these "symptoms" for what they were.

The first African maroons in North America, Aptheker informs us, predated Jamestown by eighty-two years. They were slave insurrectionists from an abortive Spanish colonizing effort in the present North and South Carolina in 1526:

> The settlement consisted of about five hundred Spaniards and one hundred Negro slaves. Trouble soon beset it. . . . Finally, probably in November, several of the slaves rebelled, and fled to the Indians. The next month what was left of the adventurers, some one hundred and fifty souls, returned to Haiti, leaving the rebel Negroes with their Indian friends—as the first permanent inhabitants, other than the Indians, in what was to be the United States.[15]

These rebels remained nameless and their numbers uncounted in official records, but in the century after the English settlements began, the maroons began to leave a more certain trail.

In their treatments of maroons, Aptheker and then Gerald Mullin[16] placed their emphases on the Black participants—the slaves who had responded to racial oppression in a fashion ignored by the racial narratives of mainstream American historiography and popular culture. American marronage, however, was not just a Black phenomenon. Indeed, American maroon communities frequently acquired the multicultural and multiracial character that liberal historians of the early twentieth century had expected of the whole nation. Underlining this observation are the writings of Hugo Prosper Leaming, a Virginian historian of Poor White and African American ancestry:

> Maroons are thought of as Black, and they usually were. Black people were the central racial group of the Dismal Swamp maroons. African ancestry among the maroons, arousing racial feelings within their enemies, heightened the ferocity of the wars in the South Carolina back country. Yet there were also many maroons who were of Native American (Indian) descent, escaped slaves or remnants of destroyed nations. And there were many other maroons descended from the European poor, escaped indentured servants and other Poor Whites for whom there was no place in plantation society. . . . All three racial groups were maroons as fugitives from bondage or from other forms of subjugation inherent to the slavery system. They joined

in struggle against a common enemy and shared elements from their respective cultures of origin.[17]

In seventeenth-century English America, the first of those significantly involved in marronage had been European indentured servants and colonists who had immigrated and settled without benefit of a charter from the crown. And once the Indian wars had reduced some of the smaller Iroquois nations to captivity and their social order to rubble, they too became maroons. But from the last quarter of the seventeenth century, African rebels, particularly in Virginia and the Carolinas, joined their number. And by the beginning of the eighteenth century, mixed communities of renegade colonists, Native Americans, and Africans were being molded. As the slave trade increased the local African population, it also added new human resources to the maroon villages and guerrilla bands.

From the beginning of official colonial records, the most frequently named leaders of the maroon bands were African. Twenty years after the county legally authorized the pursuit and killing of "outlying" slaves, Aptheker informs us, the Order Book for Middlesex County, Virginia, reported on the activities of a band of maroon raiders under the leadership of a slave named Mingoe in 1691. *Mingo* is the Algonquian term for an Iroquois or an Iroquois-speaking person, so it may be surmised that Mingoe had lived long enough in the emergent mixed-culture maroon community to learn Tuscarora (an Iroquoian language) in addition to English and his original language. (Later, several Black maroon leaders would also use the designation: for example, Captain Mingo was captured near Norfolk in 1822.) That there was a maroon community awaiting the return of Mingo's renegades is attested to by the loot the renegades sought: hogs, cattle, and guns.[18] Captain Peter was operating out of the Dismal Swamp in 1709, and by 1728 planter William Byrd II was warning the Virginia authorities about the communities sequestered in the Dismal Swamp. Byrd reminded his colleagues of a classic tale: the escaped slaves Romulus and Remus had made Rome. Unless dealt with, the maroon communities would be transformed into a formidable power.[19]

In South Carolina during the first decades of the eighteenth century, the colony was harassed by maroons. When the Yamasee War of 1715–16 was conducted, Kathryn Holland Braund reports that "some blacks were believed to have joined the Indians against South Carolina."[20] After the war, the Yamasee assisted fugitive slaves in reaching Spanish St. Augustine; meanwhile Black maroons and Yamasee allied with Spain against the Creek trade with Britain. In 1733, rewards were posted by the governor for Black fugitive raiders; and in 1744, Governor James Glen enlisted the aid of

Notchee Indians against "runaway Negroes, who had sheltered themselves in the Woods, and being armed, had committed disorders." In 1765, in fear of a general slave rebellion instigated by maroon rebels, a military force was deployed to destroy "a numerous collection of outcast mullattoes, mustes, and free negroes."[21] A similar situation arose in Georgia in 1771 and 1772. With slaves constituting nearly half the colony's population, Governor James Habersham mobilized the militia and Indian allies because he had learned "that a great number of fugitive Negroes had Committed many Robberies and insults between this town [Savannah] and Ebenezer and that their Numbers (which) were now Considerable might be expected to increase daily." For Habersham and his predecessors, it was not only the ratio of slave to colonist that was troubling; perhaps even more distressing was Georgia's proximity to Spanish Florida and particularly the maroon town of Gracia Real de Santa Teresa de Mose (henceforth Mose).

Mose was a free Black town, the only instance in North America of the kind of free Black towns that Spanish officials in the seventeenth and eighteenth centuries had begun to recognize through treaty arrangements with rebellious Blacks (the Spanish called them *cimarrones*, the origin of the English *maroon*). In Mexico, for example, were the free Black towns of San Lorenzo de los Negros (founded in 1609), San Lorenzo Cerralvo (1635), and Nuestra Señora de Guadalupe de los Morenos de Amapa (1769) in the mountains of Vera Cruz.[22] Jane Landers surmises that the possibility of taking refuge in Florida probably came about through a Spanish raiding party's attacks ("a force of fifty-three Indians and blacks") on the South Carolina settlements of Port Royal and Edisto in 1686.[23] Fugitives began to arrive the next year. Forty years later, in 1728, a slave militia commanded by Francisco Menendez assisted in the defense of St. Augustine against a British force. Menendez was one of the Black veterans of the Yamasee War who made up the militia. But despite their petitions to the Spanish crown, the fugitives remained slaves until March of 1738, when Governor Manuel de Montiano recognized their unconditional freedom.

> Governor Montiano established the freedmen in a new town, about two miles north of St. Augustine, which he called Gracia Real de Santa Teresa de Mose. The freedmen built the settlement, a walled fort and shelters described by the Spaniards as resembling thatched Indian huts . . . but later British reports add that the fort was constructed of stone, "four square with a flanker at each corner, banked with earth, having a ditch without on all sides lined round with prickly royal and had a well and house within, and a look-out." They also confirm Spanish reports that the freedmen planted fields nearby.[24]

Mose was abandoned in 1740 due to the British-Georgian attacks on St. Augustine during the War of Jenkins' Ear. The community of free Blacks, however, remained intact but moved to St. Augustine. All the while the community received newcomers—fugitives (the rebels at Stono had attempted to reach St. Augustine before they were apprehended) as well as free Blacks—and its records of fugitive life reflected the African ravages of the slave trade:

> One hundred and forty-seven black marriages were reported from 1735 to 1763, and fifty-two of those married were designated as Congos—twenty-six males and twenty-six females. The next largest group was the Caravalis, including nine males and nineteen females. The Mandingos constituted the third largest group and had nine males and four females. Also represented in the marriage registers were the Minas, Gambas, Lecumis, Sambas, Gangas, Araras, and Guineans. (27)

Mose was rebuilt in 1749, but its existence ended in 1763 when the Spanish evacuated St. Augustine and the province became British territory. The inhabitants were relocated to Matanzas, Cuba. Menendez, who had commanded the Mose militia for thirty years, eventually relocated to Havana. Spanish Florida, however, still survived as a threat to the Carolinas and Georgia, and it would play an even more dramatic role in American slave rebellions in the following century.

Compared to the Spanish settlements in Florida and the French initiatives in Canada and the West Indies, the French colony in the Mississippi delta was a minor irritant to British colonial interests. Notwithstanding, French merchants and pirates inspired their own variant of marronage in the New World. Founded in 1699, colonial Louisiana (named in deference to Louis XIV) experienced only modest development. Officially, of the 278 people listed in the 1708 census, fewer than 90 were Europeans; by 1717, the population had risen to 400. Until its concession to the Company of the West (renamed the Company of the Indies) in 1717, and its brief transformation into a penal colony between 1717 and 1720, Louisiana remained outside the global maneuvers of the great powers and the meteoric growth of an Atlantic mercantile capitalist system.[25] Even by 1726, despite the company's transportation of more than 7,000 colonists (including Germans) to Louisiana and the efforts of special police squadrons in Paris to export hundreds of "vagabonds," prostitutes, and political dissidents, the European population was still below 2,000.

Constantly under siege from the Natchez and (with British encouragement) the Western Choctaw and the Chickasaw; wracked by military mutinies; and plagued by an unhealthy environment for Europeans, the colony's value was essentially geopolitical (i.e., halting the British western expansion at the Mississippi river) rather than economic. The only reliable production was of the food crop rice; the cotton, tobacco, and indigo produced in the colony were of little market value. The only certain profit was to be had in corruption, a pursuit dominated by the LeMoyne brothers (Pierre and Jean Baptiste), the merchants-pirates-commanders who expropriated lands and labor in the French concessions in Senegambia and Louisiana, embezzled naval supplies, appropriated goods destined to resupply the colony, and employed the military garrison for the transport and protection of their slave property and other commercial goods. By 1731, the colony had reverted to crown control.

African slave laborers began arriving in Louisiana in 1709, first a mere trickle and then, in the 1720s, in such numbers that they outnumbered the Europeans. By the 1740s, New Orleans was predominantly Black as were most of the colonial Louisiana settlements (175–176). The Africans had been brought initially from Whydah and then principally from Senegambia. With them came the agrarian and textile sciences to cultivate rice, corn, cotton, and indigo. By the late 1720s, when for a time Louisiana became the sole disembarkation point for the Senegambian slave trade in Bambara, the African workers also brought a tradition of resistance. Largely constituted by those enslaved as a result of the Bambaran imperial wars associated with the rise of the Segu Empire, the new laborers transplanted the Bambara heroic tradition.

> The *fadenya* principle, validated above all in troubled times, asserted itself. They revolted at sea. After arriving in Louisiana, the Bambara maintained an organized language community, formed alliances with the Indian nations who were in revolt against the French, and conspired to take over the colony. (55)

At one time or another in the first decade of large-scale French slave-trading, the Bambara appear to have organized rebellions or conspiracies to revolt at every link in the commerce between Africa and Louisiana. In October 1723, the slaves aboard *le Courrier de Bourbon* were discovered in a conspiracy to kill the ship's crew as the vessel set sail for Louisiana from Grenada; in October 1724, the slaves held in the warehouse of the trading post at Goree revolted, killing a guard before they were subdued; and in May 1729, while *l'Annibal* was anchored at the mouth of the Gambia River, the cargo rose up, killing four crewmen, and suffered the deaths of scores (including three women and two nursing babies). Less than two months later, on the same ship now at Caye St. Louis, some Black women seized the initiative and precipitated a revolt: "a flock of our *negresses* burst into the main bedroom and punched M. Bart, sublieutenant of the ship. Being suddenly awakened, he believed that it was the *negres* [males] who had come to murder him."[26] These were some of the more dramatic efforts at liberation in Africa and the New World. But they were not the most successful. More captives were freed through slave escapes along the trade routes and rivers of Senegambia and as fugitives in colonial Louisiana. And once distributed among colonists in Louisiana, some Africans resorted to murdering their owners and applying arson to their masters' fields and domiciles.

The most effective forms of slave resistance, however, were those organized in colonial Louisiana and resulted from collaborations between Native Americans and Africans. The first of these was at Natchez settlement (now Natchez, Mississippi), a tobacco colony consisting of slightly more than 430 French settlers and 280 Africans. In late November 1729, after assuring themselves of the cooperation of the Africans, the Natchez attacked the settlement, killing 247 of the Europeans and at least one Black slave foreman. Two months later, when a contingent of French and Choctaw forces (and fifteen Blacks) successfully attacked the captured settlement, nearly half of the now liberated slaves chose to remain with the Natchez natives:

> Those blacks who were not captured fought alongside the Natchez, preventing the Choctaw from taking their powder, and giving the Natchez enough time to enter the two forts. The blacks' role was decisive in preventing the total defeat of the Natchez. The French and their Choctaw allies had not expected to have to fight the blacks as well as the Natchez. (102)

This was a reasonable expectation since the French colonists had purposively sought to use Native Americans against the Africans, and the Africans against the Native Americans. Indeed, only shortly before the attempt to recapture Natchez, the colony's governor, Perier, had sent Black military auxiliaries to assassinate a small group of Chaouchas just south of New Orleans. The killings had been "carried out promptly and secretly," but afterward the governor trumpeted the massacre in order to secure "the other little nations below the river in respect." (102) Frustrated by the relatively few colonists willing to join the militia, and military units of small size and dubious discipline, colonial officials constantly recruited Africans into the militia, promising (and delivering) emancipation for service to the state.

Notwithstanding, Indian and African slaves continued to escape together, form maroon communities near the colonial settlements, and periodically engage in terrifying the European settlers. "Documents surviving from the 1730s and 1740s," Gwendolyn Hall observes, "record the departure of Indian and African slaves, who often left together to seek refuge among Indian tribes" (115). And if they were recaptured, the fugitives proved to be a formidable problem for colonial officials and settlers. In June 1731, and later at Christmas, Bambara conspiracies were discovered involving an estimated 400 slaves. Through the use of spies and torture, the leaders of the June conspiracy (eight men and one woman) were uncovered and executed. Based on the stories of the few slaves who broke under torture, the authorities reconstructed the conspiracy. A slave fugitive from the Natchez settlement returned, appearing in New Orleans. Once among his fellows (and particularly those who had been with the Natchez for some eighteen months), he began assuring the slaves that British and Indian allies would support a rebellion. The plan was that:

all the whites from Pointe Coupee to Balize were to be massacred. All the Bambara had joined together to free themselves and take possession of the country by revolt. The other blacks in the colony who were not of the Bambara nation were to serve them as slaves." (106)

The forced testimony of the tortured slaves rang true, referring as it did to the customary social hierarchy of Bambara society and the tradition of slave militaries. Later, more support for the narrative would appear in the 1730s and 1740s with the repeated instances of alliances between war-prone Indians and rebellious Africans. Colonial French Louisiana mirrored the record of African and Creole resistance being written in the English and Spanish colonies in North America.

Diverging Political Cultures

The recitation of Black resistance during the colonial era of American history must now be brought to a close, but not without some attention to those contradictions signaled at the beginning of this chapter. That is, some discussion is required of colonial slavery's legacy in the American Revolution and the nation that resulted. As Morgan suggested, we must understand that some of the things said and done in the colonial years had a profound and enduring impact.

The resistances to slavery were the principal grounds for the radically alternative political culture that coalesced in the Black communities of the eighteenth and nineteenth centuries, the era of revolutionary, liberal, and nationalist impulses among Europeans in North America. Among Blacks, the rule of law was respected for its power rather than for any resemblance to justice or a moral order. For the slaves, the rule of law was an injustice, a mercurial and violent companion to their humiliations, a form of physical abuse, a force for the destruction of their families, and an omnipresent cruelty to their loved ones. Even for free Blacks, the rule of law was too often a cruel hypocrisy, impotent in protecting their tenuous status. For both the slaves and the free Blacks, even as revolutionary fervor increased among the colonists, the masquerades of the law were becoming more transparent: the domestic slave trade displaced the African slave trade in the late eighteenth century. With this new economy of slavery, the separation of slave families by sale and the kidnapping and enslavement of free Blacks increased astronomically.

To the very contrary, the rebellious colonial ruling class sought to invest the rule of law with a moral authority sufficient to justify their rejection of British authority. As slave traders and merchants, as slaveholders and propagandists, as lawyers, ministers, and civil authorities for slavery, the most influential men and women among the emergent American community used the rule of law as the warrant for the justness of their claims and practices. By their law they hunted, traded, bought, and sold other human beings; waged war against, whipped, dismembered, burned, hanged, and tortured their property for possessing a human will; treated their colonist servants and laboring classes with the customary disdain of the English gentle classes. Now this same law was to serve their revolutionary ambitions, their right to liberty.

On this score, the Blacks, particularly the slaves, possessed conflicting opinions. The 5,000 Blacks who fought for American independence fought for liberty, and had a very different vision of national freedom than the one imagined by their countrymen. But as we shall see, many thousands of Blacks would fight against independence, not for love of imperial Britain but because they understood that Black freedom was otherwise unobtainable. Like the Native American nations that sided with the British, the Black Loyalists sought to employ the British army to serve their own interests, for their own ends. Long after the defeated British had departed, their allies, the Native Americans and the Blacks, continued the struggle for liberty. For generations to come, Native Americans recognized America as a colonial power, and Blacks read the new nation as tyrannical. Their suspicion of and opposition toward American society survived in the political cultures of Blacks and Native Americans for the next two hundred years.

CHAPTER TWO

Slavery and the Constitutions

*   *   *

Sir, suffer me to recall to your mind that time, in which the arms and tyranny of the British crown were exerted, with every powerful effort, in order to reduce you to a state of servitude. . . .

Here was a time, in which your tender feelings for yourselves had engaged you thus to declare, you were then impressed with proper ideas of the great violation of liberty . . . but, Sir, how pitiable is it to reflect, that although you were so fully convinced of the benevolence of the Father of Mankind . . . that you should at the same time counteract his mercies, in detaining by fraud and violence so numerous a part of my brethren, under groaning captivity, and cruel oppression, that you should at the same time be found guilty of that most criminal act, which you professedly detested in others, with respect to yourselves.

—Benjamin Banneker to Thomas Jefferson

Three American Revolutions

Like most revolutions of modern times, the American Revolution was not a solitary insurrection but several simultaneous upheavals. But the shadow of a master narrative, first concocted by revolutionary publicists through public documents like the Declaration of Independence, the Constitution, the Federalist Papers, and in the private writings of various "founding fathers," and then perpetuated by professional historians and scholars, has concealed the acts of communities outside a select circle of colonial elites. We can be certain that it was not merely a preference for narrative simplicity that led generations of American historians to largely erase the other American revolutions. As Barbara Chase Smith observes, "Few historians or others approach the Revolution freshly," preferring instead to follow George Bancroft in staging the Revolution as a "culminating event" that transformed a complex colonial society "into a comfortable, democratic nineteenth-century society that was, after all, good enough for everyone."[1] The American Revolution was hardly anything of the kind, for it bequeathed civil rights on what Linda Grant DePauw estimates to be only 15 percent of the population, leaving the poorer colonists, the slaves, all women, and Native Americans to the mercies of the few.[2] This limited freedom was not what most Americans fought for—the poor, the Blacks, and the Native Americans possessed a radically different mission. And fortunately, we do not have to speculate that the majority of rebellious colonists had in mind a democracy of the many rather than a republic ruled by a virtuous few.

As Howard Zinn recounts it, the revolution of the poor colonists against the wealthy—that is, the actions of the Green Mountain rebels of Vermont, the Regulators movement of North Carolina, the Privates Committee in Pennsylvania—had been presaged by rural tenant riots in New Jersey and New York in the 1740s and 1750s. These insurgencies reached their apogee in the 1760s and 1770s.

> Mechanics were demanding political democracy in the colonial cities: open meetings of representative assemblies, public galleries in the legislative halls, and the publishing of roll-call votes, so that constituents could check on representatives.[3]

Quite unlike their predecessors in the Bacon Rebellion of a century earlier, the poor of eighteenth-century America saw Britain, more often than not, as a counterweight to the colonial ruling class. In petitioning British authorities, poor workers and the unemployed complained about "the great and overgrown rich men" (as the Privates Committee had described its foes) and mounted opposition to "the rich and powerful . . . designing Monsters" (as the Regulators' rhetoric would have it). These desperate, angry workers demanded relief. But, as Zinn recounts, their desires were to be frustrated:

> In the countryside, where most people lived, there was a similar conflict of poor against rich, one which political leaders would use to mobilize the population against England, granting some benefits for the rebellious poor, and many more for themselves in the process. (62)

For many it was a time to put their revolutionary ardor for democracy at the service of aristocratic republicans. But they did so expecting that a compromise would come with victory: with the vast colonial wealth of the British crown to disburse, the rebel victors would achieve some accommodation of property and popular government.

Among the colonial elite, the British monarchy was the direct object of their enmity. It was not merely that the presence of British authority had become a nuisance in their class warfare against the poor. Britain had, too, ceded the territory east of the Appalachia mountains to the Native Americans (the Proclamation of 1763) and protected its merchants' interests in the African slave trade (despite a late eighteenth-century slave surplus in the colonies that was depreciating the property of the colonial elites). Also, the British Parliament levied new taxes on the colonies in a desperate attempt to pay the debts incurred by imperial war (the French-Indian War). Britain was an external and distant predator, and the colonial elite and urban middle classes insisted upon it. But, as we have seen, colonial opinion was not united:

> Yes, mechanics and sailors, some others, were incensed against the British. But the general enthusiasm for the war was not strong. While much of the white male population went into military service at one time or another during the war, only a small fraction stayed. . . . John Adams had estimated a third opposed, a third in support, a third neutral. (76)

In the politics of their day and later in our historical chronicles, however, the elite had the last word. In 1776, when the Congress met in Philadelphia, it was composed of wealth, and the wealthiest among them was the Virginian slaveholder, George Washington. They disdained popular government (which one put as asking a blind man to choose one's colors) and insured that the advantage in pursuing happiness would remain with the plantocrats and their New England business partners. As Adams, the future president (1796–1800), put it, majority rule would result in "the eight or nine millions who have no property . . . usurping over the rights of the one or two millions who have."[4] And there was, of course, a more pressing agenda. Having dubbed themselves the Continental Congress (1774– 87), they suggested a less publicized ambition: to seize the whole of North America.

The third and least memorialized uprising that forged the American Revolution was that of the Blacks, slave and free. This war of the Blacks, frequently allied with Native Americans and sometimes with abolitionist colonials, provided the occasion for the liberation of what some estimate to be one hundred thousand slaves, a fifth of the Black population (who numbered 575,000 in 1780). This constituted the largest emancipation of slaves in the Americas prior to the Haitian Revolution (1791–1804) and the most significant act of liberation among Africans in North America prior to the Civil War. It is thus somewhat remarkable that such a massive emancipation should remain largely unrecounted in American historiography. But historians have treated these events much as Americans contemporary to the Haitian Revolution treated it. In 1803, the House of Representatives unanimously declared a ban on Haitian refugees because they posed a "danger to the peace and security of the United States," thus conveniently forgetting that 700 Black Haitians had fought for the United States during the American Revolution (an event generally effaced by the greater attention given to support from the French aristocracy). Similarly, the great war of Blacks against the United States has been erased.

The Black reaction to the American rebellion against Britain was a sharp escalation of the slave revolts in South Carolina in 1765 and 1768, and in Georgia in 1771 and 1772. William Loren Katz reports:

> The month before minutemen faced British muskets at Lexington and Concord [April 1775], slaves in Ulster County, New York, organized an uprising that also involved five hundred Indians. By summer 1775, patriots found armed slaves a menace from Maryland to Georgia. Hundreds, perhaps thousands, struck in three North Carolina counties but were crushed by overwhelming white firepower.[5]

Sensing from these events that the principal weakness of the American revolutionaries was the slave population in the rebellious colonies, British authorities seized the initiative. In November 1775, the British Governor of Virginia, Lord Dunmore, declared a martial law that included the caveat that "all indented servants, Negroes, or others (appertaining to Rebels) [are] free, that are able and willing to bear arms." The historian, James W. St. G. Walker, reconstructs the effects of the law:

> It seems certain that slaves fled their American masters in tens of thousands. Thomas Jefferson declared that Virginia alone lost 30,000, though there is no indication that they all went over to the British after deserting their erstwhile owners. . . .
>
> Among the Americans who were prominent in the articulation of the Declaration of Independence as a charter of human liberty, James Madison, Benjamin Harrison, Arthur Middleton and George Washington himself all lost slaves who fled to the banner of British security, many of them seeing active service against the Republican cause.[6]

As Loyalists, the slaves and their free Black counterparts (approximately one-third of them) took up arms and served as spies, couriers, guides, cooks, orderlies, waiters, personal servants, and field hands on captured plantations. Walker states that "several Black Pioneer Corps were formed of fugitive slaves, with their own non-commissioned officers, dozens of blacks served the Royal Navy as ordinary seamen or as pilots on coastal vessels, and there was even a black cavalry troop created in 1782" (6). When the British General Cornwallis surrendered to the patriots in 1781, more than 4,000 of his 5,000 seamen were Black.

Some of those who fought, however, remained slaves, reappearing as property in the slave markets of Canada and the West Indies or as reimbursement to colonial Loyalists who had lost property to the rebels. Despite what would be the American Constitution's (1787) much heralded determination to end the slave trade, four years earlier, during the negotiations over the exact meaning of the Provisional Peace Agreement of 1782 between Britain and the new nation, George Washington showed up at New York in 1783 to insist that all slaves must be returned to their American owners. Washington was unsuccessful and the final British action was the reception of 30,000 Blacks (3,000 of them free Blacks) in Nova Scotia. Many remained in Canada, others were transported to West Africa (eventually the colony of Sierra Leone), and others joined the thousands of other liberated slaves who had already been transferred to the West Indies.

As Walker testified, not all the fugitive slaves joined the British or, having done so, accompanied them to other parts of the British empire. As Herbert Aptheker informs us, some of the fugitives resorted to marronage:

> They fled, with their arms, called themselves soldiers of the King of England, and carried on a guerrilla warfare for years along the Savannah River. Militia from Georgia and South Carolina, together with Indian allies, successfully attacked the Negro settlement in May 1786, with resulting heavy casualties.[7]

A similar series of engagements was reported the next year on South Carolina's southern border. New fugitives raised alarms in Virginia in 1792, and in North Carolina in 1795 and 1802. In 1800, there was Gabriel's rebellion in Richmond; and in 1802, Sancho's conspiracy embraced Virginia and North Carolina. But it was Spanish Florida that was to prove the most troubling region for the new government and the slave interests it was resolved to protect. They followed, as the day the night, from the conspiracies of the governing classes.

Documenting Indifference and Interest

Thomas Jefferson included in the Declaration of Independence drafted for the Continental Congress in 1776 a paragraph detailing the king's guilt in imposing an "execrable commerce" on the colonies: the slave trade and slavery. That paragraph was deleted, in all probability because so many at the Congress (George Washington, Patrick Henry, and Thomas Jefferson himself) were now pursuing the domestic slave trade; that is, the sale and transfer of slaves from the upper to the lower South.[8] All that was left in the Declaration of moral judgment against slavery was the accusation that the king "has excited domestic insurrections amongst us" (a reference, it would seem to Lord Dunmore's activities). The final Declaration voiced equal anger at the King's alliances with the "merciless Indian Savages." Eleven years later, the Constitution of the new government directly referred to the servant class, the slaves, or the slave trade on only three occasions. Under Article 1, the number of representatives and direct taxes apportioned to each state was to be determined by its population: "adding to the whole Number of free Persons, including those bound to Service for a Term of Years, and excluding Indians not taxed, three fifths of all other Persons." Further along, the slave trade was taken up:

> The Migration or Importation of such Persons as any of the States now existing shall think proper to admit, shall not be prohibited by the Congress prior to the Year one thousand eight hundred and eight, but a Tax or duty may be imposed on such Importation, not exceeding ten dollars for each Person.

Finally, under Article II, the whole nation was to serve as an informer against fugitive slaves and servants:

> No Person held to Service or Labour in one State, under the Laws thereof, escaping into another, shall, in Consequence of any Law or Regulation therein, be discharged from such Service or Labour, but shall be delivered up on Claim of the Party to whom such Service or Labour may be due.

In short, just as had been the case under the British crown, the whole judicial and military might of the new nation conspired against servants and slaves. To finalize the garrison character of the new nation, the second Congress enacted the Fugitive Slave Act in 1793, condemning any who would provide aid or protection to fugitive slaves.

One of the most recently celebrated apologists for the Founding Fathers has argued that it is mere "presentism" to have expected a more critical contemplation of slavery among eighteenth-century revolutionaries. The American Revolution, Gordon Wood maintains, was a radical revolution. Even though the Declaration of Independence, for one example, "did not mean that blacks and women were created equal to white men (although it would in time be used to justify those equalities, too). It was radical in 1776 because it meant that all white men were equal."⁹ In his Pulitzer Prize– winning study, *The Radicalism of the American Revolution*, Wood insisted:

> For a century or more the colonists had taken slavery more or less for granted as the most base and dependent status in a hierarchy of dependen- cies and a world of laborers. Rarely had they felt the need either to criticize black slavery or to defend it. Now, however, the republican attack on depen- dency compelled Americans to see the deviant character of slavery and to confront the institution as they never had to before. It was no accident that Americans in Philadelphia in 1775 formed the first anti-slavery society in the world.¹⁰

In supposing that the colonists had a cavalier disposition toward slavery, Wood mimics his colonial subjects by paying scant attention in his study to the slaves: the only sustained attention Wood gives the subject was a single paragraph about Colonel Landon Carter's complaint that his slaves bore him great contempt (153–54). Thus, for more than three hundred pages of colonial and revolutionary history, Wood cites no slave fugitives, no slave insurrections, no maroons. Furthermore, he erases colonial oppo- sition to slavery.

The recorded instances of colonists objecting to slavery are, in fact, multiple. In 1736, William Byrd wrote to the Earl of Egmont concerning the "many bad consequences of multiplying these Ethiopians amongst us":

> They blow up the pride, and ruin the Industry of our White People, who seeing a Rank of poor Creatures below them, detest work for fear it shoud make them look like Slaves. . . .
>
> But these private mischeifs are nothing if compared to the publick dan- ger. We have already at least 10,000 men of these descendants of Ham fit to bear Arms, and their Numbers increase every day as well by birth as Impor- tation. And in case there shoud arise a Man of desperate courage amongst us, exasperated by a desperate fortune, he might with more advantage than Cataline kindle a Servile War. . . .
>
> It were therefore worth the consideration of a British Parliament, My Lord, to put an end to this unchristian Traffick of making Merchandize of Our Fellow Creatures.¹¹

In his own diary in 1739, the Earl of Egmont recorded why Robert Hows opposed the legalization of slavery in Georgia: "He feared they would take the work from white men's hands and impoverish them"(595). The next year, the Earl recorded Captain Dempsey's objections: if slavery was allowed in Georgia, "there would not be 50 out of 500 [slaves] who would be found remaining after two months, for they would fly to the Spaniards at Augustine"(595). And in 1742, Colonel William Stephens wrote Benjamin Martyn concerning Georgia's safety, even with the formation of Troops of Rangers:

> Nevertheless Negroes, seeking for liberty, were they now among us, would soon find means, by untrodden paths thro' Wilderness of thick Woods, to flee to Augustine so near us as tis; more especially when they will not only obtain their promised freedome, but also have Arms put into their hands, and become a part of their Army to fight against us. . . .
> I have always professed my own natural Aversion to keeping Slaves. (604)

Forty years before the American Revolution, then, Byrd had remarked upon the "unchristian Traffick." And more than thirty years before him, in 1700, the Puritan merchant and judge, Samuel Sewall of Boston, had published his sermon "The Selling of Joseph," which appealed "for the Redemption of our own enslaved Friends out of *Africa*."[12] John Hepburn's 1715 pamphlet denouncing slavery as a sin was an early Quaker voice in the controversy. In the 1730s and 1740s, proponents as well as opponents of the Great Awakening recognized contradictions between their interpretations of Christianity and slavery (some credited the 1741 slave conspiracy in New York to the agitation of the Great Awakening);[13] and in the period before the Revolution, Quakers like John Woolman and Anthony Benezet became prominent antislavery advocates. From a very different perspective, we have seen that colonial officials and settlers were constantly mindful of the public peril posed by slavery. Of "Negroes rising and cutting [our] throats," as Hows had bluntly declared. The historical evidence, then, hardly concurs with Wood's flimsy assertions marginalizing the contradictions of slavery before the Revolution.

Thus, two years into the existence of the United States, Benjamin Banneker (1731–1806) could confidently approach the subject of slavery with Thomas Jefferson, the Secretary of State. Banneker was a free Black who was a scientist (of bees), a mathematician (his was the first almanac produced by a Black in North America, 1791 to 1802), an astronomer (he predicted the 1789 eclipse), a mechanic (he constructed a wood clock), and a civil employee (he was commissioned by George Washington to survey and plan the new capitol, Washington, D.C., in 1790, with Major Andrew

Ellicott). His grandmother was Molly Welsh, an Englishwoman and indentured servant who had obtained a farm in Maryland, then freed and married one of her native African slaves. Banneker's father, born in Africa, had married Mary, one of Molly's four children.[14]

It is far from certain that Banneker was aware of Jefferson's original draft of the Declaration of Independence, the one that read: "We hold these truths to be sacred & undeniable; that all men are created equal & independant, that from that equal creation they derive rights inherent & inalienable." But Banneker could only have reminded Jefferson of this stronger, original version: "created equal & independant." Two hundred years later, Wood would shrink from the task, but Banneker had a personal stake in the matter: "Sir, I freely and cheerfully acknowledge, that I am of the African race." Thus he joined his name to those of slaves like Felix, Peter Bestes, Sambo Freeman, Felix Holbrook, Chester Joie, Prime, Prince, Pomp, and Ned Griffin, who filed general petitions for freedom addressed to state legislatures, governors, and federal officers. To the Massachusetts Bay legislature in 1777, Prime and Prince presented the following:

> The petition of A Great Number of Blackes detained in a State of slavery in the Bowels of a free & Christian Country Humbly sheweth that your Petitioners apprehend that they have in Common with all other men a Natural and Unaliable right to that freedom which the Grat Parent of the Unavers hath Bestowed equalley on all menkind and which they have Never forfeited by any Compact or agreement whatever. . . .
>
> they Cannot but express their Astonishment that It have Never Bin Consirdered that Every Principle from which Amarica has Acted in the Cours of their unhappy Difficultes with Great Briton Pleads Stronger than A Thousand arguments in favours of your petioners that therfor humble Beseech your honours to give this petion its due weight & consideration & cause an act of the Legislatur to be past Wherby they may be Restored to the Enjoyments of that which is the Naturel Right of all men—and their Children who wher Born in this Land of Liberty may not be heald as Slaves.[15]

The slaves and the free Blacks petitioned but they were not heard. And so the young republic descended into the deepest of moral hypocrisies.

The Slaves' Revolution Continues

Slave conspiracies continued throughout the national period until the ending of the Civil War. Some, like the fabled Underground Railroad, succeeded admirably both in reality as well as in the popular imagination. Frequently credited with the emancipation of some 60,000 slaves, the "railroad" most frequently consisted of aid and protection extended by individual free Blacks and non-Black abolitionists to fugitives who had begun the journey to freedom on their own. But in "stations" like Cincinnati, Wilmington, Detroit, Sandusky, Erie, and Buffalo, particularly after the passage of the Fugitive Slave Law of 1850, abolitionist organizations like the Philadelphia and New York Vigilance Committee sprang up to provide support for the fugitives in their passage to Canada. Less characteristically, but the more remarkable for it, such "conductors" as the fugitives Harriet Tubman and Josiah Henson and the Quaker Levi Coffin organized and directed fugitives from the point of their escape to the safety of Canada. Henson's stature was somewhat diminished by his trading on the popular but erroneous belief that he was the model for Tom in Harriet Beecher Stowe's 1851 novel, *Uncle Tom's Cabin*. But his courage and practical sense were confirmed by his organizing of Dawn, a Black colony in present Ontario, and his forays into his native Kentucky to retrieve other fugitives.

Tubman, however, was the truly larger-than-life figure, born in 1820 or 1821 in Maryland. Small of stature, Tubman was yet a massive presence in the Black liberation struggle. Her own escape from slavery had been exhilarating: "I looked at my hands to see if I was the same person now I was free. There was such a glory over everything, the sun comes like gold through the trees." Before the Civil War, Tubman conducted nineteen "trains" out of the South, freeing some 300 slaves: "Her brothers and sisters, her aging parents and anyone else who wanted to go," according to Bennett.[16] As John Lovell, Jr., has recounted:

> In spite of redoubled patrols, in spite of increasing rewards which began at $1,000 and finally reached as high as $40,000 (at least $.5 million in today's currency), General Harriet kept returning to slave territory, kept bringing out slaves like some omniscient, unselfish, incomparably fearless and brave Pied Piper, kept marching them along to the tune of "Old Chariot," "Go Down Moses," "Steal Away," "The Gospel Train is Coming," "There's No Rain to Wet You," and "Didn't My Lord Deliver Daniel?" to freedom, to complete freedom on this earth, in Canada, if necessary.[17]

In 1859, in Troy, New York, Tubman effected the rescue of fugitive Charles Nalle by inciting a crowd and then locking her arms around his manacles. Nalle's lawyer, Martin Townsend, recorded that as the crowd surged and the police attempted to control their prisoner, Tubman "held on to him without even loosening her hold through the more than half-hour struggle. In the melee she was repeatedly beaten over the head with policemen's clubs, but she never for a moment released her hold."[18] Indomitable, the woman made plans that same year with John Brown to join him at Harper's Ferry; only illness prevented her from that martyrdom. It was just as well, because she got her chance to engage in greater militancy in the Civil War. During the conflict, Tubman employed her mastery of the terrain to guide and lead Union Army companies: "Working in South Carolina and other states, she organized slave intelligence networks behind enemy lines and led scouting raids. She also became the first and possibly the last woman to lead U.S. Army troops in battle."[19] And after the war, she established a center ("built a house") for freed men too old or sick to support themselves. Tubman and her colleagues were the actual railroad, their "stations" were often *ad hoc* rather than fixed. Nonetheless, from 1830 until the Civil War, the Black and majority press as well as Southern slave owners imagined the Underground Railroad as a vast national conspiracy. In truth, while thousands of free men and women were committed to the fugitives, it was the intelligence, desire, and courage of the fugitive slaves themselves that jolted the Underground Railroad into movement.

From 1800 on, the slave conspiracies took a rather nasty turn as far as the supporters of slavery were concerned. Unlike their counterparts in the colonial era and the Underground Railroad, the slaves began to conspire against the institution of slavery itself, starting with Gabriel's rebellion in Richmond. No longer content to escape the system, they now sought to destroy it.

In quiet colonial Louisiana—under Spanish rule from about 1769 to 1800—a slave conspiracy was discovered in Pointe Coupee in early July 1791. It was a small affair (some sixteen slaves were brought to trial) largely confined to the Mina (or Ewe) peoples in the settlement. What Gwendolyn Midlo Hall terms "a narrowly focused ethnic conspiracy involving slaves who belonged to small slave owners" would have been just another conspiracy were it not for the fact that it served as a staging ground for the Pointe Coupee Conspiracy of 1795.[20] In any case, the conspirators of 1791 were spared the excessive brutality of the French *code noir* by the intervention of Spanish colonial authorities anxious to demonstrate a more solicitous policy toward slaves and by the appearance in court of Antonio Cofi Mina, a former slave who had won his freedom in 1778. Antonio Cofi Mina acted as an interpreter for the accused. He was a resident of New Orleans, working as a shoemaker, and during the trials he constructed the defense that the confessed conspirators had not understood the language of their interrogators. Most were freed eventually, while Antonio Cofi Mina kept hidden from the court that he himself was the recognized leader of the Mina in the colony. All this would be revealed four years later: "During his trial in 1795, he testified that for over twenty years, all the Mina of the colony, even those he did not know, called him 'capitain'." (331)

The Pointe Coupee Conspiracy of 1795 was fueled by the Haitian Revolution (the earlier conspiracy in the settlement had occurred some months before the slave revolution in Haiti) and the abolition of slavery in February 1794 by the revolutionary French National Convention. The 1795 conspiracy appropriated the revolutionary momentum exploding in both France and the French West Indies. The possibility of successful conspiracy was created by the import of Haitian slaves into colonial Louisiana in the aftermath of the slave rebellion in Haiti, and then the appearance of Jacobin radicals:

> This internationalist, revolutionary effervescence among the lower classes led by seafarers, the *gens de mer*, washed up on the shores of Louisiana, radiating to New Orleans and along her major waterways. Louisiana was "blanketed with partisans of the revolution who came in many guises and colors. They appeared in the smallest outposts, among the clergy, in all the city's taverns, and among the immigrant merchant community. They were French, Saint-Domingan, and locally bred. They were white, brown, and black. . ." (348)

The influence of these ideologues was most apparent during the trials of the conspirators when slaves, free Blacks, and whites spoke knowledgeably about the rights of man, the abolition of slavery, and the resolve of colonial slaveowners to deceive the slaves about the actions of the revolutionary authorities in France. Led by, among others, Antoine Sarrasin, the Afro-Indian Creole (his mother, Marie Jeanne had sued for her own and her children's freedom in 1793 on the grounds that her mother was a pure Indian); Jean Baptist (like Sarrasin, from the Poydras estate); the English-speaking Capitain (a sixty-year-old Mande); and Antonio Cofi Mina, the conspiracy had been prepared for months by meetings in which news of the revolutions in Haiti and France, and the Declaration of the Rights of Man had become familiar discourse. (348ff.) Unlike the earlier plotters, the conspirators were drawn broadly from the slave community (the guilty included nine mulattos, twenty-six Creoles, and nineteen Africans) and included insurgents from Senegambia (five Bambara, four Fulbe, one Maniga) and the Western and Angola regions (two Mina, two Congo, two Chamba, one Ibo, one Caraba, and one Thoma). In April 1795, betrayed by a community of Tunica Indians apparently employed as spies among the slaves, fifty-seven slaves and three whites were arrested. Some twenty-five slaves were killed during the arrests. After the trials, twenty-three were hanged, their bodies decapitated, and the heads placed on poles along the Mississippi River from New Orleans to Pointe Coupee.[21] By then, the Spanish authorities were in no mood to compromise with a slave revolution informed by revolutionary creeds from Haiti and France.

In 1800, the Haitian Revolution was into its ninth year, and the revolutionary slaves and their mulatto allies were in control of most of the island. The news of the slave revolution was broadly available in the United States and particularly in Virginia. Three thousand French refugees from the island had evacuated to Norfolk by 1793; by 1795, 12,000 Haitian slaves had been transported to this country. In early 1794, responding to Haitian-led representations, the revolutionary French Convention abolished slavery. Of course, the struggle of St. Domingo's slaves both fascinated and terrified slaveholders, and it is not surprising that on May 16, 1800, the Fredericksburg *Virginia Herald* reported on the career of Toussaint L'Ouverture, the leader of the Haitian Revolution and a general commissioned by the French government. The war between Britain and France also dramatically intruded into American politics: the upcoming elections at the national and state levels pitted Francophiles like the Republicans Thomas Jefferson and James Monroe against the "British" party of President John Adams, Alexander Hamilton, and their Federalist friends. Increasingly anxious about the political furor occasioned by his war-like interventions on behalf of Britain, Adams pushed through the spurious Alien and Sedition Acts in 1798, and his administration began a series of draconian prosecutions against public misdemeanors (one drunk was jailed for not standing as the president rode by) and private behaviors (one member of Congress was convicted for comments in his personal correspondence). In Virginia, a Republican stronghold, Adams's enemies struck back. The assembly passed legislation (Vice President Jefferson was the anonymous author) encouraging other states to join in nullifying the acts as unconstitutional; the more extreme Republicans suggested secession. Indeed, a civil war appeared imminent only a little more than a decade into the new nation's history.[22]

In the midst of this tumult, the slaves in and around Richmond began to plan a general uprising. Led by Gabriel, a tall, powerful, literate bondsman born in 1776 on the tobacco plantation of Thomas Prosser, the plan for the insurrection spread from its origins among slave artisans to field hands. The plan also enlisted the aid of such resident aliens as the radical Frenchman Charles Quersey and the probably German Alexander Beddenhurst, and Lucas, a non-Black worker. Gabriel envisioned the conspiracy as the promised realization of the American Revolution, the struggle of oppressed workers as well as slaves against the "merchants." Gabriel committed his followers to this vision. As Douglas Egerton relates:

> Their revolt need not be the prelude to a race war; the black and white insurgents he expected to recruit would spark a class struggle that had a recognized purpose and might force specific concessions from the state authorities. "Quakers, the Methodists, and [all] Frenchmen . . . were to be spared," Gabriel insisted, on account of "their being friendly to liberty." The blacksmith "intended also to spare the poor white women who had no slaves." (49)

From the spring of 1800, Gabriel and his older and younger brothers, Martin and Solomon, enlisted men like the giant slave Jack (the) Ditcher from among the slave and freemen workers in the tobacco storehouses in Richmond and the plantations in southern Henrico county. On the day of the "business," a powerful storm broke, impeding the planned gathering of the conspirators. The insurrectionists were betrayed. Some of the conspirators resisted arrest, but most fled only to be captured by the mobilized state militia and armed vigilantes. Twenty-six of the revolutionists, including Gabriel, Martin, and Solomon, were hanged before the judicial frenzy ended in November ($8,899.91 was paid in compensation to their owners). On Vice President Jefferson's advice ("there is a strong sentiment that there has been hanging enough"), nine were "transported" to Louisiana (New Orleans). But the plot was found to be so extensive that the trials were suspended on October 13. According to the *Commercial Advertiser* on October 13, 1800, "this measure is said to be owing to the immense numbers, who are implicated in the plot." One of those who survived was Sancho, a Black ferry operator on the James and Roanoke rivers. In 1802, he resumed the conspiracy, extending it to North Carolina by employing his network of contacts among the mariner community. The plot was discovered and ten conspirators were hanged in Virginia, fifteen more in North Carolina.

In 1811, the slaves in Louisiana mounted another major revolt against slavery. Indeed, the nineteenth-century historian, Francois-Xavier Martin, described the formation of a virtual slave army:

> The slaves of a plantation, in the parish of St. John the Baptist . . . revolted and were immediately joined by those of several neighboring plantations. They marched along the river, towards the city [New Orleans], divided into

companies, each under an officer, with beat of drums and flags displayed, compelling the blacks they met to fall in their rear; and before they could be checked, set fire to the houses of four or five plantations. Their exact number was never ascertained, but asserted to be about five hundred.[23]

Again, mulattos were prominent in the revolt. One of them, Charles Deslonde, and another slave, Jupiter, were among the leaders.[24] Though poorly armed, the slave army drew the attentions of a United States detachment in Baton Rouge, a New Orleans militia led by General Wade Hampton (South Carolina), and a settler militia. Sixty-six insurgents were killed in the confrontation, and another sixteen executed after short trials in New Orleans. "Their heads were placed on high poles, above and below the city, and along the river as far as the plantation on which the revolt began, and on those on which they had committed devastation." (349)

The slaves of South Carolina were active as well. In September 1800, during the first weeks of the trials of Gabriel's comrades, the area outside of Charleston experienced an uprising during which several citizens were killed. In June 1816, another conspiracy was uncovered, this time in Camden. Six years after, on May 30, 1822, Denmark Vessey, a sixty-year-old freeman, was betrayed as the head of a planned insurrection. Denmark (originally named Telemaque) was a Charleston carpenter who had lived as a freeman for twenty-two years. Originally from the island of St. Thomas, Denmark had been enslaved for a time in Haiti (around 1781). San Domingo proved to inspire Denmark's work. According to one of his comrades, Jack (a slave owned by Purcell), "He was in the habit of reading to me all the passages in the newspapers that related to St. Domingo." Denmark assured his friends that Haiti would aid their insurrection and provide them asylum. However, Gullah Jack, another conspirator, relied on alternative resources. Deemed a necromancer during his trial, Jack was from Angola where he had specialized as a "conjurer and physician." At the conclusion of his trial, the court seemed particularly incensed at this man who, after "fifteen or twenty years in this country . . . appeared to be untouched by the influences of civilized life."

In the prosecution of your wicked designs, you were not satisfied with resorting to natural and ordinary means, but endeavored to enlist on your behalf, all the powers of darkness, and employed for that purpose, the most disgusting mummery and superstition. You represented yourself as invulnerable; that you could neither be taken nor destroyed, and that all who fought under your banners would be invincible. . . . Your boasted Charms have not preserved yourself, and of course could not protect others. "Your Altars and your Gods have sunk together in the dust." The airy spectres, conjured by you, have been chased away by the special light of Truth, and you stand exposed, the miserable and deluded victim of offended Justice.[25]

Nevertheless, it was concluded that most of the conspirators were members of the "African Church" (the secessionist Methodist Episcopal Church).

Denmark and the other leaders of the conspiracy, Ned (Bennett), Peter (Poyas), William (Garner), Rolla and Batteau (also the property of Governor Bennett), and Jesse (Blackwood), did their recruiting from among the skilled slaves and free Black artisans of Charleston, the slave shopkeepers, and domestics. Jesse's confession summarized their mission: "[Denmark] said, we were deprived of our rights and privileges by the white people, and that our church was shut up, so that we could not use it, and that it was high time for us to seek for our rights, and that we were fully able to conquer the whites, if we were only unanimous and courageous, as the St. Domingo people were." The scale of the trials reveals that the conspiracy was as extensive as the Gabriel and Sancho rebellions: 131 conspirators were tried. Thirty-five were hanged; thirty-four were sentenced to banishment, nine were acquitted but banished, and fifty-two acquitted and discharged.

Joshua Coffin wrote that at New Bern, Hillsboro, and Tarboro in North Carolina, insurrections were uncovered in 1826. "The people of Newbern, being informed that forty slaves were assembled in a swamp, surrounded it, and killed the whole party!!" But the discomfort of these citizens was nothing compared to that of their countrymen in Southampton, Virginia, five years later.

Gabriel, Denmark, and their countless predecessors had been intelligent, cunning, and rhetorically powerful figures, but in 1831 a truly charismatic leader emerged from the slave social order. Gabriel was a resistance leader and Denmark had been a preacher, but Nat (Turner) was a prophet. Nat signaled the appearance of a new historical, psychological, and cultural phenomenon, a personality forged from a cultural fusion coincidental to the enslavement of Africans in the New World. Many accused slaves had only court lawyers for their perfunctory trials; Nat's lawyer was a William Parker. But Thomas Gray, an enterprising lawyer who had no official role in the trial, sought and received permission from the jailer to interview Nat. Gray's intervention provided us with "The Confession of Nat Turner," one of the most important historical documents of American slavery. Since the document originated from an accused slave rather than an accused Boston Brahmin or Virginian plantocrat, historians have agreed that it was a "confession" and not a "declaration" (even though, at his trial, Nat pleaded "not guilty"). But if one were to employ the terms interchangeably, many similarities link the Declaration of 1776 and the Confession of 1831: They both were authored by insurgents, gave a narrative to the imperative for action, and constructed a moral universe within which their authors actions were just. What was "self-evident" to the American rebels was equally sensible to Nat: "I had too much sense to be raised, and if I was, I would never be of any use to anyone as a slave."

In Nat's consciousness, as he revealed to Gray, one could discern the cultural materials of the messianic narratives of Christianity and African beliefs in the transmigration of the soul, the coincidence of moral order and genuine authority, and what Michel Foucault would term the "archaeology of knowledge." But Nat's warrant came from God and the Holy Spirit. Nat's African-born mother and father read the marks on his head and breast as confirming that the child was a prophet who could both recount tales of events before his birth as well as foretell the future. His grandmother taught him he could "never be of any use to anyone as a slave." As a child, Nat provided other signs: his voracious appetite for knowledge ("there was nothing that I saw or heard of to which my attention was not directed"), his spontaneous acquisition of literacy ("I have no recollection whatever of learning the alphabet, but, to the astonishment of the family, one day when a book was shown to me to keep me from crying, I began spelling the names of different objects"), and his treatment by other children ("they would often carry me with them when they were going on any roguery, to plan for them"). All these instances were the signatures of destiny and impressed his family, his community, and Nat himself. "Having soon discovered to be great, I must appear so, and therefore studiously avoided mixing in society and wrapped myself in mystery, devoting my time to fasting and prayer."

Several years before the August 1831 rebellion, Nat began to experience visions and inner voices. While at the plow, the spirit spoke to him: "Seek ye the kingdom of Heaven and all things will be added onto you." Having reached maturity according to the reckoning of slave discipline, Nat was now placed under an overseer. He promptly ran away, spending thirty days in the wilderness before returning. The other slaves, thinking he had made a successful escape, ridiculed him for coming back. Then visions began coming that foretold his purpose: scenes of battles between black and white spirits. Nat was told to look for "the signs," and the spirit reminded him "of the things it had already shown me, and that it would then reveal to me the knowledge of the elements, the revolutions of the planets, the operation of tides, and changes of the seasons." All around him the spirit constantly gave him encouragement: drops of blood on the corn, hieroglyphic writings and numbers in blood on leaves, and more visions. Meanwhile, he preached to the slaves, converted a white man through miracles, and waited. The eclipse of the sun in February of 1831 was the final signature of the Holy Spirit.[26]

On August 22, sixty to eighty slaves and free Blacks rose up to join Nat. For two days they ravaged Southampton, killing some fifty-five adults and children of the slave-holding classes. Lovell comments:

> To read the Southern papers for the summer and fall of 1831, from the time when Nat Turner's murderous assaults were first reported, is to receive a lesson in the ways the Southerners had of terrifying themselves. The long weeks when Nat could not be found were a period of fearful excitement all over the South. Not just that he had to be caught and hanged, but who knew when he would explode from some nearby swamp and strike again?[27]

But the terror was not all rhetoric. The Navy and Federal troops were mobilized along with Virginia's militia; between them and the mobs, several hundred Blacks were massacred, hundreds of others terrorized. In the *Richmond Whig*, the editor wrote that "men were tortured to death, burned, maimed and subjected to nameless atrocities."[28] Mrs. Lawrence Lewis, a niece of George Washington, wrote to the mayor of Boston: "It is like a smothered volcano—we know not when, or where, the flame will burst forth but we know that death in the most horrid forms threaten us. Some have died, others have become deranged from apprehension since the South Hampton affair." For more than two months, Nat avoided capture, but eventually he surrendered. The trials of his confederates (including one Black woman, Lucy Barrow, who was hanged) had begun in September, before he was caught, and ended with his own on November 5. In 1831 and the next year, the state legislatures renewed their bans on teaching literacy to slaves, on possession of books by slaves, on preaching by slaves, and on prayer by slaves, banishing anything that might fortify slave knowledge and resolve. One satisfied Virginia legislator declared: "We have, as far as possible, closed every avenue by which light might enter their minds"(Coffing 33). He was in error.

Until the Civil War and even more so during it, slave fugitives were an everyday phenomenon in the slaveholding states. Some of those who escaped were caught and returned, some were killed, some committed suicide, and some became the reality of the Underground Railroad. Still others went not to the North and Canada, but remained in the local forests and swamps. Maroon communities continued to be a vibrant alternative for the slaves, frequently providing inspiration and support for nearby revolts. Herbert Aptheker documented their nineteenth-century presence: in 1818, in Princess Anne County, Virginia, and Wake County, North Carolina; in 1819, in Williamsburg County, South Carolina; in 1820, in Gates County, North Carolina; in 1821 near Georgetown, South Carolina, and in Onslow, Carteret, and Bladen counties in North Carolina (reputedly led by a slave named Isam who took the nom de guerre General Jackson); in 1822, in South Carolina (fugitives from Jacksonborough gathered who might have been followers of Denmark); in 1823 in Norfolk, Virginia, ("lurking assassins" harassed by killings and written threats); in 1827, in Mobile County, Alabama ("A maroon community consisting of men, women, and children was broken up by a three-day attack made by armed slaveholders of Mobile County, Alabama": the fugitives were building a stockade fort at the time of the attack); in 1830, in Bladen and Onslow counties in North Carolina (maroons once again were reported, fueling "uncontrollable" slaves in Sampson, Jones, New Hanover, and Dublin counties, and establishing camps in the Dover Swamp, on Gastons Island, and on Price's Creek); in 1836 and 1837, in the Cypress Swamp near New Orleans, (Black outlaws were credited with the deaths of several white men); in 1841 in Wilmington, North Carolina ("Armed runaways repulsed an attack after killing one of the whites"); again in 1841, about forty-five miles outside Mobile and in Terrebonne Parish in Louisiana (where fugitives were attacking whites); in 1844, near Hanesville, Mississippi (maroons were ambushed); in 1846, in St. Landry Parish, Louisiana ("a considerable gang of runaway Negroes" was surprised); in 1856 in the large swamp between Bladen and Robeson counties in North Carolina (the governor was informed that a "secure retreat" of maroons for several years had existed and when it was besieged, "the negroes ran off cursing and swearing and telling them to come on, they were ready for them again"); in 1857, near Bovina, Mississippi (authorities did succeed in destroying a Black camp); in 1859 in Nash County, North Carolina (a similar success was reported); and in 1860 in Talladega County, Alabama (an "'organized camp of white men and Negroes' was held responsible for a servile conspiracy, involving whites, which was uncovered").[29]

But unlike the visions presented by Gabriel and Nat Turner, these incidents, in practical terms, constituted resistances to slavery rather than attempts to overthrow the social order. Of course, they had impact and significance. For the slaves, acts of resistance and the lore that swelled around them in tales and songs provided the integument of a Black culture, the materials for a historical consciousness and a sense of community, and a moral system for determining how the lord of the cosmos negotiated the existence of good and evil. These new narratives provided them with stories for their children's instruction, a way of using lessons from the New World's experiences to flesh out the catechisms of their older traditions. For parents, employing intelligence and creativity was necessary in training children to survive. Both adults and the young had to invent the means of preserving terrains of autonomy and dignity in the face of the intrusive oppressions of slavery. Thus, in a social order obsessed with domination and the policing of the spirit, resistance was the antithetical core, the soul of Black life. But the secret languages, the furtive acts, even the covert taxes on non-Blacks exacted through sarcasm, word-play, indirection, and humor were not sufficient to themselves. They required a more outrageous space at their source. As Frantz Fanon would recognize a century later, a monstrous center of overt acts was imperative: murdering masters paid so much more handsomely in the social-psychology of the slave community than work slowdowns or breaking tools. The enveloping violence of conspiracies and rebellions, thus, provided the most profit of all. There was, however, a higher plane of political consciousness. Ironically enough, it was most deliberately arrived at by slaves largely associated with Georgia, the state whose colonial origins were the most ambivalent toward slavery.

The War of 1812 reinvigorated the alliance between Blacks, Native Americans, and Britain. But by then the Native American ethnographic subdivisions enlisted two new amalgamations of peoples, the Creek and the Seminole nations. Incited by the British proclamation of 1763, the historian J. Leitch Wright, Jr., reports that British authorities "insisted that most of the Muscogulges belonged to the Creek nation. . . . In this same fashion British authorities made an increasing number of Muscogulges in Florida admit that they were Seminoles."[30] But each of the terms was a derivative, an invention to stabilize the fluidity of migrations and marronage encouraged by native and colonial wars: *Muskogee* was an Algonquian word for "people of the swampy ground": that is, the Yuchis, Alabamas, Shawnees, Tuskegees, and others who in southern migrations had joined the Coweta, Kasihta, Coosa, and Abihka; *Creek* was an English reference to the topography of the southeastern territory; and *Seminole* was the closest pronunciation the Hitchiti-speaking Oconees, who originated from the Georgia tidewater, could give to the Spanish *Cimarron* when encountering English speakers in their new Florida domicile. (3–6) Eventually, each term was adapted to include the arrivals of fugitive Africans and Blacks among them: the terms Lower Creek, Black Muscogulges, and Black Seminoles would become signatures of African–Native American settlements.

In the War of 1812, British officers in Florida revisited the stratagem introduced by Lord Dunmore during the American War of Independence:

> Freeing southern slaves seemed appropriate, and British commanders encouraged Negroes—and Creeks and Seminoles—to rally around King George. During the conflict several hundred Negro soldiers could be seen drilling in the streets of Pensacola or at the British (Negro) fort on the Apalachicola River. They, the Indians, and a few British troops were to invade Georgia's interior and liberate the slaves. This project and the attack on New Orleans failed, and in 1815, at the conclusion of the war, Britain withdrew her forces from the Gulf and Atlantic coasts. Disbanded soldiers remained on the scene, however, still arming and drilling Negroes, Creeks, and Seminoles, still helping them to protect or recover their lands. (92–93)

Negro Fort at Prospect Bluff on the Apalachicola River survived, serving as a rallying point for slave fugitives in Florida and potential fugitives on plantations in Georgia. The fort was largely occupied by some three hundred Spanish-speaking Blacks originating from Pensacola. Its commander was a Black man named Garcia. Above and below the fort, extending for fifty miles along the river, Black fugitives from the American plantations established farming settlements. Encouraged by Georgia planters, the American general, Andrew Jackson, ordered an attack on the fort in July 1816. "I have little doubt of the fact, that this fort has been established by some villains for the purpose of rapine and plunder . . . destroy it and return the stolen Negroes and property to their rightful owners."[31] The fort and nearly all of its inhabitants were destroyed by the American expedition, but the Blacks in the settlements escaped. Many of them fled to the Seminoles on the Suwannee River, coming under the protection of chief "Bowlegs" and his heir Mikonopi (Micanopy), and they reconstituted their farming settlements in several Black villages like Pilaklikaha.[32] Thus began the First Seminole War (1816—no treaty), which was largely suspended after Bowlegs's Town was sacked in 1818 (its inhabitants and their surrounding dependencies had already evacuated deeper into Florida).

One of the refugees from Negro Fort was Abraham, a slave whose origins have been traced to Pensacola by Kenneth Wiggins Porter. Upon his arrival in Bowlegs's Town, Abraham became a dependent, "slave," or vassal of Micanopy. As part of the Seminole delegation to Washington, D.C., in 1825–26, Abraham accompanied Micanopy as his interpreter. Upon their return to Florida, Abraham's dependency was ended, and during the Second Seminole War (1835–42) he was to distinguish himself as a war counselor and warrior. This war was precipitated by General Jackson's constant ambition to remove all Native Americans west of the Mississippi into Indian Territory (present-day Oklahoma) to the benefit of slaveholders in Georgia, Alabama, and South Carolina; farmers in Illinois and Wisconsin; and American settlers in Florida.

In 1830, the Congress enacted the Indian Removal Act, supplying now President Jackson (1829–37) with the legal tool to realize his imperial and economic interests. Already experienced in the diplomatic contrivances and legalistic trickery habitual to American officials in their conduct with natives, the majority of the Seminole opposed removal and chose war. The Blacks among them provided the most obdurate opposition to removal. Joshua Giddings, the abolitionist congressman who published his *Exiles of Florida* in 1858, discovered in his research that the highest-ranking American officers recognized their strategic predicament: "These and other officers of Government united in the opinion, that these '*negroes*,' as they were generally called, exerted a controlling influence over the Indians, and that it would be in vain to attempt the removal of the Indians under these circumstances."[33]

Osceola, the principal Seminole war chieftain, was reputedly part Black, and one of his wives was Black. Wright informs us that

> For whatever reason Seminole-Negroes deeply concerned Osceola. As whites saw it, Osceola and the Seminoles were refractory in part because of the Negro influence. . . . Blacks at the Negro Fort on the Apalachicola River, even some of those . . . taken back to Georgia and sold, in one fashion or another made their way to the Seminole country, never forgetting what the Negro Fort had symbolized.[34]

Certainly Abraham was among the latter, pushing and cajoling the lethargic Micanopy into resisting to removal. Indeed, in the enemy American camp, he was repeatedly accused of controlling his chief. "Abraham, who is sometimes dignified with the title of 'Prophet' . . . is the prime minister and privy counselor of Micanopy; and has through his master, who is somewhat imbecile, ruled all the councils and actions of the Indians in this region," noted one American officer. "We have a perfect Talleyrand of the Savage Court in the person of a Seminole Negro, called Abraham," wrote another.[35] General Thomas Jessup, one of the American commanders in the Second Seminole War, had no illusions about it. "This, you may be assured, is a Negro, not an Indian war," he wrote in 1836, "and if it be not speedily put down, the South will feel the effects of it on their slave population before the end of the next season."[36] Giddings succinctly concurred: "The Exiles endeavored to stimulate the Indians to deeds of valor. In general council, they decreed that the first Seminole who should make any movement preparatory to emigration, should suffer death."[37]

The Native American response to the Indian Removal Act was mixed. The Cherokee and many of the Creek in Georgia undertook the Trail of Tears (with their Black slaves and dependents) to Indian Territory in the early 1830s, but the Sac and Fox in Illinois and Wisconsin (involved in the Black Hawk War), some of the Creek, and thousands of the Seminole responded by guerrilla warfare. The Seminole proved to be the most formidable force because of their tactics, and the United States prosecuted the war at the eventual expense of $40 million and the deaths of some 1,500 troops. The keys to the Seminoles' protracted resistance were the plantations and the swamps. Black Seminoles like Abraham, Cudjo, Ino, Gopher John Cavallo, and John Caesar recruited slaves to the war from the plantations of Georgia. Abraham also directly commanded five hundred Black warriors while enjoying considerable influence over Micanopy and his allied chiefs. John Caesar, who must have been near sixty when the war began, was equally influential with his own chief, Emathla (King Phillip to the Americans), the second in authority to Micanopy and his brother-in-law. After Emathla had withdrawn from the fray, John Caesar campaigned with other Black guerrillas (among them the fugitives Andrew Gay and Stephen Hernandez, and the free Black Joe Merritt) in the vicinity of St. Augustine until his death in January 1837.[38]

General Jessup concluded his first "peace" with the Seminole in March 1837, persuading Abraham and several Seminole chiefs that both the Seminoles and their allies in the war would be allowed to emigrate together to Indian Territory. Abraham was employed as a surveyor of the Seminole section in the Creek Reservation of the Territory and was delegated to persuade other Black Seminoles to surrender. He remained in the Florida region until 1839, when he and his family were transported west. He was returned to Florida in 1852 to assist in the persuasion of still-recalcitrant Seminoles, visiting New York before his return to the Territory where he died sometime after 1870.[39] However, under pressure from officials in Washington and Florida slaveholders, Jessup reneged on allowing other Black Seminoles to emigrate, attacking those whom Abraham and others had failed to influence. The war was renewed by Black subchiefs like John Cavallo and Tony Barnett, and Seminole chiefs like old Arpeika and Wild Cat, all of them persisting in the recruitment of slaves from the plantations. Their surrenders were realized later in 1837 or by 1839, but others remained in the field until the early 1840s. Eventually, the resistance groups had been reduced to such small bands that the U.S. commanders declared an end to hostilities in 1842.

In the Indian Territory, militant Seminole and Black Seminole leaders continued their struggle. In 1850, Cavallo and Wild Cat fled with their followers into Mexico, where they served for ten years in military campaigns against Mexican Indians (most returned to the Territory in 1861, but some founded the town of Nacimiento de los Negros in Coahuila). During the American Civil War, the Seminole split their loyalties between the Confederates and the Union: the pro-Confederate group emigrated to Kansas and enslaved their Black fellows; the pro-Union group resettled near Fort Gibson in the Cherokee Reservation. The Blacks returned after the war, founding settlements in the northern part of the reservation with their comrades from Fort Gibson. In 1866 they were granted as Seminole Freedmen "all the rights and privileges accruing to tribal members."[40] Ironically, they would reappear in history as Indian fighters in the American wars against the Apache and Comanche (1873–1881), their scouts winning four Medals of Honor.[41] Presently, the descendants of the Black Seminoles are found in Mexico, Texas, Oklahoma, Florida, and on Andros Island in the Bahamas (refugees from the First Seminole War).

In one sense, then, the Second Seminole War was the most extreme resistance to slavery, eventually transporting some of the rebellious Black slaves into an American identity. In the attempt to distance themselves from slavery, and to destroy the United States if possible, the Black Seminoles first allied with Native Americans. But in the end they negotiated their own freedom at the expense of Indians. Their courage and intelligence were exemplified at both extremes of the continent, in Florida and in the Southwest, but eventually Black slaves succumbed to the most narrow construction of their historical and social identity. One could effectively argue, however, that they did the best they could given the circumstances: they fought an unwinnable war and in the process salvaged thousands of Black and Native American lives from the horror of the slave plantations. They bequeathed a legacy, ultimately, of brave loyalty to a United States different than the one they opposed. On that score they were superior to the patriots who employed the might of the American government against the Seminole for their own selfish ends. In that sense, they never descended to the moral degradation and hypocrisy of the governing classes, made so rich by the blood of slaves.

Having reviewed the slaves and their most visible resistances to tyranny, we now must attend to free Blacks of the early national period. While many fewer in number than their slave counterparts, they had the task of bringing into intellectual focus the contradictions of American slavery and American freedom.

CHAPTER THREE

Free Blacks and Resistance

*   *   *

If any wish to plunge me into the wretched incapacity of a slave, or murder me for the truth, know ye, that I am in the hand of God, and at your disposal. . . . For what is the use of living, when in fact I am dead.

—*David Walker's Appeal to the Coloured Citizens of the World*

Beyond the immediate world of the slaves and the slaveholders, the response to slavery and racial oppression in the pre–Civil War period took many and sometimes conflicting forms. In the diverse communities where free Blacks and fugitive slaves resided, all manner of opinion was possible save indifference. The same must be said of non-Blacks, even among those who opposed slavery. The range of contradiction in these two parts of the nation's political culture was represented, at one extreme, by those free Blacks in Louisiana who themselves owned slaves and, at another, by the insurrectionary army of whites, free Blacks, and fugitive slaves gathered by John Brown at Harper's Ferry in 1859. Some Blacks supported colonization to Africa, more opposed it; some Blacks planned and executed emigration to the West Indies or Canada; more opposed it. Some antislavery northern whites endorsed the social and political equality of Blacks; a few prominent Federalists (for examples, Chief Justice John Jay, Vice President Daniel Tompkins, Treasury Secretary Alexander Hamilton) joined such associations as the New York Manumission Society dedicated to the legal defense of fugitive slaves; still others like John Quincy Adams, the former president, secretary of state, and member of Congress, assisted in the defense of the Mendi mutiny on board the *Amistad* in 1840–1841; but the majority of whites in the antislavery camp merely opposed the further expansion of slavery into the West. In short, there were only local consensus. In the absence of any more exact evidence, we can surmise that the vast majority of Blacks opposed slavery, while whites were divided by class, religion, and region on the question of support for the system.[1] As Edmund Morgan has suggested, slavery was profoundly interwoven with the popular and public perception of the identity of the new country.

Among those opposed to slavery—the abolitionists, as they were called—one strain of thought was that the Constitution of the United States institutionally and judicially embraced slavery: William Lloyd Garrison, one of the most influential and prominent of the white abolitionists, saw the Constitution as a proslavery instrument and all political parties as necessarily proslavery parties.[2] Generally recognized by their contemporaries as part of the extreme wing of the antislavery movement, Garrisonians dismissed political organizing and, eventually, championed the dissolution of the federal polity. According to Stephen Symonds Foster, a Garrisonian, the Constitution's encoding of slavery into its articles on representation, taxation, and interstate commerce had subordinated national power to the South:

> [The South] commands our armies. It controls our treasury. It dictates law to our judges. It expounds the gospel to our churches. It has bound the conscience of the nation by an oath to participate in its crimes, and thereby rendered its opposition impossible, or powerless. At its command we trample the law of God under our feet, and refuse to hide the outcast. Thus has it made us at once a nation of atheists and an empire of slaves.[3]

On the other hand, there were those whom Robert Cover has called the "Constitutional Utopians." Gerritt Smith, Garrison's most ardent abolitionist critic and rival, and Frederick Douglass, the most famous fugitive slave (who did not break with Garrison until the late 1840s), argued that the Constitution outlawed slavery.[4] Federal courts, they urged, would provide legitimacy to abolitionist activists and eventually judicial rulings would destroy slavery. That this was utopian was revealed when James Madison's notes on the Constitutional Convention were published for the first time in 1840. As Staughton Lynd puts it, the convention's records made it obvious that the delegates had deliberately manufactured "a sordid sectional compromise" with slavery. They had knowingly produced a Constitution that one of them, Luther Martin, had characterized as an *"insult to that God . . . who views with equal eye the poor African slave and his American master."*[5]

Nevertheless, in 1860, while opposing Foster's urgings of revolution and Garrison's plea for a dissolution of the Union, Douglass declared:

> I have much confidence in the instincts of the slaveholders. They see that the Constitution will afford slavery no protection when it shall cease to be administered by slaveholders. . . . [T]here is no word, no syllable in the Constitution to forbid that result. . . . There was one Free State at the beginning of the Government: there are eighteen now. . . . Within the Union we have a firm basis of opposition to slavery. It is opposed to all the great objects of the Constitution. . . . My position now is one of reform, not of revolution. I would act for the abolition of slavery through the Government—not over its ruins.[6]

Douglass was, of course, correct that reform had been consequential: gradual abolition had been enacted successively in Vermont (1777), Massachusetts/Maine (1780), Pennsylvania (1780), New Hampshire (1783), Rhode Island and Connecticut (1784), New York (1799), and New Jersey (1804). But these triumphs were less an opposition to slavery than a resolve by merchants and manufacturers to inaugurate a purer capitalism dependent on wage labor.

Douglass was mistaken, then, to believe that it was the moral authority or even the internal logic of the Constitution that compelled these changes. The Supreme Court's Chief Justice, Roger B. Taney, for one, perceived nothing remotely like opposition to slavery in the Constitution when in 1857 he rendered his Dred Scott decision that Blacks "were not regarded as a portion of the people or citizens of the Government then formed."[7] And Douglass and Smith, both indicted by Virginia authorities for their complicity in the John Brown affair, were not wholly candid in their public professions on behalf of legal methods. By 1860, the sectional conflict between the North and the South, at base a contest between two forms of property and commerce, required an extreme government policy. Thus, the oppositions to slavery that had earlier propelled the nation toward revolution or reform, and that were grounded on alternative and contradictory conceptions of America, had alarmed the rulers of the South to the point of revolution.

Abolition and Free Blacks

Abolitionism can be said to have manifested itself in three phases: the elitist phase, militant-populist phase, and the revolutionary phase. These transitions were not neatly chronological nor did the body of abolitionists cohere as factions metamorphosed from one tendency to another while others strengthened or dissipated. Abolitionism and abolitionists changed. In the American Revolutionary era, the most visible abolitionist societies first appeared in the urban centers of the North: Philadelphia in 1775, New York in 1785, and so on. In 1794, five of these societies coalesced into the national organization, the American Convention for Promoting the Abolition of Slavery and Improving the Condition of the African Race. This formal, organized opposition to slavery was led by an educated and largely wealthy elite drawn from the ranks of both the merchant and manufacturing capitalists. For half a century, these moderate leaders created and sought to maintain a sedate antislavery, projecting the end of slavery as the result of a gradual process of moral (that is, Christian) "suasion" rather than by force or insurrection. But, as the abolitionist movement acquired deeper and different social roots, its ideology changed. By the 1830s, the movement drew much of its white membership from the rural rather than urban areas (thus embracing small Ohio communities like that of Owen Brown's, the father of John Brown); and the numbers and resources of free Blacks in the North were sufficient for some to emerge as the movement's new leaders. The growing domination of these social elements produced a second, militant, abolitionist movement, signaled by the appearances of organizations that used the term "Anti-Slavery" to distinguish their militancy from the moderate "abolitionist" organizations of the first period.

In its rural redoubts and small towns of the North and South (Louis Filler recounts that in 1827, 106 of 130 antislavery societies were in slave states), a largely religious opposition to slavery achieved some modest impact on opinion and cultivated some rather remarkable white adherents (Benjamin Lundy, Frances Wright, Angelina and Sarah Grimke, Lydia Maria Child, John Rankin, and Elihu Embree, to name some).[8] Some were poets, others early suffragettes, others merchants, and two (the Grimkes) the children of eminent slaveholders. More, however, were small farmers, quietly pursuing the dictates of their consciences.

Religious principles, however, pushed some of these white abolitionists into "precipitous" action; specifically, actions the laws of several slave states signified as "slave stealing." For example, in 1841 three members of the Mission Institute in Quincy, Illinois—Alanson Work, James E. Burr, and George Thompson—crossed the Mississippi River into Missouri to encourage slaves to escape. The three were betrayed and sentenced to twelve years in the state penitentiary for slave stealing (they were pardoned in 1846). In June of 1844, Charles Torrey, the editor of the *Albany*

Patriot and a Congregationalist minister, was arrested in Baltimore for assisting slaves to escape. He was sentenced to six years in the state penitentiary, where he died of tuberculosis in 1846. In September of 1844, Reverend Calvin Fairbank (of the Methodist Church) and Delia Webster, the principal of the Lexington Female Academy in Kentucky, were apprehended by a Kentucky posse after the two had rescued Lewis Hayden and his family. Fairbank was sentenced to hard labor for fifteen years, Webster was given a two-year sentence. Webster was pardoned after serving two months; but Fairbank, pardoned in 1849 (Hayden led the campaign), was arrested again in 1851 for "abducting" a female slave and remained in the penitentiary for thirteen years, until 1864. Johnathan Walker, a sailor and shipwright, was also arrested in 1844 after he returned from Cape Cod to his former home in Pensacola, Florida, in order to escort his former slaves to freedom. He was imprisoned for a year (his fine of $600 was paid by abolitionists) and had the letters SS (slave stealer) branded on his hand. In 1848, William L. Chaplin, Torrey's successor at the *Patriot* and a lawyer, was implicated in the escape of seventy-seven slaves being transported to freedom aboard the schooner *Pearl*. The schooner was intercepted, and its captain Edward Sayres and his coconspirator Daniel Drayton were convicted and fined $20,000 (they received pardons in 1852). Chaplin was not indicted, but in August 1850, while assisting two escaped slaves from Washington, he was arrested and charged with "larceny of slaves."[9] While their actions were short of John Brown's guerrilla war, these "fanatics," "extremists," nevertheless put their lives on the line. And the Black abolitionists honored them, along with their own: Tubman, Hayden, William Still, David Ruggles, the imprisoned Leonard Grimes, Elijah Anderson, Samuel Burris, Oswald Wright, and Samuel Green.[10]

Johnathan Walker was reputed to have friends among his slaves with whom he behaved "on terms of perfect equality with his family"; Fairbank preached in Black churches; and Torrey attended only Black churches in Washington and was active in the Black community in Philadelphia.[11] But with these few exceptions, the whites who opposed slavery were not conspicuous in their sympathies for Blacks. Leon Litwack writes, "It was possible to be both 'antislavery' and anti-Negro," a reality obvious to many observers.[12] The Black Philadelphian abolitionist, Sarah Forten, gave some contemporary evidence of this when she "recalled a white friend who told her that when walking with a Negro 'the darker the night, the better Abolitionist was I'" (139).

What was generally true of the abolition movement was, of course, even more transparently present in the slaveholder aristocracy. Indeed, it was a hatred of the Black that caused some members of the Southern ruling class to hatch the most radical scheme to prolong slavery: African colonization. Not surprisingly, colonization attracted broad support and even Congressional approval.

> [In December 1816] there was a meeting in Washington, composed almost entirely of Southerners. Judge Bushrod Washington . . . presided. Present also were Henry Clay, John Randolph of Roanoke, and others of mark. They set up the American Society for Colonizing the Free People of Colour of the United States, and in the face of skepticism quickly built up impressive support.[13]

Unlike the religious enterprise that characterized abolition, this scheme was engendered by those who despised Blacks, particularly free Blacks. Whatever the intrinsic merits of emigration, it was now sullied by association with some of the most rapine racists in the nation. This backing, however, was not sufficient to doom the plan, as a federal allocation of $100,000 substantiated. What scuttled colonization was that it achieved no consensus among the plantocrats, the class that had spawned it. The presence of free Blacks provided moral legitimacy to the paternalistic pretensions of the slave order, and their social and economic roles subsidized the slave economy and the ruling of slaves. Moreover, colonization offended the leadership among the free Blacks: the wealthy James Forten and his actively abolitionist daughters, Sarah and Margaret, and granddaughter, Charlotte; such prominent ministers as Absalom Jones, John Gloucester, and Peter Williams; and, among professionals, the equally impressive blind hydrotherapist, David Ruggles.[14] Some of these spokespersons even castigated Harriet Beecher Stowe for having one of her heroic Black characters in *Uncle Tom's Cabin* emigrate to Liberia. (220–21) Later, by the 1850s, some would be forced by circumstance into changing their minds about emigration (two of the most significant being Henry Highland Garnet and Martin Delany), but in the late 1820s and early 1830s, free Blacks were poised to make claims on their rights as American citizens.

The Black Abolitionists

According to the official census, by 1830 there were nearly 320,000 free Blacks in the country (compared to over 2,009,000 slaves), almost half of them residing in the northern and western states, which had abolished or were ending slavery. But, if the rate of increase is taken as a measure of the well-being of the free Black population, then it must be surmised that their lives were hard: over the next three decades, while the slave population nearly doubled to 3,953,000 in 1860, the free Black population only increased by 170,000 (in 1840, free Blacks numbered 386,303; in 1850, 434,495; in 1860, 488,070). Tens of thousands of Blacks, particularly the fugitives, had made their way into Canada (nearly 50,000 by 1860); still the different growth of the two Black populations was telling.

Although some free Blacks could always be found among the slave insurrectionists and conspirators, the majority of leading free Black abolitionists let considerations of property and civic gentility sway them toward reform. Thus, long after free Black workers had begun to sour on the new country, the free Black middle classes remained enchanted by the possibility of achieving equality in America. Indeed, as a token of their patriotism and expectations, Black men and women of influence rallied their communities to the defense of Philadelphia and New York during the War of 1812.[15] Consequently, Black businessmen, clergy, professionals, and the like took to the abolitionist movement with enthusiasm. They believed that ending slavery would secure their own rights, ensure their personal security, and add dignity to their claims. When, in 1832, Garrison proposed to publish the *Liberator*, Forten the sailmaker subsidized the project and James Vashon, a well-to-do Black barber, provided timely advances of capital. By virtue of such visible endorsements, Black support was assured. Benjamin Quarles reports that "for the first three crucial years the majority of the paper's subscribers were Negroes; in April 1834 whites comprised only one-quarter of the 2300 subscribers."[16] Indeed, Black support was Garrison's constant companion. And when, in 1833, Garrison determined to take his abolitionist message to England, Blacks rallied to him.

> Garrison had no money for the trip, but his Negro admirers took up collections, raising nearly $400. . . .
>
> When Garrison, after four months in England, prepared to return to America, he was again without funds. This time he turned to Nathaniel Paul, a Negro Baptist clergyman. . . . Paul advanced Garrison $200, "so that I could return home without begging," as he phrased it in a letter to Lewis Tappan. (20–21)

Garrison received sanctuary in Black homes when he was attacked by proslavery mobs, and during his travels around the country was received and domiciled by Blacks.

The sympathetic impulse among Black leaders toward the abolitionist movement continued despite the racial intolerance and paternalism so frequently exhibited by white antislave activists. Thus, when many of the abolitionist societies refused membership to Blacks, separate Black anti-slavery societies were formed. Nevertheless, the ambivalence of their white comrades stung: commenting on the undercurrent of racist pater-nalism among his white abolitionist comrades, the physician, dentist, and explorer Martin Delany wrote in 1852 that "we were doomed to disap-pointment, sad, sad disappointment."[17]

With the emergence of Black antislavery associations, it was only a mat-ter of time before the contradictions of being free and Black would become manifest in alternative and opposing political impulses among Black abolitionists. The options that matured were militant political reformism, "Negro sovereignty" (as Howard Bell characterized emigra-tionism), and insurrection. Even the most steadfast Black leaders found it difficult to choose the most effective means of securing the equality desired by free Blacks and the liberty pursued on behalf of the slaves. Douglass, the fugitive slave, made the most dramatic odyssey, moving from moral suasion, to militant reform, to conspiring with John Brown on insur-rection, and, on the eve of the Civil War, flirting with free Black emigra-tion (to Haiti). Delany, on the other hand, traveled a much shorter road: from militant reform in the 1840s to emigration in the 1850s. The major-ity of Black abolitionists, however, were committed to political reform, supporting movements like the Liberty Party (founded in 1839) and the Free Soil Party (1848), which opposed the expansion of slavery and counted on the gradual disappearance of the institution itself. Until the 1850s, it was much smaller factions of free Blacks who championed the radical proposals to emigrate or conspire for a general slave uprising. But then, most suddenly, as Leon Litwack reports, a change occurred:

> During the crucial decade of the 1850s, the Negro abolitionist grew ever more restive and impatient. The Fugitive Slave Act, the resurgence of the American Colonization Society, the unsuccessful attempts to win equal suf-frage, and finally, the Dred Scott decision, impressed many Negroes with the increasing helplessness of their position in the face of the white man's apparent determination to maintain racial supremacy. (150)

The Congress, the courts, and the Constitution had failed them, and many free Blacks found themselves in agreement with Delany's sentiments: "I must admit, that I have no hopes in this country—no confidence in the American people." (152) With this growing recognition of the deep cur-rent of racism in American culture, abolitionism took on its third and rev-olutionary form: the pursuit of Black self-governance, on the one hand, and an insurrection of the slaves on the other.

Black Sovereignty

The resolve to move beyond the orbit of slavery and oppression was as old as slavery. As we have seen, the Spanish and other European slave entrepreneurs encountered this form of resistance as early as the sixteenth century; in the seventeenth century, English slavers and colonists wrestled with slave fugitives, maroons, and insurrectionists. In Brazil, New Spain, Florida, the British West Indies, and elsewhere, African and then Creole peoples had established and defended mountain-based *quilombos* and "nanny-towns," hill-secured free towns, and swamp-remote maroon communities in the seventeenth, eighteenth, and nineteenth centuries. In the southeastern United States, Black Indians and Black-Indian alliances had pursued liberty through an anticolonial struggle and under the authority of Indian nations. Petitions and plans for a Christian African emigration emanated from the Black communities of Newport and Boston in the 1780s; in the mid–1820s, some 6,000 Blacks reportedly left the United States for Haiti.[18] For much of the national era, then, as the vise of slave oppression closed more securely on their brethren, free Blacks grew more acutely conscious of their own jeopardy and frustrated by their inability to end slavery. One result was that by "the eve of the Civil War," as Howard Bell reveals, "there was scarcely a Negro leader of national prominence who had not paid deference to the twin concepts of emigration and Negro nationalism." By 1861, this included Frederick Douglass, the figure who came closest to having become a national leader; William Watkins, the orator and abolitionist agitator; Martin Delany; and William Wells Brown, the former slave and author (*Narrative of William W. Brown; a Fugitive Slave,* published in 1842; *Clotel: or the President's Daughter,* 1853)—all of whom had opposed emigration for decades.[19]

The advent of a middle class among the free Blacks in the nineteenth century added some profoundly new elements to emigrationism: namely, ambitions for the economic development of the free Black community and for self-governance. The rejection by most free Blacks of the American Colonization Society's program of transporting free Blacks to Africa was so passionate that any interest in emigration was at first only tentatively expressed in public forums. In 1838 in *The Colored American,* two letters signed "Augustine" raised the issue, suggesting that the successes of Black communities in the West Indies and Canada were a basis for questioning the general resolve to die before submitting to transportation. "Augustine" reasoned that he "rather be a *living freeman,* even in one of these places, than a 'dead nigger' in the United States."[20] The next year, James Whitfield— poet, reporter, and editor—gave substantial space in *The Colored American* to an emigrationist plan developed by the Young Men's Union Society in

Cleveland. In 1847, with Liberia's declaration of independence, the free Black middle class discovered a destination for its economic and political impulses. "By 1847," Bell notes, "the National Negro Convention at Troy, New York, was ready to listen respectfully to a plan for a commercial venture involving Negroes of Jamaica, the United States, and Africa . . . a company owned and operated by people of African descent."[21]

In 1848, Black delegations from Ohio and Kentucky returned from Liberia and the west coast of Africa with favorable reports. The next year, there appeared the first prominent Black voice for emigrationism since Paul Cuffe's 1814–1816 Sierra Leone colonization project. In articles appearing in *The North Star* in January and March of 1949, Henry Highland Garnet nominated Liberia as a land where free Blacks might secure wealth and power. Garnet, however, felt it necessary to impose certain Black nationalist ethics on this pursuit, chastising those Africans in Liberia who were still involved in the slave trade. He advised them to take up "some other and honorable business."[22] With the growing consolidation of free Blacks' social organization, the stock of the nationalists began to rise and with it the impulse towards emigration: "For these individuals, a nationalistic viewpoint required the acceptance of emigration as well," Floyd Miller reports.[23]

The National Negro Convention movement had begun in 1830, fueled by a Baltimore emigrationist, Hezekiah Grice, and under the patronage of Bishop Richard Allen. From the first meeting in Philadelphia (the principal agenda was emigration to Canada), the movement spawned "annual" national and state conventions—"almost as frequent as church meetings," as *The Anglo-African* put it in October 1859—concerned with the plight of free Blacks and the slaves.[24] Both in 1849 and 1852, at the Black state conventions in Ohio (Columbus and Cincinnati, respectively), John Mercer Langston and W. H. Burnham supported emigration, but their proposals were defeated by a 4 to 1 margin in the 1852 meetings. In 1851, before the interested gaze of many Black abolitionists, two prominent fugitive slaves and writers, Samuel Ward and Henry Bibb, emigrated to Canada, from where Bibb agitated for an emigration meeting. Bibb's call resulted in the Toronto convention in September 1851, at which James T. Holly from Vermont presented his plan for a North American and West Indian Federal Agricultural Union to cooperatively purchase and distribute land in the Caribbean. In the same year, Blacks from Trenton, New Jersey, met to plan the purchase and settlement of lands in Canada. In July 1852, emigrationists met in convention in Baltimore, indicating a preference for Liberia but also a readiness to investigate other possible sites. The next year, 1853, a second meeting was held in Canada (at Amherstburgh), and it was proclaimed that "the American Negro owed no loyalty to the United States; that if emigration did not take place, revolution would; that if Canada were not an acceptable haven, then Haiti beckoned."[25]

Delany had rejected emigration as late as 1851. For the most part, his objections were based on his opposition to the American Colonization Society and his belief that the society's proposed African site, Liberia, was actually a "nominal nation" dominated by white interests. Thus, the revelation of Delany's own program for a Black nation in the Caribbean was somewhat unexpected. However, in the spring of 1852, following his own emigration to Canada, Delany issued his pamphlet *The Condition, Elevation, and Destiny of the Colored People of the United States, Politically Considered*. Delany coupled his plan with a denunciation of the Colonization Society and Liberia, a scheme that had forced him, he revealed, to abandon his earlier (1836) plan for free Black emigration to the eastern coast of Africa.[26] In the piece, Delany enveloped his concern for the fate of the slaves with Black nationalism: "The redemption of the bondmen depends entirely upon the elevation of the freeman; therefore, to elevate the free colored people of America, anywhere upon this continent, forebodes the speedy redemption of the slaves." A Black nation, Delany argued, would have a "reflex influence" on the condition of the slave. He wrote to Frederick Douglass in the same year saying, "We must have a position, independently of anything pertaining to white men or nations."[27] Delany was more than ready, then, in August 1854, when the largest ever emigrationist convention met in Cleveland. Supported by William Monroe, Reverend William Paul Quinn, and the widow Mary Bibb (Henry had recently died in Jamaica), Delany now submitted a lengthy report, "Political Destiny of the Colored Race on the American Continent."

> It denied both the citizenship and the freedom of the American Negro and contended that Freedom existed only where a racial group constituted a majority; it approved emigration to the Caribbean area via Canada as a way station; and it warned that the rights withheld by a majority were never freely given but must be seized.[28]

Delany's plan, as faithfully reported in the otherwise hostile Pittsburgh *Daily Morning Post*, was to construct empires ruled by the "nearly twenty-one millions [of] colored people of African and Indian origin" in the West Indies, Central America, Latin America, and Brazil. These empires would form the seat of "negro civilization" and to the slaves of the United States would serve as "the facility of escape, the near neighborhood of friends and aid . . . drain[ing] off from the Southern States all the most intelligent, robust, and bold of their slaves."²⁹ The convention, made up in its entirety of emigrationists, approved the proposal and met again in 1856 to continue its work as the National Emigration Convention.

Paradoxically, at this point, it was the intervention of non-Blacks that propelled the movement to its next stage. In January 1858, member of Congress Frank Blair, Jr., of Missouri, proposed that the House of Representatives initiate and subsidize a colony of free Blacks in Central America. Almost immediately, leading Black emigrationists took him up on the suggestion. James Holly had been active since 1854 in negotiating with the Haitian government of Emperor Faustin I on behalf of potential settlers; James Whitfield was nearing twenty years as an emigrationist agitator. Now, Holly and Whitfield informed Blair that Blacks were already active in the field and that his best contribution would be to secure financial support for those programs. Delany, ever suspicious of whites, made certain that Blair understood that the origin of the plan was his own.

The publicity generated around Blair's intervention helped to revitalize the emigration to Haiti programs. In 1859, James Redpath—the radical Scottish journalist, abolitionist, and associate of John Brown—traveled to Haiti and secured a pledge of $20,000 for the project from A. Jean Simon, the new Haitian Secretary of State whose president (General Fabre Geffrard) was desperately searching for agricultural specialists. Redpath returned to the United States, began publishing a weekly emigrationist newspaper called *The Pine and the Palm;* enlisted the support of Holly, Garnet, Douglass ("let us go to Hayti, where our oppressors do not want us to go"), William Wells Brown, and Watkins; hired recruitment agents (one of whom was John Brown, Jr.); and organized the Haitian Bureau of Emigration. Christopher Dixon makes it clear that the material support the Haitian government provided proved decisive:

> The first group of emigrants to leave for Haiti under the auspices of the Bureau left the United States in January 1861. By the time the final group departed in August 1862, the Bureau had despatched over two thousand African Americans to the island republic.³⁰

The Haitian scheme, however, was aborted by a constellation of factors. Some were internal: Redpath's mercurial temperament and revolving ideology (in 1861, he renounced violence as an instrument of slave liberation, rededicating himself to religion); illness among the emigrants; mismanagement on the ground in Haiti; and opposing objectives among the emigrants and the bureau's leaders. Others were external, such as the Civil War and President Lincoln's semiliberatory proclamations on slaves as confiscated property; the threat of war between Haiti and Spain (which seized the Dominican Republic in 1861); and the criticisms of Black emigrationists like Delany (who believed himself the better organizer), Mary Ann Shadd Cary, and William Newman. The more principled opponent was Cary, an editor of the *Provincial Freeman* who had herself emigrated to Canada in the 1850s and was the daughter of Abraham Shadd, an early emigrationist. She had warned that climate and disease made Haiti a death trap and the scheme merely another permutation of the American Colonization Society.[31] In any case, many of those emigrants who survived returned to the United States and the Bureau closed in 1862. Holly, who was to become the first Black Episcopalian Bishop, had accompanied one colony of emigrants to Haiti and remained there until his death in 1911.

An earlier expression of organized emigrationism also matured. In 1858, the National Emigration Convention met for a third time. As president, Delany was now replaced by William H. Day (who then abandoned emigrationism) while Delany secured the position of foreign secretary. In that capacity, Delany set about planning and seeking funding for the Niger Valley Exploring Party, an expedition to western Africa (Delany would eventually include Liberia along with the Yoruba region of present-day Nigeria as a destination). And for that purpose he organized a new enterprise, the African Civilization Society of Canada, largely a paper entity. Meanwhile, in Philadelphia, Henry Highland Garnet organized a rival African emigrationist organization, the African Civilization Society of New York, with the intention of exploring the Niger River region for free Black colonies. Garnet's group was aided by sympathetic whites (such as Benjamin Coates of the American Colonization Society), and it was somewhat disturbing to Delany that this meant it achieved the funding for its Niger expedition more quickly. Even more annoying to Delany was that Garnet's group designated Robert Campbell as its leader. Campbell, a Jamaican-born chemist and a teacher in the Institute for Colored Youth in Philadelphia, had been nominated by Delany to the Board of Commissioners of the National Emigration Convention in 1858. Fortunately, they were reconciled when Delany, bowing to financial expediency, was compelled to compromise with white colonizationists in New York. (194–97)

Delany disembarked in Liberia on July 10, 1859; Campbell's ship anchored off Lagos on July 21, 1859. In early November, the two met at "Abbeokuta," and from that moment they traveled together on horseback: "We proceeded to Ijaye, population 78,000, reckoned by the white missionaries and officers of the Niger Expedition of Her Majesty's service; . . . Oyo, population, 75,000; Ogbomoso, population 70,000; Illorin, population 120,000; returning back, *via* Ogbomoso to Oyo."[32] The two departed

Lagos on April 10, 1860. Delany and Campbell both wrote accounts of their expedition: Delany's entitled, "Official Report of The Niger Valley Exploring Party"; and Campbell's "A Pilgrimage to My Motherland: An Account of a Journey Among the Egbas and Yorubas of Central Africa, in 1859–60." These works constituted two of the first deliberate contributions to ethnography by New World Blacks. Delany, always mindful of the historic and moral import of Black American emigration, recorded some memorable nationalist injunctions. To the free Black emigrationists, he warned:

> Africa is our fatherland and we its legitimate descendants, and we will never agree nor consent to see . . . the first voluntary step that has ever been taken for her regeneration by her own descendants—blasted by a disinterested or renegade set, whose only object might be in the one case to get rid of a portion of the colored population, and in the other, make money. (110)

And, like Garnet, Delany addressed himself to the slavers, both Black and white:

> We do not leave America and go to Africa to be passive spectators of such a policy as traffic in the flesh and blood of our kindred, nor any other species of the human race. . . . We will not live there and permit it. . . . We will bide our time; *but the Slave-trade shall not continue!* (114)

Eventually Campbell returned to Liberia to settle in 1862, while Delany remained in America. In the next months, Delany began recruiting Blacks for the Civil War (joining the efforts of Tubman, Mary Ann Shadd Cary, and Garnet) and became the first Black major in the armed services. After the war, Delany emerged as a political figure in South Carolina but still held to his nationalist/emigrationist beliefs.

Emigrants both preceded and followed the expedition of Delany and Campbell. "Between 1820 and the beginning of the Civil War, some ten thousand free blacks and newly emancipated slaves sailed to Liberia," we are told by Shepard, Pollard, and Schwartz. (96) Among the earliest were the former slave, Lott Cary, the first Western educator in the country, and Joseph Jenkins Roberts, a free Black who became Liberia's first Black governor and first elected president.[33] But it would not be until long after the Civil War, Reconstruction, and the advent of American apartheid (Jim Crow) that Africa would beckon again in the form of a mass movement. Meanwhile, an even smaller minority of radical free Black abolitionists chose a different path to the ending of slavery, conspiring to provoke a general slave uprising.

Insurrection

In his Appeal, David Walker urged a general slave revolution in 1829.[34] In 1831, Nat Turner attempted to organize such an uprising. In Florida, in the mid-1830s, the Black Seminoles prosecuted a series of slave insurrections. In 1843, Henry Highland Garnet came within one vote of winning a Black convention's endorsement of violence to end slavery. In the mid-1850s, following his second and third tours of the South, James Redpath, under the pseudonyms of "James Ball, Jr." and "Jacobius," reported in the abolitionist press on his secret interviews with free Blacks and slaves: "At Richmond and at Willmington . . . I found the slaves discontented, but despondingly resigned to their fate. At Charleston I found them morose and savagely brooding over their wrongs." In the September 8, 1854, issue of Garrison's *Liberator*, Redpath recounted one Charleston slave's declaration to him: "All [slaves] that I does know *wants to be free very bad*, I tell you, and *may be will fight before long if they don't get freedom somehow*."[35] During the 1840s and 1850s in Louisiana, Mississippi, North Carolina, and Alabama, the resistances of slave fugitives, maroons, and radical white abolitionists plagued the slavers of the South, documenting Redpath's reports.

Even Harriet Beecher Stowe, disappointed by the social impact of her popular *Uncle Tom's Cabin* (over 300,000 copies sold the first year), took up the necessity of a slave uprising in her second novel, *Dred, A Tale of the Great Dismal Swamp* (published in 1856). In her nonfiction work between the two novels, *A Key to Uncle Tom's Cabin* (published in 1853), Stowe first defended the factual basis of her first novel and then proceeded to examine the laws of slavery, which progressively increased the oppression of the slaves and inspired fear among free Blacks. Propelled by the stark honesty of Judge Thomas Ruffin's declaration in *State v. Mann* (1829) that "the power of the master must be absolute, to render the submission of the slave perfect,"[36] Stowe came to accept, as Lisa Whitney concludes, that the "slaveholder's power . . . both inspires and justifies rebellion on the part of slaves."[37] In her second novel, drawing on Nat Turner, Stowe's Dred spurred his fellow conspirators by recounting how the law legitimized the murder of slaves. In real life, Simeon Souther (*Souther v. Commonwealth*, 1851) took twelve hours to torture his slave Sam to death: "Whilst the deceased was so tied to the tree, the prisoner did strike, knock, kick, stamp, and beat him upon various parts of his head, face, and body; that he applied fire to his body . . . that he then washed his body with warm water, in which pods of red pepper had been put and steeped."[38] Souther was convicted of only second-degree murder and sentenced to the Virginia penitentiary for five years. Stowe's fictive slaveholders exercised the same absolute rights

("Dey's all last night a killing of him"). Dred, by referring his comrades to the *Declaration of Independence*, assured them of the justice of their conspiracy to liberate themselves.[39]

As we have seen, in the real world of slavery Nat Turner was succeeded by hundreds of Black rebels, slave and free. Their numbers swelled to nearly 200,000 during the Civil War, when self-liberated slaves and free Blacks joined the Union forces to bring slavery to the fore of the war. But nearly a century would pass before the maroons and Black-Indian warriors and their struggles were restored to American history. Meanwhile, history recorded two white figures as icons and explanators of the struggle against slavery: the madman, John Brown, and the tragic president, Abraham Lincoln. Among Blacks, however, it was never accepted that Brown was insane; nor, as we shall see later, did they believe that it was Lincoln who had ended slavery.

A week before the execution of John Brown, "some colored ladies" of New York sent a letter to his wife, Mary, announcing their intention to make contributions to her family: "Tell your dear husband then, that henceforth you shall be our own!"[40] On the day of his execution, December 2, 1859, Blacks by the thousands congregated in northern churches to declare their debt to John Brown. In Detroit, William Lambert spoke for the crowd at Second Baptist Church: "Resolved, That we hold the name of Old Capt. John Brown in the most sacred remembrance, now the first disinterested martyr for our liberty." In Boston, the pastor at Tremont Temple, the former slave J. Sella Martin, spoke of Brown, who, "like John the Baptist, retired into the hard and stony desert of Kansas, and there, by the weapons of heroism, by the principles of freedom, and the undaunted courage of a man, wrung from that bloody soil the highest encomiums of Freedom, and the most base acknowledgments of slavery, that the one was right and the other wrong." The free Black support for John Brown's "business" was not just talk nor just after the fact.

Twelve years before the expedition against Harper's Ferry by Brown's army, he divulged his plan of attack on slavery to Frederick Douglass. Douglass recounted their 1847 discussion:

> "These mountains [the Alleghenies], he said, "are the basis of my plan. God has given the strength of the hills to freedom; they were placed here for the emancipation of the Negro race. . . . My plan, then, is to take at first about twenty-five picked men, and begin on a small scale; supply them with arms and ammunition and post them in squads of fives on a line of twenty-five miles. The most persuasive and judicious of these shall go down to the fields from time to time, as opportunity offers, and induce the slaves to join them, seeking and selecting the most restless and daring." . . .

[T]hey would run off the slaves in large numbers, retain the brave and strong ones in the mountains, and send the weak and timid to the North by the Underground Railroad."[41]

Before divulging the plan, Douglass remembered Brown saying that "he had been for some time looking for colored men to whom he could safely reveal his secret, and at times he had almost despaired of finding such men; but that now he was encouraged, for he saw heads of such rising up in all directions." (105) By the time that Brown's men stormed the arsenal at Harper's Ferry, he had found his "colored men": the free Blacks John Anthony Copeland, Lewis S. Leary, and Osborn Perry Anderson;[42] and the former slaves Dangerfield Newby and Shields Green.

Douglass was one of Brown's closest confidantes in the free Black and former slave communities of the North; Delany and Tubman served as his principal resources for recruitment among the 40–50,000 Black emigrants in Canada. Delany was on his African sojourn when Brown's army struck in 1859. But the year before, in Chatham, Canada, he had met with Brown and organized his meeting with other Blacks. Delany had also been at the May 1858 conclave of thirty-four Blacks and twelve whites during which Brown unveiled his plan and his Provisional Constitution. They had expected Douglass, Garnet, J. W. Loguen, and Tubman (of whom Brown had written: "*He Harriet* is the most of a *man* naturally; that I *ever* met with"), but, in their absence, Brown had been elected as commander-in-chief and Osborn Anderson as a member of congress in the proposed revolutionary state. The conferees also agreed that their objective was not to dissolve the United States but to submit it to "Amendment and Repeal."[43]

Douglass was absent again when Brown's army struck and was defeated. Once again a fugitive, now sought for his role in the conspiracy, Douglass castigated himself in his Canadian retreat:

> In a letter to the Rochester *Democrat and American*, Douglass confessed that, "tried by the Harper's Ferry insurrection test," he was "most miserably deficient in courage . . . when he deserted his old brave captain, and fled to the mountains." . . . "Posterity will owe everlasting thanks to John Brown," for he "has attacked slavery with the weapons precisely adapted to bring it to the death." (315)

Douglass's self-criticism is understandable: for twelve years he and Brown had been friends and confederates and he mourned for the loss of "the old captain." But in their last meeting in August 1859, they had disagreed on the merits of the proposed action. Doubtless, Douglass, the escaped slave who for decades had faced violent, hostile mobs, had shown more than sufficient courage in the struggle.

Alongside Douglass, Tubman, and Delany, the number of prominent free Black leaders linked to Brown's plan was rather impressive. In Brooklyn, there were Dr. J. Gloucester and his wife; in Syracuse, J. W. Loguen, a Black minister; and in Philadelphia, the Reverend Stephen Smith, William Still, Frederick Douglass, and Brown's old friend and fellow revolutionary, Henry Highland Garnet. Brown had held conferences with the Philadelphians in March 1858 and Brown left Philadelphia fully expecting these men to raise money and Negro recruits for the coming revolution." (240–41) Their efforts at support had meager results, but without them there would likely have been a much smaller Black contingent at Harper's Ferry.

By the next year, some Blacks did make their way to Brown's farm in Maryland: in July, Newby, who hoped to free his wife; in August, Green, who hoped to free his son; in late September, Osborn Anderson, the emigrant printer; in mid-October, Copeland, the carpenter, and Leary, the harness-maker (both Oberlin-trained).[44] When the firing began in the morning hours of October 17, "Newby was the first of the raiders to die and the last hope of his slave wife whose letter he carried in his pocket: 'Oh dear Dangerfield, com this fall without fail monny or no Monney I want to see you so much that is the one bright hope I have before me.'" (294) Leary and Jeremiah Anderson, too, were killed as were Oliver and Watson, Brown's sons; John Kagi, a reporter; Stewart Taylor; William Leeman; William Thompson; and Dauphin Thompson. One free Black, Copeland, and one fugitive slave, Green, were captured, tried, and sentenced to be hanged.

> "I am not terrified by the gallows," John Copeland, the Negro college student, wrote his parents in Oberlin. "Could I die in a more noble cause? Could I die in a manner and for a cause which would induce true and honest men more to honor me, and the angels more ready to receive me to their happy home of everlasting joy above?" Shields Green retained a quiet dignity as he waited for the gallows like the others; even some Virginians had to concede that the two Negroes were "persevering" and "manly" (although Governor Wise refused to give up the bodies of Green and Copeland after they were executed, unless "white men came after them"). (338)

Osborn Anderson escaped, surviving to fight in the Civil War and provide what DuBois considered the best account of what happened at Harper's Ferry. Of the rest of the raiders, four escaped: Owen Brown (the third of

John's sons involved in the raid), Francis Meriam (to serve as the captain of a Black company during the Civil War), Charles Tidd (killed in the Civil War), and Barclay Coppoc (killed in the Civil War). Captured were Barclay's brother Edwin, Aaron Stevens, John Cook, and Albert Hazlett.

Brown, too, was captured. Despite an insufficient number of slaves coming to his aid, and the death of his sons Oliver and Watson (a third, Owen, escaped), Brown maintained that what he had done was right. Fifty-nine years old, a participant in the Underground Railroad in Ohio's Western Reserve, a veteran of the free-state war in Kansas (where his son, Frederick, had been killed), and a "slave-stealer," Brown knew only that his attempt at "Amendment" had proven inadequate. He had been ill often with "ague" in the previous three years, and at his hastily arranged trial he was carried in on a cot, his wounds still apparent. It might be reasonably expected that he would not be up to the ordeal. The trial, however, went badly for the slaveholders. First Brown rejected "as a miserable artifice" the case for insanity so carefully crafted by his friends and defense counsel (Lawson Botts and Thomas Green) from the official construction of Brown's capacity for judgment. His eloquence on that score immediately dampened his image as a madman. The American and foreign journalists took note, angered perhaps by the scent of a ruse in the authorities' characterization of Brown.[45] But what persuaded most observers, near and afar, of his sound judgment was Brown's extraordinary rejoinder to his sentence of death. Reminding his audience that the authority for his actions was the Bible ("a book kissed here"), and describing how the Southern courts had countenanced the most heinous crimes on behalf of slavery ("had I interfered in behalf of the rich, the powerful, the intelligent, the so-called great . . . it would have been all right"), Brown stood his ground by saying:

> Now, if it is deemed necessary that I should forfeit my life for the further-ance of the ends of justice, and mingle my blood further with the blood of my children and with the blood of millions in this slave country whose rights are disregarded by wicked, cruel, and unjust enactments,—I submit; so let it be done![46]

On the day he was hanged, on the walk to the gallows, he handed a note to an attendant:

Charlestown, Va, 2d, December, 1859.
I John Brown am now quite *certain* that the crimes of this *guilty, land: will* never be purged *away;* but with Blood. I had *as I now think: vainly* flattered myself that without *very much* bloodshed; it might be done.

In his 1970 biography of Brown, Stephen Oates declared Brown's operation a "dismal failure." Echoing the self-deceit of Andrew Hunter, the
state prosecutor at Brown's trial, Oates presumed, "No uprisings had taken
place anywhere in Virginia and Maryland, because the slaves there . . . had
been both unable and unwilling to join him."[47] But sixty years earlier,
DuBois had seen the event differently, mirroring the slaveholders' terrified
view: "Fifteen or twenty Negroes had enlisted and would probably have
been present had they had the time. Five, probably six, actually came in
time, and thirty or forty slaves actively helped."[48] The trials of Brown and
his comrades had begun on October 27, nine days after their arrests. During those nine days, while the militias and the federal army marshaled
thousands to stand watch over the slaves and proslavery mobs began their
long terror, the slaves employed arson: "five incendiary fires in a single
week after the raid," DuBois recorded. Over the next months, the slaveholders' activities testified to their understanding of the threats they faced.

In Virginia and Maryland, slave sales increased, reducing the slave population in the counties adjacent to Harper's Ferry (352–54). Throughout
the South, recounts Seymore Drescher, "especially incomprehensible were
the campaigns to intimidate people of color and white outsiders. . . .
Motions introduced in southern legislatures to expel or enslave resident
free blacks seemed signs of a society gone out of control."[49] In the Senate,
James Mason (of Virginia) chaired a special investigating committee (Jefferson Davis of Mississippi was the chief counsel) hoping to indict and
punish Brown's influential supporters, the "Secret Six" who had financed
much of the operation: Samuel Gridley Howe, George Luther Stearns,
Garrit Smith, Thomas Wentworth Higginson, Theodore Parker, and
Franklin Sanborn. Ironically, a proposed Thirteenth Amendment was
passed through Congress from the House of Representatives, which would
have given "a perpetual commitment to the sanctity of slave property in
states as opposed to territories."[50] Lincoln publicly asserted he neither
would nor could raise an objection to the amendment. Four years later, the
actual Thirteenth Amendment would state: "Neither slavery, nor involun-
tary servitude, except as a punishment for crime whereof the party shall
have been duly convicted, shall exist within the United States, or any place
subject to their jurisdiction."

For the masters and merchants of the slave economy, however, neither
Congress nor the presidents (Buchanan and then Lincoln), neither the Federal army nor their own militias could insure them against the slaves and
their allies. Thousands of abolitionists all across the nation had met to
plead for Brown's life following his extraordinary performance in the trial;
after his execution, they continued to meet to honor their new martyrs. In

1860, as another troubling sign, the American Anti-Slavery Society had taken the audacious step of publishing Joshua Coffin's thirty-six-page pamphlet, *An Account of Some of the Principal Slave Insurrections*, an act that reflected the new radicalism now flashing from the abolitionist camp. Besieged by what they now believed to be "the Abolitionist North" (on the evidence of Brown's connections with prominent Republicans, white abolitionists, and free Blacks), the slaveholders and their allies accelerated their movement toward secession.

There was, then, much that was true in Brown's prophetic final note; but what Douglass concluded about the matter was even truer: "If John Brown did not end the war that ended slavery, he did, at least, begin the war that ended slavery."[51]

CHAPTER FOUR

The Civil War and Its Aftermath

* * *

The bringing of the African to America planted the first seed of dis-Union.

—D. W. Griffith, *Birth of a Nation*

The secessions of slave states, which led to the Civil War between the Union and the Confederate forces, were commenced by South Carolina in December 1860. Only seemingly paradoxical, it was this Civil War that dismembered the slave regime. By March of 1861, Mississippi, Florida, Alabama, Georgia, Louisiana, and Texas in fraternity with South Carolina had initiated the Confederate States of America. In April, when Lincoln mobilized Union troops to put down the rebellion, Virginia, Arkansas, North Carolina, and Tennessee joined the Confederacy. The slave (or "border") states of Delaware, Kentucky, Maryland, and Missouri, however, remained within the Union, evidence that loyalty to the Union and slavery were compatible. The Southern planters and their middling classes saw their causes as the preservation of their rule over a thriving slave economy, the maintenance of a societal stratification based on slavery, and the defense of the master/slave culture from the predations of manufacturing capitalists and abolitionist liberalism. The Union government and its merchants saw their cause as the preservation of the union; that is, retaining their political and commercial provenance in the South and western territories. For the seventy previous years, the Southern plantocracy and its banking and merchant allies had dominated the federal government and national policy. For pro-Unionists, it was now the turn of the industrial bourgeoisie—with its appetite for protective tariffs, a national banking system, labor regulation, and federal corporate and stock supports—to dominate.

The majority of the civilian and military leaders on both sides expected a quick, three-month conflict. They anticipated no major battles, rather a few decisive skirmishes that would demonstrate the cause of secession as being too tenuous militarily (as loyalists anticipated) or the Union as without the resources or resolve to end the rebellion (as Southerners hoped). That the war extended into a protracted struggle spelled the end of only one side, however: the slave regime was undone. Being a slave regime, constantly on alert for threats from the domestic enemy, the white South had the advantage in military readiness and the habit of mobilizing armed militias.[1] But they mistakenly imagined that they could call up a good portion of the white males without disrupting the economy; that black coerced labor would release sufficient free laborers and small farmers for war duties; that their human property would manage the production of staple crops, construct fortifications, transport supplies, and serve as support in the battle camps; that slaves would go on, according to the Southern racist mantra, being dependent, loyal, and simple. But Southern white expectations were unreal. Once the slaves gained the knowledge that the slaveholders were confronted by a second enemy, they carried out defections, insurrections, and empowering maneuvers (for example, negotiating for wages). Even more heretical, most slaves rejected the slaveholders' deliberate characterization of the Unionists as Yankees (New England industrial capitalists and their agents in Kansas) and as devils. As one abolitionist put it: "I once heard a negro say: 'When my massa and somebody else quarrel I'm on the somebody else's side.'"[2] Within days of the beginning of the war, few could go on pretending that slaves were a constant labor source or social pedestal of the white South. They were on "somebody else's side." Contrary to the official wishes of the Union government, they forced their way into the Civil War in ways unimagined except by the most radical abolitionists and the most frightened plantocrats. The overwhelming majority of Blacks who served in the Union army (179,000) and navy (10,000) were slaves.[3] For a time, the slaves transformed the Union military into an army of liberation and the conflict into a war for freedom.

Opposing Objectives: Accumulation vs. Liberty

War was inevitable once the secessionist impulse betrayed the political sovereignty and economic vision installed by the American Revolution. Since both the emergent rulers of the North and the South shared the same ambition—control of the surplus capital produced by slave labor—

one or the other of the oligopolies had to be humbled, subordinated by force. Certainly, the South's profitable and constantly diversifying economy was an enviable one. Between 1840 and 1860, labor productivity in service and manufacturing doubled the comparable increase in agricultural production; cotton production itself had doubled between 1850 and 1860; and cotton profits for planters were substantially above normal; slave labor was 70 percent more productive than free agricultural labor, and during the spring, summer, and fall, slaves worked an average work week of 57 to 60 hours. In addition, slaves constituted nearly 80 percent of the South's artisan class. Consequently, as Robert W. Fogel observes, "The southern plutocrats were considerably richer, on average, than their northern counterparts (by a factor of roughly 2 to 1).... Nearly two out of every three males with estates of $100,000 or more lived in the South in 1860." (101) This distribution of wealth was achieved despite the population of the white South (nearly 6 million) being less than one-third that of the North (more than 21 million). The Civil War, however, would end the Southern elite's dominance of wealth: by 1870, 80 percent of the super rich would now be northerners (84).[4]

Ironically, it was only the abolitionists, or at least the bulk of them, who championed the peaceable dissolution of the Union. Garrison and many other antislavery activists were persuaded that the South's rulers could not sustain a slave regime without the power of federal troops and federal fugitive slave laws. They despaired at the cloak of progress bestowed in international opinion on the slave South by its association with the North and the complicity of northern-based capital in slave labor and slave-produced commodities. No such timidity infected northern capitalists in the last months of 1860.[5] In Boston, Buffalo, New York, Utica, Rome, Auburn, and elsewhere, concern for their Southern debtors, slave mortgages, and stocks compelled northern merchants, bankers, and lawyers to lead mobs into violent disruptions of abolitionist meetings. But abolitionists like the Garrisonian, Samuel May, Jr., thrilled to secession: "Let the South go—put not a *straw* in her way—interpose not even an objection or a regret; let her go." (33)

The incitement of mob violence against abolitionists and Blacks in 1860 and earlier, foretold the events of the summer of 1863 when New York City white and immigrant working class mobs added the Republicans, the federal government, and its agents (police officers, fire fighters, and draft officials) to their targets.[6] Fueled by the first federal Conscription Act—March 1863—which sought to bolster the Union army drained by casualties and desertions (100,000 by 1862) and faced with the radical decline of volunteers—laborers from the building trades and docks initially and then from manufacturing sectors took to the streets to express their opposition to the war and to Black equality. Their language of choice: lynching, arson, looting, and brutal violence. For five days, starting with July 13, mobs terrorized Blacks, federal officials, and Republican groups, chanting slogans that expressed the fear that Black emancipation would displace whites in the work force (Blacks had been used as strikebreakers in the city; of course, as noncitizens, Blacks were not subject to the draft). There were even cheers for Jefferson Davis, the Confederate president. The riots ended only with the intervention of Union troops returning from their defeat of Lee's Confederate army at Gettysburg.

The New York City Draft Riots exploded on Monday, July 13, 1863, the day scheduled for the beginning of the conscription lottery. Among the first victims were the Colored Orphan Asylum, the *New York Tribune* office, and some federal buildings. Iver Bernstein notes: "After Monday the crowds increasingly turned their attention toward the local black community. . . . The riots were an occasion for gangs of white workingmen in certain trades to introduce into the community the 'white-only' rule of their work settings."[7] The sexual mutilation, drowning, and lynching of Black men; the burning of Black tenements; and the beating of Black women (and white women associated with Blacks) characterized the actions of the midweek mobs. The corpse of the lynched Abraham Franklin, a crippled Black coach driver, was strung up twice more and finally dragged through the streets by the genitals by sixteen-year-old Patrick Butler: "After yet another hanging in this neighborhood, rioters cut off their black victim's fingers and toes."(29) Whatever the final toll of the riots (estimates range from 105 to 1,000), or the racial identities of its victims, the lesson was understood by Blacks, who for months after the riot continued to abandon the city. And, for years after the riots, "racist white contractors and work gangs collaborated to keep black wage earners away from docks, pits, and quarries and terrorize those actually hired." (233) Thus, twenty years after the beginnings of blackface minstrelsy among these same white artisans, their most adored entertainment dehumanized Blacks, particularly the Black male. The immediate circumstances of the war, the draft, and popular culture wrought their social consequence: "The alliance of urban working people with the planter interest in the South."[8] Convinced that the war was merely a plot by powerful Republicans to reduce white labor under the heels of Black labor, the mobs rejected the wealthy, the federal government of the plutocrats, Blacks, and the war.

Abraham Lincoln and his comrades in the young Republican party also felt that neither the fates of slavery nor the "Africans" were compelling reasons to tear the South from the Union. Indeed, in his debates with Stephen Douglas in 1858, Lincoln declared he would not interfere with slavery and that he had no inclination to do so. But if it came to abolition, Lincoln maintained then and later, freed slaves would be transported to Liberia. For the moment, "while [the black and white races] do remain together there must be the position of superior and inferior, and I as much as any other man am in favor of having the superior position assigned to the white race."9 Thus when secession did come, Lincoln pursued the union and not slavery, and when he first confronted emancipation, he balked not once but several times. When that obstacle had been breached, he still dreamed of Black colonization. As late as August 1862, in a meeting with Black leaders, Lincoln appealed for support for voluntary emigration: "Not a single man of your race is made the equal of a single man of ours."10 In December, Lincoln signed a contract "with a dubious character for the settlement of 5,000 blacks on an island off Haiti."11

The abolitionists were sorely disappointed in the president. Wendell Phillips, perhaps the leading white abolitionist orator, who had cautiously championed Lincoln's election ("not an abolitionist, hardly an antislavery man, Mr. Lincoln consents to represent an antislavery idea"), now characterized him as "stumbling, halting, prevaricating, irresolute, weak, besotted." In August of 1862, Horace Greeley, the editor of the *New York Tribune*, wrote to Lincoln: "We think you are strangely and disastrously remiss." Frustrated by the president's inability to seize the moral high ground, abolitionists mounted petition campaigns supporting emancipation (by 1864, 400,000 signatures had been forwarded to the Congress).12 For the moment it all appeared to be of no avail. The federal behemoth would be persuaded not by moral urgency but by contradictions.

It was the slaves and the exigencies of war that changed Lincoln's mind and provided the abolitionists in Congress, the military, and various loyal state governments with the leverage required to secure emancipation. Slave insurrections broke out in Mississippi (by the end of 1861, forty slaves had been executed in the environs of Natchez; twenty-seven or more at Second Creek) and Virginia (seventeen were hanged in Culpeper County); and Herbert Aptheker documented an additional twenty-five conspiracies in Arkansas, Virginia, South Carolina, Louisiana, and Kentucky. Escaped slaves in the lower and upper South made for the nearest Union forces (for example, of the 112,000 slaves in Missouri, 22,000 had escaped by 1862).13 As W.E.B. DuBois recounted:

Every step the Northern armies took then meant fugitive slaves. They crossed the Potomac, and the slaves of northern Virginia began to pour into the army and into Washington. They captured Fortress Monroe, and slaves from Virginia and even North Carolina poured into the army. They captured

Port Royal, and the masters ran away, leaving droves of black fugitives in the hands of the Northern army. They moved down the Mississippi Valley, and if the slaves did not rush to the army, the army marched to the slaves. They captured New Orleans, and captured a great black city and a state full of slaves.[14]

Every Union army camp in or near slave territory became a site for fugitive slaves; every military campaign into the Confederacy secured tactical intelligence from slaves on the movement of Confederate troops, on rivers and roads, on pockets of loyalists. Escaped slaves almost immediately began to undertake military adventures. DuBois reckoned that the revolt of the slaves "was a general strike that involved directly in the end perhaps a half million people." (67)

The historical archives and studies are swollen with documentation detailing how the Lincoln Administration and the majority of Republicans in Congress sought to limit the objectives of the war to warding off the rebellion of the Confederate states while preserving property in Blacks. As one Washington, D.C., newspaper, the *National Intelligencer*, put it on June 12, 1861, "Commanders of the federal forces seem to have vied with each other in repelling all suspicions of an unfriendly purpose toward the peculiar domestic institution of the Southern states."[15] Dudley Cornish reports Brigadier General Benjamin Butler, in Maryland in late April, offered troops to the governor to put down a rumored slave insurrection; in late May, General George McClellan in West Virginia told his colonels: to "repress all attempts at negro insurrection"; and General Robert Patterson in Pennsylvania instructed his troops before their march on Harper's Ferry that one of their duties while in the South was "to suppress servile insurrections."[16] Thus, in the border states and even while occupying rebel terrain, most (but not all) army commanders assisted slaveholders (and the Confederate cause) by actively returning fugitive slaves to oppression. Even the passage by Congress in August 1861 of the First Confiscation Act, authorizing the seizing of Confederate slaves as "contraband," dissuaded few Union officers from supporting slavery. The war had begun, as Frederick Douglass put it, "in the interest of slavery on both sides . . . both despising the Negro, both insulting the Negro."[17]

Union generals, however, with abolitionist histories or with sound tactical reasons for supporting Black mobilization and emancipation, sought to conspire with the insurgent slaves. On August 30, 1861, Major General John Charles Fremont, the Republican nominee for president in the 1856 election and commander of the Western Department in Missouri, declared martial law and then proclaimed: "The property, real and personal, of all persons in the State of Missouri who shall take up arms against the United States . . . is declared to be confiscated to the public use, and their slaves, if any they have, are hereby declared freemen." Lincoln rescinded Fremont's order, compelled him to restrict his authority to the Confiscation Act, and then replaced him with a West Point graduate, Major General David Hunter.[18] In September, Gideon Welles, the Secretary of the Navy, ordered the enlistment of Blacks (with ratings as "boys"). This order did not initiate a policy (Blacks were already employed by the Union navy and made up a substantial proportion of the Confederate mariners), rather Welles was acceding to tradition and expediency. However, Simon Cameron, the Secretary of War, had enthusiastically supported Fremont's initiative and, in October of 1861, authorized Brigadier General Thomas Sherman to use fugitive slaves as Union soldiers and to compensate loyal slaveholders. Sherman, a West Point graduate and a veteran of the Second Seminole War, had been appointed commander of the Department of the South, actually a small force on Hilton Head and the Port Royal islands off the coast of South Carolina. Sherman had fought against Black Seminoles and one might surmise he did not trust "contraband" to fight for any American government. Whatever his reasons, he did not use this authority, preferring to employ fugitives as plantation laborers. Sherman's corruption of his orders, however, did not save Cameron. In November, Cameron publicly declared his support for Black mobilization and then in December included a passionate defense of the idea in his annual report, employing terms like "duty" and "right." Lincoln ordered him to expunge that section of the report and in January exiled Cameron by making him ambassador to Russia.

The third challenge to Lincoln's deteriorating policy of conciliation toward slaveowners in the border states and elsewhere came from General Hunter, Fremont's replacement. In March 1862, Hunter succeeded Sherman as commander of the Department of the South. And, although Lincoln would later deny it publicly, little was surprising in Hunter's first significant order. For Hunter's abolitionist disposition was well known, both fugitive and native Blacks on the Sea Islands had already displayed a ferocity toward slavery, and Hunter had inherited a desperate military situation.[19] On April 13, Hunter declared as free the slaves of the rebel slavers at Fort Pulaski and on Cockspur Island in Georgia. On May 8, arguing that "slavery and martial law in a free country are altogether incompatible," Hunter ordered: "The persons in these three states, Georgia, Florida, and South Carolina, heretofore held as slaves are therefore declared forever free."[20] Lincoln negated the order on May 19, claiming for himself the authority to free the slaves, and then contradicted himself by declaring that he had never heard of Hunter's decree. Others, however, had heard, and along with Confederate battle victories, the order sealed the doom of Lincoln's attempt to con-serve the war as a fight merely to preserve the Union.

On May 13, 1862, the Southern steamer, *Planter*—large enough to carry a thousand troops, armed with a thirty-two pound pivot gun and a twenty-four pound howitzer, carrying four smooth-bore cannon—and the head-quarters ship of Confederate General Roswell Ripley, sailed out of Charleston, was surrendered to the Union navy blockading the port. The ship had been commandeered by insurgent Blacks: the pilot Robert Smalls; the engineer Alfred Gradine; the sailors John Smalls (no relation), Samuel Chisholm, Abraham Allston, Gabriel Turno, Abraham Jackson, and William Morrison; and their families—sixteen people in all. As Willie Lee Rose writes, "The news of the military emancipation proclamation [had] traveled swiftly through the Union lines and struck iron resolve."[21] Smalls and his companions were taking their place in the tradition of rebellion laid down by the Black mariners who conspired with Gabriel and Sancho around Charleston sixty years earlier.[22]

The tale of Smalls and his companions, and the similar military exploits of Black slaves and freemen (William Tillman commandeered a captured Union ship, sailing it into the New York harbor), were reported by news-papers in both the Union and the Confederacy. Smalls's defection was referred to by an agitated *Charleston Courier* and pictures and stories on the twelve slave fugitives appeared in the *New York Tribune* and *Harpers*. Con-gress enacted a bill authorizing a portion of the appraised value of the *Planter* to be paid to Smalls and his companions. The ship was evaluated at $9,168, one-eighth of its actual value. Thus, at the beginnings of the war, the slaves' bravery was betrayed as it would be at its conclusion. Neverthe-less, Smalls conducted himself with honor as a pilot and captain of Union ships throughout the war.[23]

> Just before Thanksgiving 1863, the *Planter* was ambushed by Confederate
> batteries in a narrow stream. The white captain, a New Englander, wanted to
> surrender, but Small[s] would not do so. He knew the Confederates did not
> treat blacks as prisoners of war but would hang him and every black crew
> member as an object lesson. Ordering the guns of the *Planter* to return the
> Confederate fire, he ignored his white superior officer and ran the steamer
> past the battery. . . . The white captain hid in the steel-clad coal bunker. . . .
> Small[s] bolted down the hatches to keep him there until the *Planter* returned
> to her base.
>
> The cowardly white captain was dismissed and the black hero was
> appointed captain of the *Planter*.[24]

By that time, hundreds of other Blacks had joined Smalls in serving with the Union forces.

The political pressures on Lincoln and his proslavery general-in-chief, McClellan, continued to mount. In May, Hunter had begun to recruit and impress free and slave Blacks for a Black regiment, the First South Carolina Colored Regiment. In June, in Kansas, another of Lincoln's commissioned abolitionists, Senator and then Brigadier General James Lane, began recruiting Black volunteers and Native Americans. At the beginning of the war, Kansas had a Black population of 800; by 1865, that population was 13,000, drawn largely from fugitives from Missouri and Arkansas. By August 1862, 500 Black volunteers made up the First Kansas Colored Volunteers; by October, they were in combat in Missouri.[25]

Finally in July 1862, under General Butler's command (now at New Orleans) but in opposition to Butler's policies toward the "contraband," Brigadier General John Phelps began raiding and recruiting fugitive slaves from the surrounding plantations. Thus, when Phelps wrote to Butler requesting service uniforms and equipment, he was rebuffed. Butler wrote his wife: "Phelps has gone crazy." Phelps resigned, but two weeks later, in late August, Butler issued a call for volunteers from the "Native Guard (colored)" of Louisiana. The consummate politician, Butler had learned from the Secretary of the Treasury Salmon Chase that the administration was now wavering on arming Blacks and former slaves and from Mrs. Butler that the abolitionist cause was advancing ("Hunter is kept in his place, and carries out all his Proclamation put forth. The President's veto was not decisive. Phelps' policy prevails instead of yours"). Butler—who in April 1861 had volunteered troops to support the slave regime in Maryland and the next month, in Virginia, had begun the practice of employing fugitive slaves as "contraband" laborers (thus exciting Congress to pass the First Confiscation Act)—in August 1862 once again reversed himself. He started recruiting slaves under the fiction that they were the "free coloreds" of the Native Guard. From the beginning, Butler had been impressed with its leaders: "In color, nay, also in conduct they had much more the appearance of white gentlemen than some." The unit had originally formed in New Orleans and applied to fight for the Confederacy.[26] Rebuffed on caste terms by their white Confederate peers (many of the free colored's owned slaves), and initially by Butler himself, the coloreds' unit now served as a deceit for the recruitment of fugitive slaves and Black workers.[27]

A few weeks after Butler's maneuver, Lincoln publicly displayed one of his own. On September 22, 1862, he issued the preliminary Emancipation Proclamation, serving notice that on January 1 he would declare then, and thenceforward, and forever free all the slaves in those states still in rebellion. . . . Lincoln also renewed his call for voluntary, gradual, and compensated emancipation in the border states, voiced support for colonizing freed slaves "upon this continent or elsewhere," and promised to recommend that all loyal owners be compensated for the loss of their slaves.[28]

This, as Howard Zinn reasons, gave the South four months to end its rebellion while implicitly "promising to leave slavery untouched in states that came over to the North."[29]

In July 1862, Lincoln had informed his cabinet of his intention to issue an emancipation of slaves in the Confederacy (as Mrs. Butler had surmised). By September, Lincoln was still opposed to the use of Black troops, but he had determined that the Union could not win the war unless it threatened to totally alienate the slaves from the Confederacy. So he promised that the Union forces would assist any slave insurrection. Meanwhile he preserved his conciliatory policy toward the border states and persisted in his conviction that Blacks would have no permanent place in the restored Union. Notwithstanding the president's indecision on arming Blacks, the Congress authorized his use of Black troops on July 17, 1862. In February 1863, Congress passed Thaddeus Stevens's legislation authorizing the raising of 150 regiments of African troops. By then, Lincoln had authorized Butler's three Louisiana regiments, Lane's Kansas regiment, and Governor Andrew's Massachusetts recruitment.

The Blacks' War

McClellan went to Richmond with two hundred thousand braves,
He said, "keep back the niggers and the Union he would save,"
Little Mac, he had his way, still the Union is in tears,
And they call for the help of the colored volunteers.[30]

Of the approximately 189,000 Blacks in the uniform of the Union army and navy, 33,000 enlisted from the free states. The slaves were, by far the more numerous. Berlin and his coauthors report that:

The border states of Delaware, Maryland, Missouri, and Kentucky accounted for a total of nearly 42,000, more than half from Kentucky. Tennessee contributed 20,000; Louisiana, 24,000; Mississippi, nearly 18,000; and the remaining states of the Confederacy accounted for approximately 37,000.

Most enlisters were slaves, then. Although they were now legally unshackled from slavery, Blacks were subjected to new humiliations by military authorities. In Louisiana, the Black commissioned officers of the Native Guard were decimated by administrative maneuvers and replaced by white officers; not until June 1864 did free Blacks (but not the former slaves) receive equal pay; they were used as cannon fodder by some generals; and many of their white comrades-in-arms insulted them in camps, on the battlefields, and elsewhere. Not surprisingly, their treatment by the Southern military was even worse. Black prisoners of war were slaughtered by the Confederates or re-enslaved; and white officers commanding Black troops were summarily executed by the Confederates as "outlaws." In 1888, George Washington Williams, the Black veteran and historian, put the matter baldly: "The Confederate soldier came to understand that it was his privilege and his duty to murder Negro prisoners of war. . . . The world over will rejoice that such a cause has perished from among the governments of mankind."[32] Notwithstanding these horrors, the overwhelming majority of Black troops were volunteers (in contrast, the majority of 2 million non-Black Union soldiers were drafted). Still, both sides slandered Blacks with the invention that they would not or could not fight.

The invention of Black cowardice or infantility was muted by events during the summer of 1863. On May 23, in a catastrophic assault on Port Hudson, Louisiana, the First and Third Louisiana regiments (Black) were repeatedly ordered to advance against what Joseph Wilson, another Black Civil War veteran, described as a Confederate position that "only abject cowardice or pitiable imbecility could have lost." And while the First and Third were sacrificing hundreds, the First Louisiana Regiment of Engineers (also Black), equipped only with picks and shovels and under constant cannon barrages, strove to support the attack by building breastworks or blowing up enemy fortifications. One journalist described the assault as reminding "the lookers on of just so many cattle going to a slaughterhouse."[33] A wounded white officer of the First exclaimed: "I have been in several engagements, and I never before beheld such coolness and darring."[34] In early June at Milliken's Bend in Arkansas, the Ninth and Eleventh Louisiana and the First Mississippi, all Black except for their officers, repelled a larger Confederate force in hand-to-hand combat. Black casualties were 123 killed, 113 murdered (the Southern assault had echoed with cries of "No quarter! No quarter to negroes or their officers").[35] And on July 18, at Fort Wagner in South Carolina, the Fifty-fourth Massachusetts (predominantly free Blacks) under the command of Colonel Robert Shaw led the assault in the evening. After the battle, nearly half of the regiment was dead, wounded, or missing. "Here the brave Shaw, with scores of his black warriors, went down, fighting desperately," one journalist recounted.[36] But another correspondent, Nathaniel Paige of the *New York*

Tribune, testified to a War Department commission in February 1864 that the carnage of Blacks was intentional. Paige recalled that when asked by his superior, General Gilmore, how he planned the attack, General Seymour had replied, "Well, I guess we will let [General] Strong lead and put those d—d niggers from Massachusetts in the advance; we may as well get rid of them, one time as another."[37] Gilmore had laughed and concurred, but after the battle, he ordered that the Black troops under his command would receive the same respect as whites. In their first three major battles, the former slaves and the free Blacks destroyed the invention of their docility, their stupidity, and their cowardice.

Discrimination in the form of unequal pay and the Confederate policy of murdering or enslaving captured Black soldiers and sailors were equally determined. In September 1863, James Henry Gooding, a free Black corporal in the Fifty-fourth Massachusetts, wrote Lincoln, reminding him of the service of Blacks at Fort Wagner: "Now Your Excellency, We have done a Soldiers Duty. Why cant we have a Soldiers pay?" (462) Free Black troopers in the Fifty-fourth and Fifty-fifth Massachusetts, the First African Descent Regiment Volunteers (of Iowa), and other units refused payment for over a year until they were granted equal pay. In late 1863, Sergeant Robert (or perhaps William) Walker of the Third South Carolina Infantry led a mutiny against unequal pay and was shot for upholding the principle.[38] Eventually the issue was settled: in June 1864, Congress provided for equal pay and backpay retroactive to January 1864—but only for the free Blacks! Not until near the end of the war, in March 1865, were the former slaves (and all other Blacks) granted equal pay and payment from their enlistment date. Dudley Cornish, Jr., ninety years later concluded: "It is impossible to measure the harm caused by the federal government's shortsighted and parsimonious policy toward the pay of colored troops. It is impossible to measure human suffering, humiliation, distrust, or the cancer of disloyalty bred of the conviction of having been treated unfairly."[39]

Regarding the Confederate treatment of Black prisoners, Blacks fought until the war's end with the memory of the Massacre at Fort Pillow, Kentucky. On April 13, 1864, General Nathan Bedford Forrest's Confederate forces overran the Union forces, numbering some 557 at Fort Pillow. The Union forces consisted of the Thirteenth Tennessee Cavalry and the Sixth United States Heavy Artillery Battery (Black) supporting a civilian settlement in the fort. According to sworn testimony before a Senate Joint Committee by eyewitnesses, few of the Union forces were killed during the Confederate attack. But, after the surrender, the Confederate forces began systematically killing soldiers, white and Black, as well as the civilians. Jacob Thompson, a Black civilian who fought in the fort and was wounded, testified: "They just called them out like dogs, and shot them down. I reckon they shot about fifty, white and black, right there. They nailed some black sergeants to the logs, and set the logs on fire." James Walls, a white enlisted man with the Thirteenth recounted: "I saw them make lots of niggers stand up, and then they shot them down like hogs. . . . The secesh [secessionists] . . . would come to a [wounded] nigger and say, 'You ain't dead are you?' . . . Then they would make them get up on their knees, when they would shoot them down like hogs." John Nelson, a white volunteer and hotel owner, estimated "that there were not less than three hundred and sixty negroes killed and two hundred whites." In his chronicle of the war, the Black veteran Joseph Wilson observed: "Later on during the war the policy of massacring was somewhat abated, that is it was not done on the battlefield."[40]

Confederate General S. D. Lee believed the motivation for the massacre was obvious: "You had a servile race armed against us." (353) Like other Confederate generals, he was shocked when the "servile" responded in kind to the massacres. The Union general Washburn, however, was not. When, of all people, the leader of the massacre, General Forrest, complained to Washburn that the Blacks had instituted what one of his officers termed "a hunt for wild game," Washburn replied on June 19, 1864:

> You say in your letter that it has been reported to you that all the negro troops stationed in Memphis took an oath, on their knees, in the presence of Major General Hurlburt and other officers of our army, to avenge Fort Pillow and that they would show your troops no quarter. I believe it is true that the colored troops did take such an oath, but not in the presence of General Hurlburt. From what I can learn this act of theirs was not influenced by any white officer, but was the result of their own sense of what was due to themselves and their fellows who had been mercilessly slaughtered. (348)

On April 30, 1863, at Jenkins Ferry, in Arkansas, the Second Kansas Colored made good the pledge. With shouts of "Remember Poison Spring," the Black troops overran a rebel battery: "Confederate casualties were high—about 150 killed or mortally wounded; the 2nd Kansas Colored lost only 15 men killed, and 55 others wounded. One prisoner was taken, by mistake."[41] At Brice's Cross Roads, Mississippi, in June, with Union forces under General Sturgis in retreat from Forrest's army, Blacks from the Sixth United States Cavalry formed the rear guard and "kept firing until their ammunition was expended, then fought with bayonet and clubbed musket, and finally either picked up new weapons and ammunition from the road along which the rest of the Union forces were fleeing, or died." (176)

The shock to the Confederate side was palpable. The conceits of slavery had disintegrated. Armed slaves—displaying none of their heralded docility—were now in the field, positioned to achieve exactly what Confederate propaganda had predicted: the extermination of the white race. The Southern ruling class, largely exempted from military service by a conscription that excused holders of twenty slaves or more, responded to the deteriorating military situation by transporting their slaves out of state (nearly 150,000 to Texas, for example) and themselves to the relative security of Confederate strongholds. And as they fled the Union army and the avenging Black troops who were despoiling slavery even in the unoccupied South, these oligarchs pressed for sacrifice and extreme conscription of Southern white farmers and laborers. No wonder the race-patrolled ties between the Southern white classes began to disintegrate. There were already scores of loyalist communities in the South, particularly in the upcountry; and now they were joined by 100,000 deserters drawn largely from the poorest white Southern class.[42] As DuBois stated: "The poor white not only began to desert and run away; but thousands followed the Negro into the Northern camps."[43]

The concerns that Confederate officers and enlisted men expressed regarding the arming of the slaves and the free Blacks were proven to be well founded. Over the course of the war, Black troops fought in some 449 engagements, according to Frederick Dyer, and Cornish reports that official records indicate that more than 68,000 uniformed Blacks were killed in combat or by disease.[44] Black casualties accounted for some 16 percent of the 360,222 Union killed (of the 800,000 Confederate troops, an estimated 258,000 were killed). The reasons for the disproportionately high number of Blacks killed or wounded are variously named as the valor of the Black troops, the frequent tactic of placing them in the advance of assaults and at the rear of retreats, and the Confederate military policy of "no quarter." But instead of describing Black achievements in major battles, as Cornish does, to counter the conception that Blacks were cowardly, the more economic method might be to excerpt remembrances of command officers and news reports. Recalling that many of the Union officers were indifferent, even hostile, toward the recruitment of Blacks, their comments are illuminating.[45]

Concerning the October 1863 engagement at Baxter Springs between three Union companies (one Black) and the forces of the Missouri guerrilla called Quantrill, Lieutenant James Pond of the Third Wisconsin Cavalry observed: "The darkies fought like devils." After the battle on December 3 and 4, 1863, at Wolf River Bridge near Moscow, Tennessee, General Hurlburt issued a General Order that read in part: "The fact that colored troops, properly disciplined and commanded, can and will fight well . . . [is] due to the officers and men of the Second Regiment west Tennessee Infantry of African Descent." At Olustee (near Jackson, Florida) on February 20, 1864, during a Union defeat, Sergeant Stephen Swails's "coolness, bravery, and efficiency during the action" provided grounds for his later promotion as the first Black to receive a commission in the Fifty-fourth Massachusetts. On June 21, 1864, the Leavenworth *Daily Conservative* reported from Virginia: "The hardest fighting has been done by the black troops. The forts they stormed were the worst of all. After the affair was over General Smith went and thanked them; told them he was proud of them, their courage and dash." At Chaffin's Farm in September 1864, fourteen of the thirty-seven Congressional Medals of Honor awarded for the battle were received by Blacks; and General Butler concluded, naively, "that the capacity of the negro race for soldiers had then and there been fully settled forever." In December 1864, Major General George Thomas observed on the battlefield of Nashville "the bodies of colored men side by side with the foremost on the very works of the enemy," and concluded rashly, "Gentlemen, the question is settled; negroes will fight." Even in the last month of the war, after Lee's surrender on April 9, the question was not yet settled for some. Following the battle for Mobile on April 14, General James Steedman was compelled to praise the Fourteenth United States Colored Troops for their "brilliant charge on the enemy's works" on Overton Hill, despite enormous losses: "I was unable to discover that color made any difference in the fighting of my troops." In the same battle, Colonel Charles Gilchrist, the commander of the Fiftieth United States Colored Infantry, reported from the siege and assault of Fort Blakely guarding Mobile that he had received "convincing proof that the former slaves of the South cannot be excelled as soldiers."

Hundreds of thousands of former slaves and free Blacks participated in the war as Union soldiers and civilians. A few served as Confederate soldiers, while many more thousands were pressed into support services for the rebels. The efforts of the loyalist Blacks won the partial emancipation provided by Lincoln, then made applicable to all by Congress with the Thirteenth Amendment adopted on January 1, 1865.[46] With the Fourteenth Amendment (in 1868), their service was further recognized by the granting of citizenship. With Lincoln assassinated in 1865, Blacks had avoided exile. But as the Reconstruction sputtered and finally was subverted, the majority of Blacks descended into the new slavery, the American apartheid orchestrated by federal and local state officials. Within seven years of the ending of the war, the pendulum swung away from liberty. The original northern objective of the Civil War—to reappropriate the human, capital, and natural resources of the South—had been restored. For more than 130 years, the struggle for freedom and equality was fought against the social impulses and interests revealed in the Draft Riots in New York: a ferociously racist culture, fearful white laboring classes, and the agents of greed. The spectacle of Black sacrifice in the Civil War and the wars that were to follow provided no lasting relief for Blacks, no enduring justification for their freedom, no national resolve for racial justice. Rejection, however, did not kill the desire.

White Reconstruction and Black Deconstruction

With the assassination of Lincoln in April 1865, his vice president, Andrew Johnson, inherited the presidency. Johnson, the only senator of the slavocracy to oppose secession, had been appointed by Lincoln as military governor of Tennessee in 1862 and had joined the Republican ticket in 1864. His selection was no sop to the Confederacy (he displayed the white lower-class contempt of Southern aristocracy), but it did place a man close to the presidency whose obsession with miscegenation would drive him into the camp of conservative capitalists and reviving plantocrats. Once he became president, Johnson pursued policies that ensured the preservation of a subordinate Black labor as the foundation of the Southern economic revival, now orchestrated by northern capital. Rebuffing the "scalawags," the derogatory term for white Southern antisecessionists, and giving evidence of his enduring hatred for Blacks, Johnson carried through Lincoln's Presidential Reconstruction by relinquishing the governments of the defeated states to "rehabilitated" Confederates. And they, forced to recognize the *de jure* status of the Fourteenth Amendment, promptly subverted it in practice, launching a series of "black codes" focused on vagrancy and labor contracts, as Foner details:

> Mississippi and South Carolina enacted the first and most severe Black codes toward the end of 1865. Mississippi required all blacks to possess, each January, written evidence of employment for the coming year. Laborers leaving their jobs before the contract expired would forfeit wages already earned, and, as under slavery, be subject to arrest by any white citizen. . . . To limit the freedmen's economic opportunities, they were forbidden to rent land in urban areas. . . . [And] criminal offenses included "insulting" gestures or language, "malicious mischief," and preaching the Gospel without a license. . . .
>
> South Carolina's Code was in some respects even more discriminatory. . . . It did not forbid blacks to rent land, but barred them from following any occupation other than farmer or servant except by paying an annual tax ranging from $10 to $100 . . . [and regulated] relations between "ser-

vants" ar   "masters" including labor from sunup to sundown and a ban on leaving the plantation, or entertaining guests upon it, without permission of the employer. (199–200)

In Florida, "Blacks who broke labor contracts could be whipped, placed in the pillory, and sold for up to one year's labor." In Louisiana and Texas, labor contracts were interpreted to include "all members of the family able to work." And in Virginia, all labor activism was forbidden. (200) Violence, of course, orchestrated these recreations of slavery, culminating in the riots of 1866 in Memphis (forty-six of the forty-eight killed were Black; five Black women were raped) and New Orleans (thirty-four Blacks, three white Radical Republicans killed). (262–63) Disdaining all economic aid to Blacks on the grounds that it would encourage indolence, Johnson vetoed the congressional attempt to extend the life of the Freedmen's Bureau in 1866; then, confronted with a congressional attempt to extend political privileges to Black males (the Civil Rights Act of 1866), he vetoed that legislation as well. In the meantime, Johnson pardoned over 7,000 rebel leaders: the class he had once despised he now believed was necessary to rule the South, to rule the Blacks.

For Johnson and the business strata that now commanded him, rule over the Blacks was assuming some urgency. In the waning months of the war, and even more so in the first months of the post–Civil war period, the many communities of freed slaves were engaged in self-emancipation. At first unaware of the sinister machinations being concocted in Washington and the nation's commercial capital, New York, the former slaves went about securing their newly won status and testing the prerogatives of free men and women. Foner reports:

> At Mitchelville, in the South Carolina Sea Islands, blacks, under army supervision, had elected a mayor and city council, who controlled local schools and the administration of justice. On Amelia Island, Florida, blacks voted alongside whites in a local election. Other examples of local self-government could be found at Davis Bend and in contraband camps from Virginia to Mississippi. (76)

In accordance with the African culture that they had brought with them, many Blacks created new names for themselves to signify their new identities as free men and women. They drew from American political culture such names as "Jefferson" and "Hamilton," which signified power and authority; they appropriated words and phrases like "Deliverance," "Hope," and "Chance Great" to signify their expectations and dreams.

They confiscated abandoned plantations and houses, the clothing of their former masters, and the land they had worked. In celebration, they held mass meetings and organized religious services.

Hundreds of thousands of former slaves abandoned their plantations, some just to wander freely because that was now possible, but many thousands in search of lost family, separated wives, husbands, children, and family elders. Not all the migrations were away from the sites of their enslavement. Former fugitives returned to their home districts in the thousands; former slaves transported to Texas by slaveholders set forth for their past homes. With the restoration of families, many Black women extracted themselves from the work force so as to raise their own children, care for their own homes, and construct the new Black communities that were appearing all over the South. After family, the second priority was the building of communities, and at the physical and spiritual center of these social bases were churches and schools. Black civilians were not the only agents of the change. "Black troops helped construct schools, churches, and orphanages, organized debating societies, and held political gatherings where 'freedom songs' were sung and soldiers delivered 'speeches of the most inflammatory kind'." (79–80) And, as the realization of what was aborning in Washington began to seep into Black consciousness, the new institutions became the grounds for a new politics. But the freedmen and women would need help against the behemoth of Johnson's federal government.

In Washington itself, disgust for Johnson, his policies, and the audacity of the former rebels propelled his opposition, the Radical Republicans, into a short-lived dominance of the contending political forces in the Congress. In March 1862, the Radical Republican members of Congress had constructed the law forbidding Lincoln's policy of having the Union army return slaves; and in April 1862, it was they who legislated the freeing of slaves in the District of Columbia, eight months before Lincoln's partial emancipation order. Now they took on Lincoln's successor and his northern Democrat allies. Forging what historians have termed the "Congressional Reconstruction" around the Union army and the Bureau of Refugees, Freedmen, and Abandoned Lands, the Radicals constructed a legalist and militarist architecture for the liberation of Blacks and assistance to poor whites. For four years, with much of the ex-Confederacy under martial law, the congressional radicals directed policies that disestablished the Johnson state regimes, provided sporadic judicial and law enforcement of protections to Blacks and other southern Unionists; distributed millions of dollars of food and clothing assistance to poor white and Black Southerners, facilitated the development of public schools, and attempted to create a stable economy.

Established in March 1865 under the Department of War, the Freedmen's Bureau was charged with stabilizing three sectors of Southern life: the white refugees (both poor whites and displaced property owners), the former slaves, and the land confiscated from rebels (approximately 850,000 acres). Initially, it had no authorized budget. Even more damaging, though, the whole project was poised against northern capitalism's war ambitions and visions for the peace. Since it was also dependent upon a dwindling Union army (down to 152,000 by the end of 1865, and 38,000 a year later) and Union officers appointed by Johnson who were often indifferent or hostile to Blacks, the bureau could only partially achieve its more radical objectives: the transformation of Black labor from slave to free labor, the disenfranchisement of former rebels committed to insurgency, land grants to the poor, and political equality. Pinned between the competing objectives of securing Black labor for the restoration of cash crop, plantation cultivation, and the necessity of protecting the freedmen and freedwomen from renewed oppression, the bureau and the army achieved a mixed result.

On the negative side of the ledger, Reconstruction reneged on the promises of generals William T. Sherman and Rufus Saxton to distribute confiscated land to the freedmen, a betrayal of particular frustration to the freedmen in South Carolina, Georgia, and Florida, where appropriations had already begun. Of equal importance, on the related matter of labor contracts, the army and the bureau tended to support the sorts of oppressive labor contracts legislated by the Johnson state regimes. In the interest of both policies, the army frequently arrested Blacks striking against the near-slavery of labor contracts and used force against Blacks unwilling to surrender land they were now cultivating; the bureau insisted that all unemployed Blacks (but not unemployed whites) had to submit to labor contracts. Away from the cities and centers of occupation troops, the army achieved less and less protection for Blacks. As James Sefton recognized, "The melancholy fact was that no amount of troops could have prevented assaults on Negroes when the crimes took place on remote stretches of country roads by disguised men."[47] On the positive side of the ledger, the bureau did relieve starvation among poor Blacks and whites in the months immediatly after the closing of the war. The bureau law courts did provide relief to Blacks contesting white contract cheats and provided some symbolic support to the legal equality of whites and Blacks under (federal) law. Finally, the bureau most definitely advanced public education. Under the auspices of the bureau and the American Missionary Society, hundreds of white and Black teachers (some males, but predominantly females) rushed to the South to begin schooling and literacy campaigns. Their efforts built more than 3,000 schools and reached more than 150,000 Black children. Under the watchful eyes of the industrial capitalists who dominated the bureau's commission, corporate philanthropy "founded and staffed the first black colleges in the South, including Berea, Fisk, Hampton, and Tougaloo."[48]

Conservative Southern whites, however, were in no way passive spectators of the interventions of the Union army, the Freedmen's Bureau, abolitionist volunteers, or the freed human property. With their ally Johnson either neutralized by congressional action on Black suffrage or at least somewhat less effective in the disciplining of Black labor, the violence once held in check by the status of Blacks as property now crescendoed into a campaign of terror. "'I saw white men whipping colored men just the same as they did before the war,' testified ex-slave Henry Adams, who claimed that 'over two thousand colored people' were murdered in 1865 in the area around Shreveport, Louisiana."[49] In North Carolina, "Carpetbagger Judge Albion W. Tourgee counted twelve murders, nine rapes, fourteen cases of arson, and over 700 beatings (including the whipping of a woman 103 years of age) in his judicial district." In Jackson county in Florida, 150 Blacks were killed. In South Carolina the violence was so extensive that one victimized Black leader, Elias Hill, organized an emigration to Liberia with sixty families. (430–31) Ironically, the organization of Southern white mob violence through the instruments of the Ku Klux Klan, the Knights of the White Camelia, the White Brotherhood, the White League, and similar secret societies reinvigorated radical reconstruction, for a time rescuing it from an increasingly negligent Congress. Responding to a surge of violence between 1868 and 1871, the Congress was forced to revive, much more than its majority intended, the enforcement of the martial law imposed on the former Confederacy in 1867.

The immediate targets of the Klan and its familiars were, expectedly, the emerging civil rights coalition: the former slaves, Freedmen's Bureau, scalawags, and Republicans. What was most threatening to the conservatives in the North and the South was the coalescing of these several elements into a radical political party, the Union League. Organized during the war as a patriotic club, after the war satellites of the league began to flourish all over the South in support of Black suffrage and Republican office holders. Combining the elements of a political mission, recreational clubs, and secular religion, the Union or Loyalty League bound the progressive white and Black members of hundreds of Southern communities through ritual, ceremony, and objectives. As the elections of 1866, 1868, and 1870 demonstrated, where the leagues thrived Blacks exercised voting privileges and Republican victories ensued. By unloosing murder, rape, beating, and arson upon the members of the league, the Klan sought to intimidate Black and white Republicans from participation in the polls, destroy Republican political influence, terrorize Republican office holders, subvert the juridical and physical protections of Blacks secured by the Freedmen's Bureau and the Union Army, and retard any development of Black economic independence. The Klan was, as Robert Gleeds, the ex-slave and Mississippi state senator, put it, a party based "on the principle of the open slaughter of human beings."[50] In two years, the Klan slaughtered 20,000 men, women and children.

The Klan made its first appearance in Pulaski, Tennessee, in 1865. Originally organized as a social club for former Confederate officers, by 1867 its more permanent character was apparent in Nashville at its first convention. Selecting none other than General Nathan Bedford Forrest as its first Grand Dragon (Robert E. Lee had declined the office while sending his "invisible" support), the secret fraternal order pledged its members to the support and protection of the United States Constitution; to chivalry, humanity, mercy, and patriotism; and to "maintain[ing] the purity of the white blood, if we would preserve for it that natural superiority with which God has ennobled it."[51] In pursuance to its truer mission, it proceeded to violate every one of these precepts. The innumerable rapes of Black women, the murders of Black women and children, the violent expulsion of elected officials, the killing and intimidation of voters, and even robbery made a mockery of the official Klan creed of race purity and constitutional fealty.

The ideological shield that concealed the Klan and blinded many of them from their own inhumanity and lawlessness was white supremacy. Over the next half-century, the stuttering pseudoscience of white supremacist doctrine would achieve its most formidable development in the hands of scientists and intellectuals like Louis Agassiz (of Harvard), scholars like John Burgess and William Dunning (both at Columbia), Walter Fleming (Vanderbilt), the wealthy scion James Ford Rhodes, and Woodrow Wilson (Bryn Mawr, Wesleyan, and Princeton). Like their lesser-known colleagues, these founding figures in the formation of American natural science, political science, and history transported scientific racism into the highest realms, helping to implicate not only the most prestigious institutions of education and government with this formalist variant of racism, but also to cultivate and transmit the formidable genus of hatred to their social inferiors (33ff) Of equal importance to the Klan and its successor organizations was that from its beginnings the secret order was founded and led by eminent local personalities and defended by intellects with international and national reputations. In his multivolume American history, Woodrow Wilson, the future president, wrote that the Klan emerged among whites "by the mere instinct of self-preservation" only to happen across "the delightful discovery of the thrill of awesome fear which their sheeted, hooded figures sent among their former slaves."[52] Characteristically, when the "best people" were not denying the very existence of the Klan, they were celebrating its existence, invoking the standard of a racial morality that transcended Christianity and the Constitution.

The real Klan was neither instinctual in its origins and objectives, as Wilson suggested, nor "white trash." Moreover, their disguises as the ghosts of dead Confederate soldiers were not convincing. Though his remark that "few freedmen took such nonsense seriously" related to the masquerade for the dead, Foner's observation might be taken as a rebuke for all three claims:

> The group that attacked the home of Mississippi scalawag Robert Flournoy, whose newspaper had denounced the Klan as "a body of midnight prowlers, robbers, and assassins," included both poor men and property holders, "as respectable as anybody we had there." Among his sixty-five Klan assailants, Abram Colby [a Black Georgian legislator who had organized Georgia's Equal Rights Association] identified men "not worth the bread they eat," but also some of the "first-class men in our town," including a lawyer and a physician.
>
> Personal experience led blacks to blame the South's "aristocratic classes" for violence and with good reason, for the Klan's leadership included planters, merchants, lawyers, and even ministers. (432)

Smith Watley, another Black victim, testified simply, "I counted sixteen men. I knew them all almost. . . . I didn't make no mistake because I have known some of them twenty years."[53] Knowing the reality of the Klan, some of its victims retaliated: in Blount County, Alabama, white Union Army veterans formed and threatened the Klan with reprisals; in Bennettsville, South Carolina, armed Blacks patrolled the town; on an Alabama plantation, Blacks challenged Klan attackers to "fight it out"; in Arkansas in 1871, three whites involved in the killing of a Black lawyer were lynched by freedmen; in Grant Parish, Louisiana, in 1873, Black veterans and militia held the county seat of Colfax for three weeks before being overpowered and slaughtered (280 dead) by Democrats intent on destroying the local government.[54]

As the events in Colfax demonstrated, state militias or the federal army were needed if the Klan was to be stopped. In only two states, Arkansas and Texas, did governors respond effectively. In the rest of the South, state governors and local officials vacillated, hoping to win over white voters to

*too little
too late*

the Republican party through moderation and compromise. The tactic
failed dismally. By 1870–71, when the Congress intervened with the Fifteenth Amendment, the Enforcement Acts, and the Ku Klux Klan Act of
1871, the Klan's terror had achieved its objectives. Southern Unionists and
the Union Leagues had been decimated. The new president, Ulysses
Grant, did have his military round up and imprisoned Klansmen in North
Carolina, South Carolina, and Mississippi in 1871, but this was the last
forceful imposition of Reconstruction. From that moment forward, Blacks
and their comrades fought a losing, rear-guard action as the Republican
party accommodated itself to the reemergence of the Southern Democrats
and the dictates of capital. When in 1877, President Rutherford Hayes at
least symbolically removed the army from the South, Black peonage had
become the new social and economic order.

The most potent Black response to the subversion and eventual ending
of Reconstruction was populist Black separatism. Although its most palpable form was emigration, it differed rather significantly from the antebellum nationalism of Delany (now a South Carolina legislator), Mary Ann
Shadd Cary (who penned a literacy pamphlet on Black history for the
Freedmen's Bureau), or Henry Garnet. One difference was the sheer scale
of the movement. As Nell Irvin Painter records, between 1879 and 1880,
some 60,000 Blacks emigrated from Alabama, Louisiana, North Carolina,
Texas, and Mississippi to Kansas and Indiana.[55] Another was the clandes-
tine character of the movement, which began as early as 1869 in some
parts of the South and only publicly surfaced in 1877. A third distinction
was that the movement occurred outside the orbit of elite Black leaders,
particularly those who had sought and still hoped to mirror the class and
social development of the "responsible" strata of Euro-America. All of this
was confirmed, V. P. Franklin reports, when a Senate committee began its
hearings in January 1880: "One hundred fifty-three black and white wit-
nesses were examined from North Carolina, Georgia, Alabama, Mississippi, Louisiana, Texas, Missouri, Kansas, and Indiana."[56]

"To my own knowledge," Henry Adams testified, "two thousand colored
people [were] killed trying to get away, after the white people told us we
were free, which was in 1865." Adams's knowledge was extensive, for "in
1870 Adams and several other black Civil War veterans formed 'the Committee,' whose purpose was to collect information on Afro-American
social, economic, and political conditions and 'to look into affairs and see
the true conditions of our race, to see whether it was possible we could
stay under a people who had held us under bondage or not'." (128) The
Committee, which at its largest had included 500 members, recruited 150
or so field researchers to go throughout the South, live and work with

Black separatism

the Committee

other Blacks, and collect observations: "We worked some of us, worked our way from place to place and went from "State to State and worked . . . amongst our people in the fields, everywhere, to see what sort of living our people lived."[57] The Committee had also banned Black politicians from its organization: "No politicianers didn't belong to it, because we didn't allow them to know nothing about it, because we was afraid that if we allowed the colored politicianer to belong to it he would tell it to the Republican politicianers, and from that the men that was doing all this to us would get hold of it, too, and then get after us." (164)

In 1875, a Black national convention was held in New Orleans to which Adams was a delegate. The convention endorsed emigration to the North, the West, or Liberia. In 1876, the Committee renamed itself, becoming the National Colored Colonization Council: "Well, we found ourselves in such condition that we looked around and we seed that there was no way on earth, it seemed, that we could better our conditions there, and we discussed that thoroughly in our organization along in May."(166) The council now began to gather the names of potential emigrants while petitioning Congress and President Hayes:

> Then, in 1877 we appealed to President Hayes and to Congress, to both Houses. I am certain we sent papers there; if they didn't get them that is not our fault; we sent them. . . .
>
> We asked for protection, to have our rights guaranteed to us, and at least if that could not be done; we asked that money should be provided to send us to Liberia. . . .
>
> In 1877, too, we declared that if we could not get a territory we would go anywhere on God's earth; we didn't care where. . . .
>
> Yes, anywhere to leave them Southern States. We declared that in our council in 1877. We said we would go anywhere to get away. (166–67)

By August 1877, Adams testified, 69,000 Black men and women had enrolled; by April 1879, the council had gathered over 98,000 names (mostly from Louisiana, but some from Texas, Arkansas, and Mississippi). By 1877, public meetings of the council were being held (with some 5,000 in attendance at one) in Shreveport, Caddo Parish, Madison, and Bossier Parish. Notwithstanding the detailed testimony of Adams and others, the majority report of the Senate committee concluded that the movement was the result of "outside agitators."[58]

In South Carolina, the Liberian Exodus Joint-Stock Steamship Company pursued a similar solution. In Tennessee, emigration was also in the wind, leading to the inauguration of such organizations as the Edgefield

Real Estate Association. But, as that organization's name implied, the objective was not Liberia but Kansas. The association was one of several organizations with which Benjamin "Pap" Singleton would be associated, the man who claimed to be "the father of the exodus." In time, from the mid-1870s to the late 1880s, Singleton would be involved with a number of groups, the majority concerned with emigration. But Painter maintains that Singleton and his associates, despite their attempts at appropriation of the emigration movement, played only a partial (and secondary) role in the Black migration to Kansas, which as early as 1870 had brought almost 16,000 Blacks to the state and in another decade would swell that number to over 43,000. This migration, like the one that would grip several thousand Blacks in the spring months of 1879, was "a spontaneous, popular movement." Neither had required a "single great leader."[59] Kansas, itself, was their inducement, just as post-Reconstruction society was their catalyst. For the landless Black agrarians, the bitter antebellum struggle that had marked the securing of Kansas's Free Statehood, the abundance of the state's fertile land, and the memory of John Brown sufficed.

Adams testified that Black "politicianers" and ministers had opposed the emigration. He supposed it was because the Black migration would decrease the power of Black politicians and local churches. Implicit in his observations, however, was not merely a class-based critique. Quite obviously, Adams recognized that the interests of the emergent Black elite differed in some ways from what he termed "laboring men." Adams and his comrades had appealed to the federal government to either protect their rights and privileges or provide them a territory, "somewhere where we could go and live with our families."

Q. You preferred to go off somewhere by yourselves?
A. Yes. . . . If that failed, our other object was to ask for an appropriation of money to ship us all to Liberia in Africa; somewhere where we could live in peace and quiet.[60]

But the choice laid before the president and the Congress by the council was either to substantiate their citizenry or to facilitate their separation. And separation bore none of the ambitious political designs encrusted onto antebellum Black nationalism by Delany and his cohorts. Here was a complete void of the desire for a nation or a nation-state—just a utopia of peace, quiet, and families.

While hundreds of Southern Black political leaders were ensnared in the enervating struggle of political maneuver within the nexus of electoral and institutional politics, the Black laboring class was imagining a totally alternative future, one that evoked the statelessness of their African ancestors and, more immediately, the culture of New World marronage. As Nell Irvin Painter observes:

> In the South . . . where most Blacks were slaves, they shared a rural, non-literate folk culture, which of course endured well past the Civil War. Firmly egalitarian and marked by strong racial cohesion, they commonly spoke of "our race," "the colored people," and "our color," manifesting an enduring communal identity. [61]

Thus if Adams appeared to his Senate interrogators to be surprisingly untroubled by the failure of the president and Congress to respond to his people's appeal, it may have been because American civil rights were only a second-best alternative. The council had not taken official America at its words (the Emancipation Proclamation, the Thirteenth, Fourteenth, and Fifteenth Amendments), but merely provided a final opportunity to fulfill them: "We sent papers there; if they didn't get them that is not our fault; we sent them." The expected failure—failure and not betrayal—had been realized.

There remained, however, among the Black elites some smidgen of the light of liberation, as founded in their liberal concept of the fight for the slaves' freedom. Delany had moved from the Freedmen's Bureau to state politics in South Carolina; Smalls, the talented slave captain, took state and congressional offices there; Alonzo Ransier and Richard Gleaves served as lieutenant governors; and Francis L. Cardozo served as secretary of state and state treasurer in South Carolina. In other locales, men like A. K. Davis (of Mississippi), Oscar J. Dunn, P.B.S. Pinchback, and C.C. Antoine (all three of Louisiana) also served as lieutenant governors. At the federal level, Black leaders such as Hiram R. Revels (completing Jefferson Davis's term) and Blanche K. Bruce (both from Mississippi) served in the Senate; and John Roy Lynch (Mississippi), Benjamin S. Turner (Alabama), Robert C. DeLarge, Robert B. Elliott and Joseph H. Rainey (all three of South Carolina), Josiah T. Walls (Florida), Jefferson F. Long (Georgia), and sixteen others were in the House of Representatives. From this near pinnacle of American political institutions, they futilely persevered against the collapse of their dreams of equality and freedom. Our immediate concern, however, is that these "representative colored men" were largely irrelevant to the Black masses as the latter took upon themselves the project of evolving a vital community life. "In actual fact," Painter argues, "when uneducated Blacks needed to take public community action, they invariably reached commonsense conclusions hammered out in mass meetings." (22)

With this historic juncture—the dismantling of Reconstruction—the competing paradigms of Black American politics were established, never to be quite the simple cycle among "Negro intellectuals" of assimilation, nationalism, and separatism that some have taken Harold Cruse to signify. As we have seen, some like Delany could without warning jockey from one position to another. Most of the disparate movements of the late nineteenth century and the present, however, have profound grounds. Thus, while they might be catalyzed by their immediate historical circumstances, their bases are in alternative world views germinated from radically different Black experiences. From among the antebellum free Blacks, historical consciousness emerged that mirrored the liberal, aristocratic American classes. From among the slaves, older African sensibilities were preserved, fertilized in the New World by marronage and the work regimes of plantation slavery.

CHAPTER FIVE

The Nadir and Its Aftermath

* * *

Being a problem is a strange experience. . . .

One ever feels his two-ness,—an American, a Negro; two souls, two thoughts, two unreconciled strivings; two warring ideals in one dark body, whose dogged strength alone keeps it from being torn asunder.

—W.E.B. DuBois, *The Souls of Black Folk*

In the long, violent, and increasingly oppressive era that followed the Civil War and the failed Reconstruction, land (or more particularly the appropriation of land), marred, thwarted, and maimed the promise of a democratic American social contract. The land taken from the Native American, the land refused the former slaves and the poor whites, the land withheld from the poor immigrants from Asia, Europe, and Central America, formed the politics of the republic into a stark social war between the super-rich and the grubbing poor. This horrid contest between the few and the many was made even more reprehensible, in the general opinion, because of its contrast with the democratic rhetoric of the "Founding Fathers." Perhaps a genuine understanding of the ancient site of democratic politics (Greece) might have proven sufficiently instructive to temper the class war. But greed has no natural or genetic links with historical memory. It is commanded by the immediate moment. The foundling American republic, which had borrowed from Athens its rhetoric but not its institutions, now seemed destined to replicate Athens's self-subversion.

At the beginnings of Athenian democracy, nearly two and a half millennia before the American republic, the civic leader Solon, cajoled by the wealthy, rejected the demand of impoverished and enslaved Athenians for the redistribution of the land. During the extended disintegration of Athenian democracy in the fourth century B.C., the failure to equalize access to land and to habituate the wealthy few to a democratic culture propelled Athens to its own demise.[1] In the late nineteenth and early twentieth centuries, in an almost identical train of actions, America accumulated its own negations: scattered, impoverished, agrarian outposts of Native Americans; millions of Southern Black sharecroppers; hundreds of thousands of immigrant workers in the extractive and manufacturing industries; and growing urban settlements of poor Blacks, poor whites, and poor immigrants. Thus, a variegated American labor was poised to reject its masters. The staging for the radical unions, the desperately militant strikes of the same period, and even the calculated terror of workers' organizations was put in place. And just as the Irish, the Poles, the Italians, the Scandinavians, and others brought their historical cultures into the American struggle, Blacks responded to this public betrayal by those representing wealth in ways determined by their own social and ideological development.

By the second half of the nineteenth century, two alternative Black political cultures had arisen, each nurtured by a particular Black experience. Akin to the social divergences that appeared throughout slave societies in the New World, communities of free Blacks gravitated toward the privileged political and social identities jealously reserved for non-Blacks. At the same time, on the plantations and in the slave quarters, slaves tended to form a historical identity that presumed a higher moral standard than that which seemed to bind their masters.

Among the two formations in the United States, the better publicized was the assimilationist Black political culture that appropriated the values and objectives of the dominant American creed. Especially among the urban free Blacks of the colonial and antebellum periods, a liberal, bourgeois consciousness was nourished, packed with capitalist ambitions and individualist intuitions. A constant before and after the Civil War and into the new century, this consciousness manifested itself in a tendency toward an Americanist optimism about integration/assimilation. When assimilation seemed ill-conceived, the quiescent Black middle stratum of wage laborers and professionals hunkered down, and a minority and renegade species of Black nationalist desires was enjoined. But within this galaxy of liberalism, regardless of variant, a special affection for republican values predominated, grounded on a presumption that leadership was reserved for an elite defined by nature and excellence. It was, to other Americans, the more easily understood of the two political cultures, because it flowed from the political and social intercourse between this free Black "elite" and American society in general. Moreover, since bourgeois Black culture mirrored dominant political beliefs, it had the advantage of an economy of expression. Taking American material values and national ambitions for granted, liberal Black political culture could resonate with the ongoing public articulation of the American majority. Given this license, it was possible to frequently create the illusion and self-serving conceit that such values and interests represented Blacks *en masse*.

To the contrary, the Black mass movements of the late nineteenth and twentieth centuries proved both the existence and vitality of an alternative Black political culture, emergent from the brutal rural regimes of slavery and, later, peonage. Inventive rather than imitative, communitarian rather than individualistic, democratic rather than republican, Afro-Christian rather than secular and materialist, the social values of these largely agrarian people generated a political culture that distinguished between the inferior world of the political and the transcendent universe of moral goods. Separatism was the principal impulse of this culture, and over the next century or more this separatism would assume the several forms already familiar: marronage, emigration, migration, and domestic or external colonization. Although it foreclosed the possibility of integration or assimilation, separatism in its most sanguine manifestations accommodated the possibility of social coexistence, avoiding the moral squalor of Black racism. But in times of acute oppression, the impulse could assume the forms of xenophobia, including the most virulent forms of race-hatred rising from both real and imagined experiences.

At the onset of slave communities in the sixteenth and seventeenth centuries, the first mass movement of slaves was cultural. On plantations, and then in the artisanal and agrarian laboring sites, slaves set about forming a singular social and historical racial identity out of the disparate African, Native American, and European memories, languages, and customs that cohabited in the literal and cultural spaces made available by the Atlantic slave trade, colonialism, and the plantation regime. The work discipline of agrarian slave labor, the sweep of European and Euro-American wars of conquest and pacification, and the regimens of labor resistance set the stage for marronage, which further propelled and accelerated the new racial identity of the Black oppressed. Then in the nineteenth century, with the *de jure* extinction of slavery, the racial construction of Blackness opened possibilities of collective autonomy in the Reconstruction era. Marronage was converted into emigration, the search for an open rather than a secret place. Black communities sprang forth in the South, the Midwest, and elsewhere. When this quest for open self-sufficiency was frustrated—for all but the few thousands determined to reach Kansas, Indiana, points west and north—the self-reinvention of the Black millions remaining in the South once again took a cultural form. While ex-slaves undertook a slow migration from the South, their creation of a Blues people deepened, founding a secular vein out of Afro-Christian belief. Thus, on the surface, while the successive onsets of white exclusion, peonage, and then segregation seemed to numb Black desire, in actuality that desire assumed subterranean forms of expression and masked circularity.

Thus, two political impulses matured, one open, the other more fugitive. In the decades that followed the end of Reconstruction, these ideological surges at times coalesced, at others diverged, and at still other historical moments vanquished the others to the margins. As essentially ideological frameworks, they bore the capacity to transcend their historical and social origins, acquiring adherents through emotional persuasion and ideational authority rather than stemming from social inheritance, and were transmitted as oral tradition and cultural memory. Their impulses' relative vitality was determined by external cultural forces and local political circumstance, but most frequently by economic currents.

Afro-Christianity and the Exodus

During the violent, oppressive, and disheartening trial that was post–Civil War America, Black Christianity was at once the dominant social and moral philosophy, the centering source of collective and personal identity, and the conceptual marking device for the historical past and political destiny of Blacks. Even the secular religion of Radical Republicanism, which had earned affection from the Black masses during the Civil War and Reconstruction, had been largely assimilated as a trope of Black Christianity. John Brown and Abraham Lincoln were understood as saints or messiahs, inspired by the Almighty to aid his Black children, the new Israelites. For generations to come, the mythic elements of the emancipation saga were preserved in Afro-Christian prayer, sermons, spirituals, work, songs, and speech. But the times had worn the jubilation thin, compelling a reinterpretation and adjustment of the vision of the promised land. For a particular stratum of Blacks and a select few, Republicanism retained its hold on the imagination, but for the masses it lost power. For the former, America was an unfulfilled promise; for the latter, America held little special significance. It was merely one more land of troubles. With this understanding, the mass of Blacks bent to the task of rescuing family, community, and their race. Most emphatically, as historians have chorused, it was the church that rose to become the central institution, the signal agency at the core of the Black community.

The beginnings of the Black church in America have been traced to the mid- or late-eighteenth century. Initially, Black Baptist congregations formed separate churches in the South (both Savannah, Georgia, and Silver Bluff, South Carolina, have been suggested as the first sites); but toward the end of the century, separate Black Methodist and Episcopal churches appeared in the North (Philadelphia and Baltimore) under the leadership of Black ministers such as Richard Allen, Absalom Jones, and then Daniel Coker. Within the first two decades of the national era, spurred by white discrimination and ritual and doctrinal differences, separate congregations reformed into an independent Black church movement.[2] Will Gravely reports:

> Incidents of white pastors refusing to take black infants into their arms to christen them (Washington, D.C.), of blacks having to wait until all whites were served the Lord's Supper before being admitted to the table (Ohio), of conflicts over access to burial grounds (Charleston, South Carolina) and of constraints on freedom of expression in worship (Cincinnati, Ohio) served to set off black resistance.[3]

Eventually, from the organization in the North of separate congregations (the Methodist African Zoar, Philadelphia, 1794; the St. Thomas African Episcopal Church, Philadelphia, 1794; the Joy Baptist Church, Boston, 1805; the Abyssinian Baptist Church in New York, 1808; and the African Baptist Church, Philadelphia, 1809), the seed of Black denominations was sown. The African Methodist Society came into being in 1813; the African Methodist Episcopal Church (AME) in 1816; the African Methodist Episcopal Zion (AMEZ) in 1822. Gravely summarizes:

> Black denominationalism became a reality in three African Methodist organizations between 1813 and 1822. In partial forms, it expanded with the American Baptist Missionary Convention in 1840, the Congregational and Presbyterian evangelical associations and conventions of the 1840s and 1850s and in regional black Baptist associations and conventions in the midwest, like the Western Colored Baptist Convention (1853ff.) and the Northwestern and Southern Baptist Convention (1864). (69)

Largely at the behest of free Blacks and fugitive slaves living in the North, the Black church made its institutional appearance.

While historians of the early Black church have conventionally documented these events in the tradition of the great-man school of history, ironically the best known of the early Black Methodists and Methodist-

Episcopalians were Black women: Sojourner Truth and Harriet Tubman, respectively. Now, with the beginnings of intensive research into the historic role of Black women, Tubman and Sojourner have been joined by others. Within the Methodist society and its several schisms, for examples, there were the eighteenth-century slaves Mother Suma (of Boston) and Aunt Hester (of Franklin, Louisiana), whose lay ministries are part of early Methodist history; Maria Stewart (of Hartford), whose abolitionist and self-help sermons were published in 1835; in the nineteenth century, the missionaries to Liberia, Francis Burns, Lavinia Johnson, and Sarah Simpson; and Amanda Smith, who was called to England, India, and Liberia.[4] It was, however, only in the late nineteenth century that Black women from the vast underclass came to the fore.

In the language of religious historians, the term *exodus* is employed to describe the withdrawal of Black congregations from biracial worship early in the nineteenth century. Of the postbellum era, the term has also been used to capture the mass withdrawal of Southern Blacks from the Baptist and Methodist organizations dominated by whites. Thus, by the late nineteenth century, the number of Blacks in the National Baptist Convention, USA, was reportedly at 1,700,000; in the African Methodist Society, something like 400,000 Blacks were involved in the exodus (among the other Christian denominations—the Presbyterians, Quakers, and so on— the least affected seems to have been the relatively small Black Catholic community). In effect, the two Black political cultures had assumed institutional form: for the Black liberals, Methodism and Methodist-Episcopalianism; for the Black Democrats, the Baptist church. When the former slave and leading Black intellectual, William Wells Brown, visited the South in 1879–80, he was not pleased by his encounters with Afro-Christianity's purer forms and particularly the emotionalism of Baptist service. Brown prescribed an "educated ministry" as the cure, but lamented that "it is very difficult . . . to induce the uneducated, superstitious masses to receive and support an intelligent Christian clergyman."[5] Like Bishop Daniel Alexander Payne of the AME, Reverend Alexander Crummell (of the Episcopal Church), Martin Delany, and Edward Wilmot Blyden—all of whom denounced Afro-Christian emotionalism and religious ritual exuberance—Brown marked a division among Black nationalists between those for whom religion was a "rational," Republican creed and those who drew on its messianic force for a vision of liberation.[7]

The exodus occurred suddenly, coinciding with Reconstruction and what the white South deemed Redemption. Between 1866 and 1877, more than 600,000 Black Baptists withdrew to the Consolidated American Baptist Missionary Convention; in 1879, fueled by an intense revivalism, the

Foreign Mission Convention was organized by Black Baptists to take the word to Africa. Some 250,000 Black Methodists, the vast majority former slaves, severed their relationship with the Methodist Episcopal Church of the South in order to begin the Colored (later Christian) Methodist Episcopal Church (CME). By 1871, Katherine Dvorak indicates, "the pattern of joint worship that prevailed throughout the antebellum period had changed to one of virtually total racial separation."[7] Shocked by the suddenness, scale, and moral intensity of the exodus, white Christians at first "mourned," Dvorak reports, predicting that Blacks would return. Eventually, the rupture was rationalized by the conceit that the Christian community had always been and was rightly destined to be racially separated: "Later generations would assume that the relationship of black and white Christians had always been as it was. . . . Even though the early period was replete with white expressions of regret, hope for a return to antebellum biracial patterns, and ambivalence, later sentiment—which had hardened into rejection—was commonly read back in time." (181)

For Blacks, the Afro-Christianity that had seethed beneath the regime of slavery now burst forth. In the vortex of the revivalism of the late nineteenth century, the Old Testament narrative of the Israelites and their freedom gained even more power; the book of Revelations revived the eschatology of deliverance (Jesus as deliverer); and the moral and ethical creed of Black Christians seceded from what Dvorak characterizes as "the individualistic, duty-full morality advocated by whites." (186) Black women, the overwhelming majority of certainly the Baptist congregations, fashioned and organized theology and community. As Prathia Hall Wynn puts it: "It was largely through the work of women that local churches (along with the regional and national Baptist conventions) could erect church buildings and schools, provide such basic survival needs as food and clothing for the poor, and spread a gospel of self-help, self-discipline and self-determination."[8] In her study of the most publicly intellectual of these women (Mary Virginia Cook Parrish, Fannie Barrier Williams, Lucy Wilmot Smith, Nannie Helen Burroughs, and Virginia Broughton), Evelyn Brooks Higginbotham observes, "One could say that the black Baptist church represented a sphere for public deliberation and debate precisely because of women."[9] Thus, while many of the Black male leaders of the Baptists fought over institutional power (the Foreign Mission Board, the Publishing Board, local church autonomy versus the national convention, and so on), created and led organizational schisms, and indulged in financial corruption, Black women activists forged bonds with their white Baptist counterparts to champion causes like female suffrage and women's economic independence, and Black female theologians manufactured through lectures and writings a theology championing a "common concern for women's empowerment in the home, the church, social reform, and the labor force." (128)

Growing further apart from white Christianity, as the white Southern Redemption degraded into an American apartheid, Afro-Christianity plumbed new as well as ancient doctrinal forms, theologies, and ceremonies. Eventually, in the first years of the twentieth century, and concomitant with the Southern migrations to the cities of the North and South and schisms among Black Baptists, a synthesis of Africanity and Christianity was forged. In Los Angeles in 1906, Pentecostalism burst forth from the Baptist womb, inspiring Black, white, and Hispanic congregations. With its beliefs in healing, possession, speaking in tongues, ecstasy, spirit-filled objects, and the use of the drum, Pentecostalism rose to become the second largest religious community among Blacks even while it influenced the worship of the Baptists, the larger society of Afro-Christian communicants.

The historical trajectory of Pentecostalism, indeed its very emergence, was propelled by the Black experience of America in the postbellum era. Betrayal of the Civil War, betrayal of Reconstruction, betrayal of radical Republicanism, the betrayal that Jim Crow signified, all culminated with the final betrayal at the end of the nineteenth century: the forfeiture of the right to land for the majority of Blacks still inhabiting the South. Resolved that Blacks should permanently exist as a cheap, accessible agrarian labor force, American capitalists employed racism to recruit white industrial wage laborers. Thus denied the right to autonomous farmholds, the Black migrations began (accompanied, ironically, by poor whites who as agents of racism had sealed their own fate).

Black Agrarians and Populism

In the 1870s and more aggressively in the 1880s, organizations of white farmers and artisanal laborers amassed to challenge the nation's merchants, bankers, railroad corporations, and the like. While the new farmers' cooperatives were patterned in part along the organizational lines of the Patrons of Husbandry (called the Grange) that were so successful in the 1870s, they differed by drawing their leadership from local ministers and editors rather than from large planters. Still, like the Grange, they employed lecturers to spread the word and raise local orders. In this fashion they preserved a certain ideological integrity, seeking redress for the small landowners who dominated the electoral pool but seldom held sway over politicians. Spawned from local circumstances rather than from national headquarters, they nevertheless achieved a formidable unity of purpose:

the establishment of cooperative stores, purchasing initiatives, and cooperative markets for the buying and selling of cotton and other produce. They also sought a graduated income tax; a national bureau of labor; an interstate commerce commission; a flexible money supply; control over land speculation; an end to futures markets for agricultural products; the convict-leasing system; and the founding of agricultural colleges.

In Louisiana, the most successful farmers' cooperative called itself the Farmers' Union; in Arkansas, the Agricultural Wheel and the Brothers of Freedom appeared in the early 1880s; in Mississippi, the farmers organized the Great Agricultural Relief; and in Texas, the Farmers' Alliance, the most spectacular of them all, sprung up in the western regions of the state. Indeed, it was from Texas, Edward Ayers testifies, that the farmers' movement expanded and empowered the several state organizations of the deep South:

> By 1888, the Alliance had pushed farther east, into what were to be some of its strongholds in the nineties: Alabama, Georgia, and North Carolina. In 1889, the Farmers' Alliance claimed 662,000 members in the Southern states; a year later, 852,000. In 1890, Texas had 225,000 members, Alabama 120,000, Georgia 104,000, Mississippi 80,000, North Carolina 78,000. Over half of all eligible people—rural folk over twenty-one—eventually joined the Alliance in Arkansas, Florida, Mississippi, and Georgia, while more than four in ten of those eligible joined in Alabama, South Carolina, North Carolina, Texas, and Tennessee.[10]

Dominated by small and modest landowners (rather than farm tenants or large planters), the alliance created cooperatives at the local, county, and state levels, warehousing goods to position itself to bypass merchants and middlemen, striking deals with local distributors for discount or wholesale prices, and even organizing "manufacturing firms to turn out implements or household goods for farmers." (222) Unfortunately, as the alliance moved east, absorbing or allying with state-particular farmers' groups, its mission was compromised by racism and the Redemption politics of the Democratic party and muted by the ambitions of powerful pro-farmer dissidents like Leonidas L. Polk (of North Carolina), Benjamin Tillman (South Carolina), Rueben Kolk (Alabama), Frank Burkitt (Mississippi), and, most significantly, Tom Watson (Georgia).

The Colored Farmers' National Alliance and Cooperative Union also had its beginnings in Texas (Houston). Formed in 1888 on the initiative of the Alliance of the Colored Farmers of Texas, it quickly absorbed similar Black cooperatives in other southern states. By 1890–91, its membership was considerable, including 40,000 Black alliance members in South Carolina and 20,000 in Virginia. According to Reverend Richard Manning Humphrey, its white general superintendent, at its height the Colored Farmers' Alliance obtained more than one million members. (235) Like its white counterpart, the Colored Farmers' Alliance boasted a large female membership (one-fourth of its membership was female by contemporary estimates); but unlike the white alliance, it included a large but uncounted number of farm laborers.[11] Although some of its most important leaders were white, as the organization grew and confronted paternalism and even corruption among these figures, the Colored Farmers' Alliance became increasingly race conscious. Failing to obtain more than fitful support from the white alliance and the Noble and Holy Order of the Knights of Labor, the Colored Farmers' Alliance sought the "redemption of the race" and the freedom of "the toiling masses."

At the state level, the Colored Alliance organized goods exchanges, and according to Joseph Rogers, the white superintendent for Virginia and North Carolina, the Alliance taught Blacks "about monopoly, about the meaning of 'burdensome taxation,' about unequal legislation and what it had done to the Afro-American farmer, and about the reasons why money was scarce." (194) It also immersed Black farmers like E. S. Richardson (superintendent in Georgia) and Harry C. Green and George A. Gwaltney (both Virginians) into leadership in interracial politics. William Warwick, the Virginia lecturer and alliance organizer (and Rogers' eventual successor), found his way from the Colored Alliance to leadership in the People's (Populist) Party for a time. But within five years of its founding, the Colored Farmers' Alliance fell to the forces that undermined the white alliance and its political successor, the Populist Party. The racism of white farmers and the refusal to protect the Black franchise drove a wedge between the colored and white alliances, but something else spelled their end. In the preindustrial capitalism of southern farming, Ayers maintains, "most blacks remained tenants and most whites remained landowners."[12] Even more important, in the 1890s the Southern white reformers and the Democratic party appropriated segregation as the basis of their new social order.[13] As Charles Crowe understands the moment:

> In fact, white reform often meant Black repression. Populists and Progressives frequently went so far as to equip their demands for more repression and Jim Crow laws with reform credentials calling for "better race relations" or "the prevention of friction between the races." Many Black voters, who apparently grasped the fact that they had little or nothing to gain from the reformers, voted conservative as the lesser of two evils. . . . conservatives

[were] inclined to accept the status quo and to doubt any urgent need for new repressive measures.[14]

Thus ended Black mass participation in white agrarian radicalism. Here and there, pockets of biracial agrarian Democrats survived, preserving the cause in local folklore and small-scale organizations. But, for the most part, in the 1890s Blacks confronted the most oppressive conditions since the ending of slavery. "Peonage, a practice that gave employers complete control over their laborers, practically reinstituted slavery," Pete Daniel writes. "[It] infected the South like a cancer, eating away at the economic freedom of blacks, driving the poor whites to work harder in order to compete with virtual slave labor, and preserving the class structure inherited from slavery days."[15]

The Antilynching Movement

The most dramatic and terrifying instrument in the repression of Blacks was lynching. According to the Department of Records and Research at Tuskegee Institute, between 1882 and 1968 there were 4,743 cases of death by lynching in America, with the period between 1892 and 1902 recording the most intensive activity. The largest totals were for the states of Mississippi (581), Georgia (531), and Texas (493).[16] As a result of political indifference and moral abnegation, no federal agency amassed as complete a record as that at Tuskegee, so there is no "official" count. As exhaustive and meticulous as the researchers at Tuskegee were over the eight decades, it can still be surmised that the actual number of lynchings was considerably higher (for instance, the NAACP in 1919 maintained that between 1889 and 1918, the number of lynching victims already amounted to 3,224—2,522 of them Black).[17] Moreover, lynching as defined narrowly ("an illegal death at the hands of a group acting under the pretext of serving justice") did not include the varied forms of terrorism (rape, beating, torture, mutilation, arson, threats) that completed the circle of horror drawn around Black men, women, and children. The Tuskegee report indicates that a third of the lynching victims (1,297) were "white," but there were only two states during the lynching time with significant Black populations (Kansas and Oklahoma) in which white victims outnumbered Blacks.

The fear of lynching coincided with substantial Black out-migration from the South. The news of lynching terrified Black communities throughout the country, sometimes thousands of miles from the event. Lynch stories were publicized by local papers and the national press (several historians have employed national newspapers to document lynching victims), and of course by the Black press.

The *Providence Journal*, reporting a Louisiana lynching in 1893, celebrated the mob's manly restraint. "Three Negroes were lynched in a quiet, determined manner by a mob of white men on Friday night. . . . The lynching was one of the coolest that has taken place in this section." And the *New York Times* [March, 10, 1892] . . . stressed what it called the "quick and quiet" demeanor of the white men in the mob, contrasting their stern and firm behavior with that of the "shivering Negroes" who they murdered.[18]

Sensational photographs of the "strange fruit" were published, victimizing the victims with unproven accounts of their criminal acts, and impressing in the minds of the survivors, that is the whole of Black people, the unjust and oppressive character of the society within which they found themselves.

In some few instances, attempted lynchings were successfully resisted by armed Blacks. More frequently, Neil McMillan insists, Black resistance brought greater violence to these besieged communities—from state militias, from white vigilantes, and from other forms of overwhelming white force. While out-migration became the dominant expression of Black resistance to lynching, for those left behind an awful dread descended:

> In 1919, after a black was burned in Vicksburg, a local newspaper reported "a noticeable absence of Negroes on the streets"; local merchants "missed the Negro trade." Following another burning that same year near Laurel, one local historian has written, blacks minimized contacts with whites and race leaders "were silenced by their belief that a protest might result in things being made harder for the masses of their race.". . . A Delta lynching in 1930, as one young black Coahoma Countian recalled, left blacks frozen in fear: "This mob had all the niggers in town scared. . . . None of 'em would come out on the streets. . . . [That mob] went through all the niggers' houses and nobody tried to stop 'em."[19]

But much like the slave years, Jim Crow nurtured two Black communities and two traditions of resistance. Inside the curtain of violence, brutality, and the most oppressive work conditions, a Black community withdrew into itself. On their behalf, seven months after the death of Frederick Douglass in 1895, Booker T. Washington successfully claimed national leadership of Southern Blacks by giving voice to their resignation: "The wisest among my race understand that the agitation of questions of social equality is the extremist folly, and that [the] progress . . . that will come to us must be the result of severe and constant struggle rather than of artificial forcing."[20] But beyond the curtain, more insulated from the daily exercise of racial intimidation and violence and where a minimum of civil decorum was maintained, a tradition of organized protest was being spawned.

Arguably, the most brilliant and most influential of the antilynching propagandists was Ida B. Wells, a former school teacher (she began teaching at age fourteen), publisher, and investigative journalist. Wells's impact on the moral conscience and popular cultures of America and Britain equaled that of her antiracist predecessor, Harriet Beecher Stowe, and that of Frederick Douglass, who collaborated with both women. Through her writings, *Southern Horrors* (1892), *A Red Record* (1895), and *Mob Rule in New Orleans* (1900), Wells recounted the sadism of lynching, disproving the oft-given rationale for lynching: Black rape (more often, she argued white "Delilahs" were seducing Black "Samsons"). She assigned to lynching the imprimatur of barbarism motivated by commerce and the attempt to disenfranchise the Black male. As Hazel Carby explains:

> "By the right exercise of his power as the industrial factor of the South, the Afro-American can demand and secure his rights." But economic power was only one force among the possible forms of resistance, she concluded: "a Winchester rifle should have a place of honor in every black home." . . . The loss of the vote was both a political silencing and an emasculation which placed black men outside the boundaries of contemporary patriarchal power. The cry of rape, which pleaded the necessity of revenge for assaulted white womanhood, attempted to place black males "beyond the pale of human sympathy." Black women were relegated to a place outside the ideological construction of "womanhood." That term included only white women; therefore the rape of black women was of no consequence outside the black community.[21]

With the incontestable elegance of her pen and exhaustive research, Wells proceeded to expose the monster, naming the names implicated in the mobs and exposing the moral hypocrisy of Southern white males ("True chivalry respects all womanhood, and no one who reads the record, as it is written in the faces of the million mulattos in the South, will for a minute conceive that the southern white man had a very chivalrous regard for the honor due the women of his own race or respect for the womanhood which circumstances placed in his power"[22]), and the cowardice of their "accomplices" in the Northern and Southern press.

Finding her appeals largely ignored and confined to the Black press, in 1893 and 1894 she traveled to England to lecture and write in order to enlist British public opinion and the British press in the antilynching cause. She reckoned correctly that while middle-class American newspapers, habituated to treating lynching as cozy Southern folk theater, would ignore her voice, they could not withstand a campaign of criticism from their mythical homeland. As Gale Bederman indicates, Wells succeeded:

> Wells's powerful tactics mobilized the British press and reformers, who turned lynching into the season's *cause celebre*. A *Westminster Gazette* writer said he could no longer "regard our American cousins as a civilised nation." The *Christian World* thought American lynch law "would disgrace a nation of cannibals." The *Birmingham Daily Gazette* editorialized, "The American citizen in the South is at heart more a barbarian than the Negro whom he regards as a savage. . . . Lynch law is fiendishly resorted to as a sort of sport on every possible opportunity, and the Negroes are butchered to make a Yankee holiday. . . . Either they mistrust their legal institutions or they murder in wantonness and for mere lust of blood."[23]

Returning from England, Wells translated her newfound notoriety among Southern editors and officials into Black middle-class social activism. In England, she had inspired the formation of antilynching societies; plans among newspapers as well as reformers to send investigators to America; and campaigns of letter writing to Southern and Northern newspapers, churches, and federal and state public officials. She intended to agitate for an even more ambitious objective than the end of lynching: the launching of a civilizing mission that would bring the rule of law and economic rights for Blacks and women.

The existence of benevolence societies and self-help clubs organized by Black women has been confidently traced to as early as the late eighteenth century. One hundred years later, in the last decade of the nineteenth century, the two most formidable federations of urban Black female societies, the Colored Women's League (founded in 1892) and the National Federation of Afro-American Women (1895), joined to form the National Association of Colored Women (NACW).[24] In 1892, because of her opposition to lynching, Wells was forced to abandon her press (she co-owned and edited the weekly, *Free Speech*, in Memphis, Tennessee). Subsequently, she found aides among the Black women's clubs in New York and Chicago. They provided the means for the publishing of *Southern Horrors* and the organizational base and human resources for her national campaign against lynching. Indeed, the very first issue in March 1894 of *The Woman's Era* ("the first magazine in the United States to be owned, published and managed solely by black women," Wilson J. Moses records) took up the antilynching crusade. At the behest of its founder, Josephine St. Pierre Ruffin, and her daughter, Florida Ruffin Ridley, the magazine published accounts of Southern atrocities and an editorial denouncing lynching and white feminist apologists like Laura Ormiston Chant. (106ff) In 1908–1909, Wells (now Wells-Barnett) joined with Mary Church Terrell—the prominent educator, first president of the National Association of Colored Women, and Washington correspondent for *The Woman's Era*—to assist in the formation of the National Association for the Advancement of Colored People (NAACP).[25] Drawing largely from the international furor created by Wells, but quickly spurning her radical militancy, the NAACP grew to become the staunchest organized opposition to lynching.

Ten years after Booker T. Washington conceded that, in effect, constitutional protections and the rule of law did not apply to Blacks, a group of Black professionals and businessmen, twenty-nine in all, met at Niagara Falls, Ontario. Unlike Washington—whose politics of Black survival had earned him cynical respect and largesse from powerful white philanthropists (Andrew Carnegie provided Tuskegee with $600,000, some $150,000 for Washington's personal use; industrialist W. H. Baldwin announced: "I almost worship this man")—these renegades were intent on claiming "social equality."[26] Called together by DuBois and his political tutor, William Monroe Trotter (a civil rights activist who worked at insurance and mortgage brokering in Boston and, like DuBois, was a Harvard graduate), the Niagara Movement repudiated Washington's leadership and proceeded to urge Black men to reclaim the vote. They called on the federal and state governments to enforce civil justice against "peonage and virtual slavery."[27] Four years later, provoked by the mob killings of scores of Blacks in Atlanta (in September 1906) and Springfield, Illinois (August 1908), the Niagara group joined with Wells-Barnett and Terrell of the NACW, and other Black and white activists, to call for a new organization. Meeting in New York in May 1909, some three hundred delegates established the basis for the NAACP.[28]

The organization was biracial, as it was put in those days, but even more important, it ranged across a considerable ideological spectrum. Lerone Bennett, Jr. reports:

> The conference opened in an atmosphere of mutual suspicion. The white liberals, who wanted to avoid an open break with Booker T. Washington, were uneasy in the presence of the Niagara activists. They were especially concerned about Trotter and Ida B. Wells-Barnett, who were considered more militant than DuBois. During one stormy session a black woman— probably Ida B. Wells-Barnett—leaped up and cried out, DuBois wrote, "in

passionate, almost tearful earnestness—an earnestness born of bitter experience—They are betraying us again, these white friends of ours.'" After a
long and bitter debate, the breach was papered over.29

In principle, it was from the liberal Black and white middle classes that the
highly centralized NAACP would recruit its leaders and staff. Nevertheless,
it was largely through the efforts of grassroots Black women that the
NAACP grew into a national organization, one that never actually resolved
the ideological and political differences that had characterized its foundation. Despite its contradictions, its frequent political timidity, and the
active hostility of presidents, congresses, and government agencies like
the Federal Bureau of Investigation, the NAACP managed from its earliest
years to mount powerful propaganda and legal challenges to lynching;
racist courts and juries; the exclusion of Blacks from the armed services;
apartheid in public transportation, education, and housing; the violation of
human rights by American authorities in Haiti; discrimination practiced by
federal and state bureaucracies; and the narratives and images in films like
Birth of a Nation.30 Under the editorial guidance of DuBois, the NAACP published *Crisis*, the most important Black journal of its time, providing a
forum for essayists, journalists, and artists. In the 1930s, the organization
faltered in its support of the Scottsboro defendants and, even more significantly, in its delayed response to the Great Depression (in 1934, DuBois
resigned his editorship of *Crisis* over this issue). Even earlier, in the 1920s,
strains plagued the organization as it confronted Marxist radicalism and
militant Black nationalism. It recovered its reputation among Blacks in fits:
during World War II, through its campaigns against military segregation
and housing discrimination, and in the 1950s, with its legal battle against
discrimination in education and jobs (faltering once again with the onset of
the Black Depression of the 1980s and 1990s).

For a brief moment, the most eloquent and effective response to lynching was Black migration to the North. The Great Migration, as it has been
called, was dramatic both in its scale and its character. Jacqueline Jones
writes: "Compared with their predecessors, the new migrants more often
came from the Deep South; they traveled longer distances to their final
destination and relied on overland (rail) transportation rather than water
transportation, and a greater proportion than previously chose to go to
midwestern cities."31 Tragically, the migrants had no way of knowing that
in a few years they would be the victims of race wars in Chicago, Omaha,
and other northern cities. Flight from lynching, from boll weevil infesta-
tions and drought, from declining opportunities in Southern manufacturing (where white women and children were preferred to Black men and

women), and from the daily incidents of race humiliation, brought tens of thousands of Blacks into Northern cities between 1910 and 1930. Florette Henri tells us:

> Early migrations were dwarfed by the surge of black people northward after 1900, and especially after 1910. According to various contemporaneous estimates, between 1890 and 1910 around 200,000 black Southerners fled to the North; and between 1910 and 1920 another 300,000 to 1,000,000 followed. The Department of Labor reported that in eighteen months of 1916–17 the migration was variously estimated at 200,000 to 700,000.[32]

As Lerone Bennett, Jr. observes: "Between 1910 and 1930 three Northern cities, New York (91,709 to 327,796), Chicago (44,103 to 233,903) and Detroit (5,741 to 120,066), more than tripled the percentage of their black populations."[33] Competing with even larger pools of European immigrants, they nevertheless found some decent wage labor (in 1920, 12.5 percent of employed Blacks were in manufacturing and industrial occupations; in 1930, 18.6 percent or 1,025,000 were). Some Blacks, however, reckoned that no place in America could satisfy their desires and so they emigrated to the West Indies, Canada, and even to Europe. The most spectacular emigrants, most likely, were those Oklahoman emigrants organized by a Gold Coast man known as Chief Alfred Sam: in 1914, with the Atlantic Ocean patrolled by German submarines, these families chartered a ship and set sail from Galveston to the Gold Coast of West Africa.[34]

The First World War

The First World War, the war to save democracy and to end all wars, brought no democracy or peace to Black Americans. The war between the Triple Alliance (France, Britain, and Russia—and eventually, the United States and Japan) and the Central Powers (Germany and Austria-Hungary) began in 1914, but it was not until 1917 that the United States entered the war, sending troops to the Western Front (France) in order to stave off a victory by Germany. In America, the race war persisted, implicating the military, civilians, and Black soldiers. In August 1917, more than one hundred armed Black soldiers marched into Houston after two of their comrades had been beaten and jailed by a city policeman. Their crime had been to intervene in the brutal beating of a Black woman. The soldiers were Regular Army veterans of the Third Battalion, Twenty-fourth Infantry, which earlier had served in Cuba and the Philippines during the Spanish-American War. Already legendary for its battle prowess, the Twenty-fourth had also been the unit of David Fagen, a Black American corporal who had deserted to the Filipino independence army in 1899 and for two years had led Filipino troops.[35] In Houston, where the Twenty-fourth had been assigned to guard workers constructing Camp Logan, the Black soldiers were routinely taunted by white construction workers, harassed by Houston police, and subjected (frequently unsuccessfully) to Jim Crow restrictions on the city's streetcars. Seething from these persistent provocations and now incensed by the beatings, Bernard Nalty reports, "in a two-hour rampage, the mutineers killed fifteen whites or Hispanic Americans and wounded twelve, one of who later died." (103) Five policemen were among the whites killed, as well as a white military officer. In three separate trials, 211 Black soldiers were court-martialed; 19 of them executed; and nearly 70 sentenced to hard labor for periods ranging from seven years to life. (101ff.) The NAACP challenged the sentences of the imprisoned men, but it was not until 1938 that the last was freed from a federal penitentiary. In Newport News, Virginia, the Black soldiers of the Eighth Illinois who resisted Jim Crow had a "happier" fate. Cutting their training short, the army shipped them to Europe.

Unlike the Twenty-fourth Infantry, the bulk of the Black soldiers who served in the First World War —even the 42,000 who were assigned combat duty—were draftees like those who made up the Ninety-second Division and the Ninety-third Division (Provisional). Subject to Jim Crow discrimination and brutality in the states and overseas, it was somewhat predictable that these units could perform at their best only when such conditions changed. For the Ninety-third Division, the opportunity came when the American expeditionary command under General "Black Jack" Pershing saw fit to assign the Ninety-third to the French army. Desperate from the loss of more than a million French and colonial soldiers, French officials armed and quickly trained these Black replacements. In the trenches and in the towns, fear and battle fatigue suspended the racism in French culture. Fighting alongside their French allies, the 369th Infantry (formerly Fifteenth New York) became "Men of Bronze." Nalty tells us that "the regiment fought itself to exhaustion" between July 1918 and the armistice. It was under fire for 191 days straight, the longest stretch for any American unit. The Black soldiers responded to the expectations of French civilians and French officers:

> These French officers were not disappointed. The 371st and 372nd Infantry, like the 369th, played a prominent role in the Meuse-Argonne fighting during September and October 1918. This bitter, often hand-to-hand struggle cost the three regiments some 2,500 casualties. The 370th Infantry fought

alongside French troops in the Oise-Aisne offensive, September 15 to November 11; its casualties numbered 665 killed and wounded. (120)

The four units were awarded the Croix de Guerre by the French government. Meanwhile, under the direct command of racist white American officers, the Ninety-second Division amassed a much less illustrious record. Nalty comments: "Little was expected of the blacks fighting in the American Army. They were trained accordingly, and they responded by performing pretty much as the white generals expected." But even then, "in the closing days of the war one brigade of the 92nd Division gained ground against the Germans, cutting its way through barbed wire, beating back counterattacks, and even going to the aid of an adjacent French unit." (116) Harry Truman, then a young American military officer from Missouri, noted the contrast between French-led and American-led Black troops and thirty years later, as president, he ordered the segregation in the American military ended.[36]

Although more than 1 million Blacks (nearly 380,000 of them Black Americans) enlisted in the armies of Britain, France, and the United States, American race violence increased. Confronted with an increase in lynchings (thirty-eight in 1917, fifty-eight in 1918; at least forty killed in a race riot in East St. Louis), rabid and official discrimination, and the grossest acts of race injustice in the armed forces, DuBois and Black leaders of like mind (for example, Emmett J. Scott, formerly Booker T. Washington's secretary and during the war special assistant to the Secretary of War) protested to President Woodrow Wilson to no avail. In July 1918, DuBois broke with the pacifists in the NAACP and the radical Blacks in the socialist camp in order to support Black enlistment in the war. His "Close Ranks" editorial in *Crisis* instructed, "Let us, while this war lasts, forget our special grievances," but Woodrow Wilson gave no quarter. In 1915, the Virginia-born President endorsed D.W. Griffith's epic film version of Thomas Dixon, Jr.'s *The Clansman*, a film that employed the president's own *History of the American People* for some of its script ("until at last there had sprung into existence a great Ku Klux Klan, an Invisible Empire of the South"). Wilson's and Dixon's friendship went back to their undergraduate years at Johns Hopkins (starting in 1883). With Edward White, the Chief Justice of the Supreme Court (and a member of the Klan), Wilson arranged for special showings of the film for Washington's elite.[37] Wilson also brought Jim Crow to Washington, D.C., and systematically began to disemploy or segregate Black federal employees. Only when the German government began to make America's race violence part of its war propaganda did Wil-

son relent, rhetorically urging fellow Southerners to desist from race brutality. Nevertheless, while thousands of American Black troops were fighting in France, they were repeatedly subjected to racial military justice (for
instance, ordered to stay away from French women and arrested if they did
not) and insulted by officers and the news from home.[38]

The war itself consisted of a concatenation of racial impulses, so it is
hardly surprising that few powerful or influential white Americans
responded to the pleas of Black troops, Black communities, or Black leaders to desist from race policies. In Europe, the war was orchestrated in
racial terms. The combatants were encouraged to endure the most horren-
dous experiences and unprecedented numbers of casualties by an induced
revulsion to the racial degeneracy of their monstrous foes: the savage Hun,
the mongrel French, and so on. Moreover, the war was one between
empires, every one of which was implicated in the exploitation of "darker
peoples" in Asia, Africa, and Latin America. Each empire thrived on a discourse of inferior races as its rationale and employed a zero-sum calculus
of economic survival. Anticipating Lenin's thesis on imperialism, DuBois
pointed out, in May 1915:

> The present world war is, then, the result of jealousies engendered by the
> recent rise of armed national associations of labor and capital whose aim is
> the exploitation of the wealth of the world mainly outside the European cir-
> cle of nations. These associations, grown jealous and suspicious at the divi-
> sion of the trade-empires, are fighting to enlarge their respective shares;
> they look for expansion, not in Europe but in Asia, and particularly in
> Africa.[39]

Eric Hobsbawm, one of England's most thoughtful modern historians,
would appear to agree. Eighty years after DuBois's observations, Hobsbawm tackled the mystery of why the contending powers fought such a
total war (1,800,000 German losses; 1,600,000 French losses; 800,000
British losses; 116,000 American losses). Hobsbawm believes:

> The reason was that this war, unlike earlier wars, which were typically
> waged for limited and specifiable objects, was waged for unlimited ends. In
> the Age of Empire, politics and economics had fused. International political
> rivalry was modeled on economic growth and competition, but the charac-
> teristic feature of this was precisely that it had no limit. "The 'natural fron-
> tiers' of Standard Oil, the Deutsche Bank or the De Beers Diamond
> Corporation were at the end of the universe, or rather at limits of their
> capacity to expand."[40]

As such, racial prerogatives constructed as national destiny concealed imperialism and colonialism. It was not simply that "politics and economics had fused," but that race, politics, and economics conflated, releasing a nationalist anesthesia that desensitized the European and American masses. Even in America, where so many eastern and southern Europeans had relocated, the appearance of the eugenics movement made clear that the property of being white would be patrolled as vigorously against lesser European claimants as it was against the depredations of the mythical Black rapist. Thus, the empires fought each other to the death. In Europe, even among the "victors," the lives of a generation, as well as of economies, had been ruined; within the Central Powers, revolutions followed in the wake of defeat. The empires of Germany and Austria-Hungary dissolved, leaving embittered and impoverished peoples who would be seduced by fascism in a few short years. But although domestic variants of fascism would have important consequences for Blacks, it was the crumbling of the Russian Empire by revolutions that would have the most extraordinary import for Black Americans.

On the domestic front, as the war impacted capitalists' access to European immigrant labor (immigration was depressed to a third of its prewar numbers) it also siphoned off many young, white male workers. Northern manufacturers and industrialists proceeded, then, to raid the South for its rural white and Black workers. Black newspapers advertising jobs and unprecedented wages in the North and in the war-related industries (everything from munitions manufacturing to meatpacking) were directly subsidized by American businesses; railroad companies sponsored free transportation to Southern workers; and labor agents snuck into the rural South to organize migrant caravans. Robert Abbot, the editor and publisher of the *Chicago Defender*, took the lead among Black journalists: publishing letters from aspiring migrants, soliciting job advertisements, organizing travel clubs for migrants, publicizing Southern lynchings and other evidences of white calumny, and employing Pullman porters en route to the South to deliver bundles of his paper. "In news items, anecdotes, cartoons, and photos, the *Defender* crystallized the underlying economic and social causes of black suffering into immediate motives for flight," Henri writes.[41] Indeed, the *Defender* became the leading propagandist for the Great Migration, its circulation soaring to over 280,000, two-thirds of its readers outside of Chicago. Thus, while Booker T. Washington discouraged the migrants, the mood of the Black masses brooked no denying. Summarizing the hundreds of letters written to Abbott and (after Washington's death) to Scott, Henri concludes: "Help, help, help. Over and over again . . . the cry for help in getting a job, decent wages, decent treatment, education for the children, appreciation of one's manhood." (59)

Many did not need the *Defender* or the railroads or the agents. Like "Cap" Whiteside, who left Mobile, Alabama, in the late 1920s, they relied on family who had already migrated. A few like Whiteside punctuated their leaving the South with their own unique parting gestures. The white manager at the Battle House, an exclusive hotel in Mobile, had tried to exercise his sexual privileges with a young maid, Cecilia, Whiteside's wife. When Cap was told, he returned to the Battle House that evening, beat the manager up, and hung him in the hotel's cold storage. In a few days, Whiteside headed for Oakland, California. When he earned their fare, he sent for his family: Cecilia and his daughters, Clara, Lillian, and Wilma. Chastened, the manager gained a reputation as one of the best friends of the Negro in Mobile.

Much of Southern white opinion saw the Great Migration as a betrayal. Although a few blamed it on the excessive acts or articulations of white racism, most blamed it on "gullible niggers." Thus, while the Biloxi (Mississippi) *Herald* denounced the rabble-rousing governor J. K. Vardaman as "the most dangerous man that ever aspired to the governorship of Mississippi," and in Natchez the *Democrat* queried "What home is threatened with social equality with the Negro?" others resorted to intimidation, particularly with the establishment of the Second Klan, the Knights of the Ku Klux Klan.

The new Klan made its first appearance in Georgia in late 1915. The year marked the fiftieth anniversary of the ending of the Civil War; the lynching of Leo Frank, a Jew, for the murder of Mary Phagan, a fourteen-year-old Atlanta pencil factory worker; the debut of *Birth of a Nation*; the American occupation of Haiti; and the second year of the European war. The war, indeed, retarded the growth of the Klan. But with the end of the war came the return of Black veterans and the appearance of a new Black militancy. In 1919, ten of the seventy-seven Blacks lynched were former soldiers. In another instance, "one returning veteran, still in uniform, was beaten to death in Georgia, not because he had been accused of rape or murder, but because he had vowed, while in jail for ignoring a 'whites only' sign, never to yield to Jim Crow."[42] Nancy MacLean learned that "so alarmed was the Division of Military Intelligence over 'Negro subversion'—defined as black veterans' fighting 'any white effort, especially in the South, to reestablish white ascendancy'—that it undertook a secret investigation to find out whether they had a collective organization to promote their goals."[43] Then, of course, came the Red Summer, the white racist pogroms that hit Chicago, Washington, D.C., and twenty-three other

American cities. The violence was disturbing, but now the anxiety was not confined to the Black victims. Blacks had fought back. One "Southern Colored Woman" wrote the *Crisis* in November 1919:

> The Washington riot gave me the *thrill that comes once in a life time*. I . . . read between the lines of our morning paper that at last our men had stood like men, struck back, were no longer dumb driven cattle. When I could no longer read for my streaming tears, I stood up, alone in my room, held both hands high over my head and exclaimed aloud: "Oh I thank God, thank God."[44]

On another front, the Black filmmaker, Oscar Micheaux, released *Within Our Gates*, the most powerful of his more than thirty films. Responding to Griffith's cinematic slanders of Blacks, Micheaux's film depicted the lynching of an innocent Black family by a white mob of men, women, and children, and the attempted rape of a young Black woman by a white patriarch![45] Unlike his contemporaries—the brothers Noble and George Johnson, who with their Lincoln Motion Pictures Company were making Black films celebrating the Black middle class (*The Realization of a Negro's Ambition*, 1915) and Black cavalry troops chasing Pancho Villa (*The Trooper of Troop K*, 1916)—Micheaux revealed a disturbed white America, capable of the most awful villainy toward the Black.

But in the South, Nancy MacLean assures us, there were other quite different reactions to the riots of 1919 and the new Black militancy:

> Here, it seemed, was brewing the black rebellion whose specter haunted the white establishment. Not only were black soldiers trained in combat, but it appeared their civilian peers might no longer turn the other cheek, either. This, at any rate, was the message of the race riots of 1919. In them, African Americans fought back en masse, for the first time, against white assailants. Certainly local racists noticed that, according to Athens merchants, black purchases of firearms skyrocketed in these years, restrained only by limited supply.[46]

In her characterization of the collective response in the 1919 riots as a first in American history, MacLean shows that she absorbed some of the historical mythifications of her subjects. She more persuasively points out that by 1919 one indicator of liberal Black militancy was the founding of 155 NAACP chapters in the South, accounting for over 42,000 paying members. Given such perceived provocations, the Klan rose from a few thousand to 100,000 in 1920. By 1924, the Klan had grown to encompass millions in the South and in states like Indiana, Ohio, California, Colorado, New York, and even Utah. Its members were drawn from all sections of white society and, as Prohibition, industrial ruptures, and the Great Migration concussed the nation, the Klan added to its traditional racial fears a broad tapestry of targets: official corruption, alcoholism, family abuse, immigrants, Catholics, Jews, and big business.

The Klan movement reached its apogee in the mid-1920s, gaining over 4 million members and successfully running hundreds of election campaigns at the local, state, and congressional levels. Then it waned dramatically. MacLean seems closer to the reasons behind the nature, rise, and eventual decline of the movement than other recent revisionists (like Leonard J. Moore), who have maintained that the second Klan was essentially a civic reform movement, comfortably within the political and ideological bounds of mainstream America, which dissipated when its leaders were exposed by sexual scandal and corruption.[47] By designating it "reactionary populism," MacLean likens the second Klan to the European fascist movements that were its contemporaries. Thus, she maintains, it failed in America when the conditions for its survival ameliorated (as did not happen in Germany, Italy, and elsewhere). In America, an economic boom ended the postwar recession, organized labor and the Left were temporarily defeated, and the Klan and capital managed the suppression of their now perennial demon, liberal Black militancy. MacLean notes: "The NAACP lost almost 200 branches by 1923, and over 70,000 members—or more than two-thirds of its 1919 roster—over the decade." Even more suggestive, like a Hegelian negation, the rise (and fall) of the second Klan was coterminous with the flowering of Black nationalism.

Black Self-Determination

Booker T. Washington died in 1915. Since he had wielded much power as an avuncular broker between Black labor and capital, between the philanthropy of the wealthy and undercapitalized Black institutions, and between Blacks and the non-Black American public, the Black middle class and the Black intelligentsia felt his passing had left a vacuum in Black leadership. With some deliberateness, Robert Russa Moton, Washington's successor at Tuskegee; DuBois; Trotter; James Weldon Johnson, the NAACP head; and others attempted to fill the putative post. Washington's heir proved to be an immigrant West Indian from Jamaica, Malcus Mosiah "Marcus" Garvey. Acting on an invitation from Booker T. Washington, but delayed while he gathered funds, Garvey came to the United States in 1916, too late to meet with the man who had inspired him. It took him less than four years to amass a following among ordinary Blacks that surpassed Washington's influence. By the time he was imprisoned in a federal penitentiary for mail fraud, Garvey had become the center of a vast and international organizational manifestation of Black nationalism, the Universal Negro Improvement Association (UNIA).[48] But Garvey was not uncontested.

Concealed beneath the racial sameness of the Great Black Migration was the fact that tens of thousands of West Indians also responded to the appeal for industrial wage laborers. Among them were intellectuals, agitators, and organizers who pursued the dream of liberation and Black self-determination within the embrace of what they were persuaded was an international proletariat movement. In New York, Chicago, as far as the West Coast, and sometimes in the most conservative institutions of Black higher learning, they inspired young Black American radicals to imagine a vast, global army arising to overturn the slavery of wage-labor and the less metaphorical forms of oppression in the colonies of Europe, Latin America, and Asia. Some of these radicals had immediate and permanent impact on American social history. A. Philip Randolph, a Florida-born socialist and coeditor (with Chandler Owen) of *The Messenger*, led the organization of the Brotherhood of Sleeping Car Porters in 1925; forced Franklin Delano Roosevelt, during World War II, to form the Fair Employment Practice Committee; and later became a vice president of the American Federation of Labor–Congress of Industrial Organizations (AFL–CIO). Other Black socialists conspired further from the political mainstream; for example, by amalgamating into the African Blood Brotherhood (ABB), the core of Blacks in the American Communist movement (CPUSA):

> the organizational cadre of the African Blood Brotherhood consisted largely of West Indians and Afro-Americans who had developed professionally as social agitators and journalist-propagandists. Its founding organizers in 1919 were Cyril Briggs (Nevis Island), Richard B. Moore (Barbados), and W. A. Domingo (Jamaica). Later, in the period between 1920 and 1922, Otto Huiswoud (Surinam) and a number of important Afro-American radicals joined the movement, including Otto Hall, Haywood Hall (Harry Haywood), Edward Doty, Grace Campbell, H. V. Phillips, Gordon Owens, Alonzo Isabel and Lovett Fort-Whiteman.[49]

A secret, "vanguard" organization, the ABB was as Black nationalist as the UNIA, and eventually, from its vantage point in the CPUSA, it persuaded the Communist International in 1928 to consider the "Negro Question" in America as one of Black self-determination. Profoundly impressed with the enthusiasm shown by the Black masses for the UNIA program for the "redemption of Africa" and "Africa for the Africans," the ABB aspired to the creation of a Negro Soviet Republic in America.

Meanwhile, as the UNIA gathered its massive following, it pushed even its most persistent Black militant critics toward a new vision of Black nationalism. For example, W.A. Domingo, for a time, left the ABB to join the UNIA. For most, however, the influence of the UNIA was a bit more subtle. DuBois, to cite one of the most implacable and influential UNIA foes, moved from the "talented tenth" liberal elitism that had informed his and Trotter's social theory. Still incapable of embracing Garvey himself, DuBois gravitated toward the revolutionary nationalist ideology of the ABB, even besting it in his advocacy of Marxian theory and its application to the experience of Blacks in America. In the early 1930s, while he was working on *Black Reconstruction*, DuBois summarized Marx's critique of capitalism for his readers in *Crisis*.[50] DuBois and Domingo were far from unique. In 1921, Randolph, another critic, denounced the UNIA program as a "dream" while in the same breath publicizing its importance:

> A word about the value of Garveyism to Negroes today. It has done some splendid things. It has inculcated into the minds of Negroes the need and value of organization. It has also demonstrated the ability of Negroes to come together in large masses under Negro leadership. . . . Garveyism, also, has conducted wholesome, vital, necessary and effective criticism on Negro leadership. It has stimulated the pride of Negroes in Negro history and traditions, thereby helping to break down the slave psychology which throttles and strangles Negro initiative, self-assertiveness, ambition, courage, independence, etc. It has further stiffened the Negro's backbone to resist the encroachments and insults of white people. . . . It has emphasized the international character of the Negro problem.[51]

To the notions of an African Empire and to Garvey's self-serving hagiography, Randolph, like DuBois, gave a resounding no. But in a postwar world visited by revolutionary movements of self-determination in Asia (India), Europe (Ireland and Italy), and the Levant (Turkey), Randolph acknowledged that "Garveyism," like the other movements, had roots "in the subsoil of oppression and fear."

The sheer spectacle of UNIA-massed parades of uniformed men and women down the streets of Harlem; its glorious meetings at Madison Square Garden and Liberty Hall; its annual conventions; the energetic and impassioned voices in its weekly, *The Negro World* (circulation near 200,000); its pamphlets, books, and religious catechisms; and its several enterprises (including the Black Star Line with one ship, an excursion boat, and a yacht; and the Negro Factories Corporation) drew the serious attention of those who either supported or opposed Garvey's promise of a mass emigration to Africa. Garveyites numbered in the millions, and the UNIA spanned two continents. When, in 1922, Garvey met privately with Edward Young Clarke, the Acting Imperial Wizard of the Klan, and agreed that in exchange for the Klan's protection of Black Star Line agents the UNIA would continue its opposition to the NAACP, white supremacy and Black nationalism appeared on the verge of sculpting America's destiny. The UNIA had absorbed the tradition of emigrationism generated among the slaves, the freedmen of the 1870s, and the Black peons and sharecroppers of the 1890s and early twentieth century. Garvey and his intelligentsia (among them Amy Ashwood, Benjamin Burrell, Henrietta Vinton Davis, Mayme de Mena, James Eason, Arnold Ford, George Alexander McGuire, William Sherrill, Wilford Smith, Noah Thompson, and Elinor White) had embellished that tradition into a discourse of unprecedented design.

Given the social force of the UNIA, whatever its internal contradictions and utopianism, it could not be allowed to continue. Precipitated by Garvey's meeting with the Klan, the Black socialists Owen and Randolph joined with Robert Bagnall of the NAACP to inspire a "Garvey Must Go" campaign. Only partially successful in alienating Garvey's following, it was the entry of the U.S. Justice Department into the suppression of the UNIA that achieved their ends. Tried on the charge of mail fraud in 1923, Garvey was convicted, imprisoned, and eventually deported. The dream of self-determination scattered; it was preserved in UNIA fragments like the Lost-Found Nation of Islam and the lore that eventually transported Garvey into a figure of mythical proportions. Then the traces of the most vigorous expression of the long tradition of Black self-determination were erased in the popular memory by the onset of the Great Depression, by film caricatures of Black sovereignty (like Paul Robeson's *Emperor Jones* in 1933) and sentimental portraits of the Old South (capped by *Jezebel* and *Gone With the Wind* in 1939), and by the reinvigoration of liberalism in the New Deal of Franklin Delano Roosevelt.

Thus, for most of the next decade or so, the realization of Black self-determination became the responsibility of the Black Left. After his tour of the South in 1932, Langston Hughes was clear: "If the Communists don't awaken the Negroes of the South, who will? Certainly not the race leaders whose schools and jobs depend on white philanthropy.[52] During the Depression, they collaborated with the Black poor in the northern cities and Southern fields. Organizing tenant rent strikes, protest marches, and demonstrations; the mobilization of an international campaign to save the

Scottsboro boys; writers' clubs; and sharecropper and trade unions were understood as the necessary precursors of the proletarian solidarity required for the ultimate defeat of capitalism. As Robin D.G. Kelley instructs us, among the sharecroppers, tenant farmers, and industrial laborers of Alabama and the Black Belt, collective organizing did presage a social movement after the Second World War.

> A tightly disciplined, underground movement composed of poor urban and rural blacks and a handful of white folks too hungry or idealistic to let race stand in the way of fighting the bosses, the Alabama CP had become, by the 1940s, a kind of loosely organized think tank whose individual members exercised considerable influence in local labor, liberal, and civil rights organizations. . . . They had become labor organizers, civic spokespersons, and "race" leaders who belonged to SNYC, the Alabama Committee for Human Welfare, the CIO, the AFU, and other related organizations. If there was anything dubious or dishonest about their intentions, it was that they sought to do what they believed Communists should do—build a nonracist, democratic South—but understood the political limitations of identifying themselves as Party members.[53]

Thus, in the 1930s, when crises like the Italian invasion of Ethiopia occurred, it was largely the small Black Left that bore the burden of mobilizing Black support for an independent Ethiopia.[54] The next year, in 1936, when Mussolini sent military support to the fascist side in the Spanish Civil War, more than one hundred Black American revolutionists—like the nurse from Harlem Hospital, the Chicago building trades laborer, the poet from Cleveland, the Rutgers all-American, and the sharecropper from Mississippi—were there to greet the invaders who had devastated Ethiopia.[55]

These were among the "premature antifascists" (a favorite term of the post–Second World War Right) who would be the designated targets of the political hysteria that American historians call McCarthyism. But when Black leftists joined their comrades in Harlem, Chicago, Alabama, or Spain in the 1930s, their beliefs were sincere and their understanding prescient. The bonds between fascism and racism were indissoluble. When the war against fascism was thought to have been concluded in 1945, these agitators for a nonracist, democratic South resumed their work, sowing the seeds for a militant Civil Rights movement.

CHAPTER SIX

The Search for Higher Ground

*   *   *

For the moment, we reflect and regroup with a vow that the 1990s will make the 1960s look like a tea party.

—Cornel West, *Race Matters*

During the Second World War, Black Americans experienced the most profound Americanization of their collective social conscience since the beginnings of the Civil War nearly eight decades earlier. This interlude would have enduring consequences for both the Black liberal and democratic social cultures, at first drawing them into an approximation and then into a social concurrence. But, by the mid-1960s and the ending of the Civil Rights movement, when the faith in a just order in America could only be preserved by the Black privileged, they were pared, the one from the other, once again. During the "patriotic period" of the war and for a few short years afterward, Black liberalism was on the ascendancy, achieving points of purchase among America's Black political and economic elite. At the same time, the Black democratic culture resurfaced as migration, drawing millions of ordinary Black men and women into the orbit of wage labor and trade union radicalism in the North, the West, and Southern urban manufacturing centers. Mediated by civilian and military participation in the war, the two world views tangentially touched as liberalism exploited American patriotism and national unity for its agenda in race relations and the democratic tradition insinuated its concern for liberation into working-class militancy. For a decade or more following the war, both were retarded by a vigorous right-wing political and cultural counter-movement, which through anticommunism transformed the effective terrain of Black liberal initiatives to an abject dependency on elite self-definitions and stalled Black democratic activity with outright hostility. In the Civil Rights movement of the 1960s, the two distinct Black traditions achieved their closest accommodation, reinvigorating the social and moral impulses framed by the Second World War. But once again the Right responded, instituting an almost naked class warfare that seamlessly reconfigured anticommunism into a race discourse on the rule of law. Self-deceptive, Black liberalism retreated to the protected but shrinking sphere of privileges reserved for the national middle class, and Black communitarianism reclaimed the familiar impulses of separatism and emigrationism.

The Second World War and Black Struggles

In part, these ideological, social, and political oppositions were the direct results of Franklin Delano Roosevelt's symbolic and actual performance in the presidency and the orchestration of a liberal administration. On another level, they reflected the experience shared by all Americans of the real threat to national survival emanating from the global crisis of the late 1930s and 1940s. Paradoxically, Roosevelt's patrician origins and public manner seemed to authenticate his commitment to a democratic polity and a fair deal for workers. This set him above his enduring political foes: the oligopolistic interests that controlled his Republican opposition, the Dixiecrats of his own party, and their unholy alliances in the Supreme Court and the Congress. Even Roosevelt's frequent compromises were perceived as substantiations of his personal decency. Because of his long tenure as president, it came to be expected that eventually he could reclaim every terrain lost for the moment, and he repeatedly demonstrated that he had the moral will and political acumen to revisit every defeat until he could wrest some advantage from his setbacks. Most fortunately, as Blacks saw it, he was also inseparably paired with Eleanor Roosevelt. While the president had to pilot his administration between greed and race hatred in his mission of responding to the Great Depression, Mrs. Roosevelt, with some calculated prompting from Mary McLeod Bethune, could be trusted to speak aloud what was often taken for her husband's opinions and beliefs. Serving his third term as president when America entered the war, Roosevelt occupied a commanding political presence.

The arbiters of American mass culture also signaled a renegotiated race consciousness—all in the spirit of wartime national unity. While the Black national newspaper, the *Pittsburgh Courier*, promoted its "Double V" campaign—victory against fascism and victory against domestic racism—the corporate heads and producers of radio, film, magazines, and theater mysteriously discovered Black images and narratives that plotted Black people into the natural American landscape. Thomas Cripps reminds us that radio audiences of talk shows and primetime variety could hear

> Roi Ottley's *New World A 'Comin'* on Harlem's WLIP; *Men o' War*, a black show from Great Lakes Naval Station; KNX's *These Are Americans*; Blue Network's *America's Town Meeting of the Air*; and one-shots like Wendell Wilkie's reading of *An Open Letter on Race Hatred.* . . . Kate Smith on *We the People* boldly call[ed] for an end to racial antipathy, not "at a conference table in Geneva" but "in your own home."[1]

Popular soap operas began to introduce Black characters and even Black sitcoms. Films like *Stormy Weather* (released in 1943), with Lena Horne and Bill Robinson, reminded American movie audiences that Black soldiers had played a part in the First World War; and others like *Bataan* (with the Black film actor Kenneth Spencer), *Sahara* (Rex Ingram), *Lifeboat* (Canada Lee), and *Crash Dive* (Ben Carter) placed Blacks squarely in the present conflict. On Broadway, Mike Todd produced *The Hot Mikado* and Ed Sullivan did the variety show *Harlem Cavalcade*. The Federal Theatre put on *Porgy* and a version of Richard Wright's best-seller *Native Son* (with Canada Lee), while the American Negro Theatre did a Black version of the Polish play *Anna Lucasta* as well as Abram Hill's *Walk Hard* (with Robert Earl Jones). A Gallup public opinion poll suggested the mass culture campaign had been effective: whites supported a federal antilynching law, they applauded Mrs. Roosevelt's resignation from the Daughters of the American Revolution for its racial policies, and narrowly supported changes in "Southern racial etiquette." (29–30, 72)

Some few years before the war engulfed the country, some leaders of American capital sought a more nuanced treatment of Blacks that did not view them simply as cheap, unskilled labor or a temporary substitute for recalcitrant white workers. Faced with the growing militancy of the predominantly white industrial labor force, the more farsighted controllers of American business searched for a means of ensuring the loyalty of Black workers to the most powerful classes in America. Some thought that by extending to ordinary Blacks a social program modeled on the tradition of corporate philanthropy to Black higher education might construct a Black working class permanently alienated from non-Black labor.[2] Toward that pursuit, in 1937 the Carnegie Institute commissioned Gunnar Myrdal, a Swedish economist, to decipher the codes of Black ambition and desires. Earlier, in 1932, Carnegie had funded the development of a social engineering program for white workers in South Africa—in that instance to ensure social policies that would distance them from the demands of African and Indian workers.[3] Many of these South African policies were enacted in the 1930s and continued into the apartheid era begun in 1948. In *An American Dilemma: The Negro Problem and Modern Democracy*, Myrdal and his research associates (including Ralph Bunche, E. Franklin Frazier, T. Arnold Hill, St. Clair Drake, Guy and Guion Johnson) eventually surpassed the original charge and intent. But even then they played close to the racial protocols established by capital.

On the one hand, oblivious of "source criticism," Myrdal reconstructed the loci of "race prejudice" from the testimonies of his largely Southern white informants. According to them, their practices of race discrimination most demonized "intermarriage and sexual intercourse involving white women."[4] In descending order, other arenas in which prejudice was active were social discourse and etiquette; public schools and the use of public facilities; voting; law enforcement and the courts; and then land ownership, credit, jobs, and public relief. Black informants, Myrdal reported, gave inverse importance to these rankings of discrimination—ranking discrimination against them in economic arenas as their primary concern. Eschewing Ida B. Wells's analysis a half-century earlier that the white preoccupations with intermarriage and sexual and social intercourse were conceits, Myrdal made the plebeian observations that all these factors were "interrelated," constituting a "vicious circle." (75ff) Having neatly avoided the interrogation of historical causation, Myrdal preserved the reputations of his sponsors. Notwithstanding, Carnegie's heads were not well disposed to Myrdal's prescriptions: for example, his proposal for federal intervention in job market discrimination and federal provision of vocational training or the abolition of the poll tax and white primaries as a means of reasserting Black suffrage. Myrdal then completely abandoned his hosts when he observed:

> The treatment of the Negro in America has not made good propaganda for America abroad and particularly not among colored nations. . . .
>
> It seems more definitely certain that it will be impossible to make and preserve a good peace without having built up the fullest trust and goodwill among the colored peoples. They will be strong after the War, and they are bound to become even stronger as time passes. (vol. 2: 1016–17)

It was well after the war before America's race policies caught up to Myrdal's ideas. That would be when independence movements in Africa, Asia, and south of the United States coincided with the cold war and civil rights militancy. For the time being, as Stephen Graubard reports, Carnegie's officers "never really seemed to take pleasure in Myrdal's accomplishments."[5]

America's entry into the war in late 1941 proved to be the most effective answer to the Great Depression. Because of the emergency, massive numbers of the unemployed were absorbed by the military and war-related production. Production itself was centralized through federal agencies and managed by collaborations of workers, management, and bureaucrats. Industry's capital needs (for increasing production) and development needs (for radical technological innovations) were absorbed by Congress-approved spending bills (something close to $300 billion). In this war, unlike the First World War, in which the United States served merely as the cavalry coming to the rescue, America became a general headquarters and "home front." As the productive capacities of the Western/Eastern Allies (the United States; Britain and its colonies and commonwealth; Free France, the Soviet Union; and China) were being decimated by the bombardments of the Axis Powers (principally, Germany, Italy, Japan, and Vichy France), the responsibility for producing the war machines and materials—ships, airplanes, guns, cannon, tanks, munitions, and so on— transferred to the United States, whose industry was largely distanced from the broad-scale destruction.

Although Myrdal complained that the Black worker's share of the war economy was still low in 1942, there were rapid changes in some industries, particularly the automobile, shipbuilding, and aircraft industries. Changes also came in such industries as tobacco and textiles, in which Black women were already dominant in some sectors. For the northern- and western-based industries, one change was in the availability of Black workers; the same was true for Southern urban areas. During the 1940s, 2 million Blacks left the South for states like Michigan and California. Another million, though they remained in the South, moved from the farms to the cities. By January 1946, Black employment in manufacturing had increased by 135 percent over its 1940 proportion. Although 60 percent of the 1 million new Black workers were female, only 18 percent of Black women workers assumed industrial occupations (virtually equal to the 17.9 percent in nonprivate personal services such as catering or dry-cleaning), far behind the 44.6 percent in domestic service in 1944. Meanwhile, Karen Tucker Anderson calculates, Black males had risen to 25 percent of the work force in the foundries, 11.7 percent in shipbuilding, and 11.8 percent in blast furnaces and steel mills.[6]

In Detroit, employers lost the competition with the unions and leftist organizations for the loyalty of Blacks. In the automobile industry, tens of thousands of Black workers were concentrated in the foundries, print shops, and wet sanding operations of Ford, General Motors, and the Packard factories. Nine thousand alone were to be found in Ford's foundry at River Rouge.[7] Under the tutelage of Black and white CIO (Congress of Industrial Organizations) and CPUSA organizers, 100,000 Blacks joined the United Auto Workers and 20,000 became members of the NAACP Detroit chapter. In both instances, Black workers radicalized these institutions. Backed by mass struggle tactics, Black workers created a militant civil rights agenda around racial discrimination in jobs, job assignments, job rights, public housing, and law enforcement, and mounted huge campaigns to register Black voters. Robert Korstad and Nelson Lichtenstein report that "for the next decade, Rouge Local 600 proved a center of civil rights militancy and a training ground for black leaders." (795) Among those leaders was George Crockett, the future member of Congress; Coleman Young, the future mayor; and John Conyers, Sr., whose son would enter Congress in 1964.

In Winston-Salem, North Carolina, the tobacco industry in the form of R. J. Reynolds experienced an almost identical radicalization of its Black workers. In 1943, after two years of hidden organizing by Black staffers trained in the Southern Tenant Farmers Union, the CIO United Cannery, Agricultural, Packing and Allied Workers of America (later the Food, Tobacco, Agricultural and Allied Workers) succeeded in signing up about 8,000 workers, nearly half of whom were Black women. The union leaders in Local 22, Theodosia Simpson, Velma Hopkins, Moranda Smith, and Ruby Jones, then transformed the union hall into a civil rights and cultural center (classes in labor history, Black history, and so on):

> Local 22 sponsored softball teams, checker tournaments, sewing circles, and swimming clubs. Its vigorous educational program and well-stocked library introduced many black workers (and a few whites) to a larger radical culture few had glimpsed before. "You know, at that little library they [the city of Winston-Salem] had for us, you couldn't find any books on Negro history," remembered Viola Brown. "They didn't have books by Aptheker, DuBois, or Frederick Douglass. But we had them at *our* library." (791)

The CPUSA was a power in the new union and, as in Detroit, the majority of its new members were Black. Soon the unionized Black workers poured into the local NAACP chapter, propelling its membership from 100 in 1942 to 1,991 in 1946. Like their counterparts in Detroit, the traditional Black middle-class leadership of the chapter was displaced, and the newly radicalized local organization undertook mass campaigns for voter registration, voter education, and improved social services to Blacks, utilizing political rallies and citywide mass meetings. In 1944, the surge of Black voters helped reelect John Folger, a New Dealer and in 1947, Kenneth Williams, as alderman, became the first Southern Black official in the century to defeat a white opponent.

The war itself was a vast social undertaking for Americans in general as well as for Blacks. The Second World War functioned as a colander, draining the tangled social and political protocols of the racial order in America. It plunged the country into a dramatic contest between conflicting constructions of civilization and the ordering mechanism of race. One contributing factor was the significant participation of Blacks in the military and the war economy. In the United States, nearly 1,200,000 Blacks were inducted or enlisted in the armed forces (there were 3,600 Blacks among the 190,000 in the prewar armed forces), and Black laborers made up 8.3 percent of the war production work force.[8] In colonial Africa, Black recruitment took on many of the aspects of forced labor, and service as far as the Africans were concerned was "unrelated to notions of patriotism and loyalty," but in the United States Black motives mixed economic and patriotic impulses. Notwithstanding this important difference, on both continents the compelling fact of the critical involvement of Blacks in the war exaggerated the opposition between ideologists who saw empires and nations as expressions of a master race and those who embraced civilization as a liberal missionizing instrument. Finally, among militant Blacks and leftists, an increasing amalgam of social forces forwarded the notion that civilization was both the legacy and inheritance of all humanity. In nearly every eddy of war activity, the protocols of race order were violated, injuring its claim as a fact of nature.

For comparative purposes, consider the dilemmas of the armed forces in South Africa and the United States, the two most highly developed race orders. In both the South African and American military establishments, the reigning sentiment was that described by Louis Grundlingh in the official files of the Union Defense Force (UDF) in Pretoria: "The military authorities were concerned that the black soldiers' participation in the Second World War might be a threat to the control the white people had over the black people as well as the social structure of South Africa."[9] Concomitant with the recurrent worries over exposing white civilians, communities, women, and privilege to wartime fraternization with Blacks, novel and equally excessive fears appeared. For example, Simon Buckner, a U.S. officer in Alaska, imagined one horrifying consequence if Black American engineering troops who had been mobilized to build the Alaska Highway were to remain and settle in that territory after the war: "They would be interbred with the Indians and Eskimos and produce an astonishing objectionable race of mongrels which would be a problem here from now on."[10] Thus, "where possible, black troops were assigned tasks in regions remote from large population centers."[11] An identical policy was pursued by the UDF in Egypt, Britain, and elsewhere, complemented (as was the case in the U.S. military) by the assigning of white officers to Black units; the racial segregation of troops in combat, housing, hospitals, and on leave; and the augmentation of the military justice system with unique crimes based on race.[12] As Colonel Mockford, the UDF deputy director of non-European Army services, put it for both militaries when contemplating the assigning of Black troops to duty in Europe and the Middle East, "the longer they operate in that area the graver will be the problem of fitting them back into our social structure."[13]

These fears were not unwarranted, for inevitably the attempts to control the war experiences of Black troops broke down despite all the precautions. Two revealing entries in the official records of the South African and U.S. armed forces confirm the anticipated subversion of war fraternization. Sometime in 1941, one Black South African recorded his odyssey:

> I was in the British hospital. I have enjoyed the best time which has never [sic] been enjoyed by any person in South Africa. We were dining on one table, getting the same type of food, sleeping in one ward, one cinema, same showers and same "equality" of opportunity without slightest distinction. You must always come in touch with the Tommies and Anzacs [American, New Zealand, Australian, Canadian soldiers], they have no animosity for other people. (547)

Somewhat less warming reports of encounters between white officers and Black enlisted men come from the censored letter of a Black U.S. non-commissioned officer:

> In this unit we have a new major, from Texas. The boys really almost got out of control. They disobeyed, object[ed] and showed what would happen if he kept saying and acting as he did. Any day I'm looking for a report to come in stating the major had been killed. The boys really hate him and he knows it. When the major was at Belvoir he was a Lt. Col. One day Gen. Davis [a Black] visited the post and the major wouldn't salute him. Because of this incident he was reduced to major and he has hated colored every sense [sic]. [T]hen, we have captain just the same.
>
> One day he told a boy if he didn't be quite [sic], he make him. The boy

told him that the first time he tryed [sic] to close his mouth he would cut his throat. The boy really meant it."[14]

There are more eloquent expressions of the war's corrosion of racial domination—say, Frantz Fanon's *Black Skins, White Masks*—but the proof is history. Raised exponentially by the millions of Asian, African, and West Indian participants in the war effort, these sentiments served as a basis for what Imanuel Geiss termed the acceleration and intensification of Asian and African nationalism.[15] Just beyond the reach of military authorities, Black civilians made it even clearer that the cracks in the racial order would be widened in the postwar era.

Not too surprisingly, during the war both South Africa and the United States were swept by domestic upsurges of racial violence and Black militancy. In the United States, Lerone Bennett, Jr., reports,

> In the summer of 1943, America exploded in the worst series of riots since the summer of 1919. The National Guard was called out to put down a riot that started when blacks were upgraded at a Mobile, Alabama shipyard. Two persons were killed and martial law was declared in Beaumont, Texas, on June 16. Thirty-four persons died in the Detroit race riot, which started on June 20. In the same year, in August, there was a riot in Harlem.[16]

After the war, it was returning Black veterans who were most often the catalyst for race riots (e.g., those in Alabama, Mississippi, Tennessee, and Philadelphia)[17] and lynchings (in 1946, seven actual and seventeen attempted lynchings were reported).[18] In South Africa, the working class was overwhelmingly a Black working class, and so the Democratic movement that eventually came to power in 1994 was inseparable from the interests of the majority. In America, the violent reception accorded to the returning Black veterans provided evidence that the war's challenge to the racial social order had inspired the fear of a loss of status among white workers.

In February 1946, two Black ex-servicemen were killed by white police officers: Timothy Hood in Bessemer, Alabama, and Kenny Long in El Campo, Texas.[19] The largest body count, however, was awarded to Birmingham's all-white police force: in the first six weeks of the year, Commissioner Eugene "Bull" Connor's men killed five Black military veterans. On February 12, upon receiving his discharge from an army base in Georgia, Isaac Woodard headed for his home in North Carolina by bus. Following an argument about "racial etiquette" with the driver, Woodard was removed from the bus at Batesburg, South Carolina, by the local police chief and some of his deputies. Woodard was beaten and blinded: "Doctors finally determined that a blunt instrument (a billy club, as it turned out) had been jammed into his eye sockets so violently that both of his eyes were mutilated beyond repair."[20] On February 25, in Columbia, Tennessee, James Stephenson, a navy veteran, was arrested for attempted murder after he had defended his mother from a physical attack by a white department store clerk. After Stephenson posted bond, a lynch mob formed, threatening to invade Mink Slide row, the Black residential area. Armed Black veterans responded, setting up lookout posts and extinguishing lights in the streets. When a force of Columbia police entered Mink Slide, four were wounded, one seriously. The next day the National Guard was sent into Mink Slide on a search and destroy mission, "shooting into businesses, destroying property, cleaning out cash drawers and taking other valuables, ransacking scores of homes, and seizing about three hundred weapons." (364) One hundred Blacks were arrested and three days later patrolmen murdered two of the jailed Black males, seriously wounding a third. In April, forty Black draftees were arrested and beaten in Columbus, Georgia. (363–66) Other Black servicemen or veterans killed in this period were Private Charles Ferguson (by a Freeport, Long Island, policeman); Private Nathaniel Jackson (by a Granville, Wisconsin, barracks guard); in France, two white guards at Camp Lucky Strike killed Private Allen Leftridge and Technical Specialist 5 Frank Glenn for talking with French women; and George Collins, a Black shore patrolman, was killed by a McAlester, Oklahoma, policeman.[21]

In that summer, veteran Leon McTatie was lynched near Lexington, Mississippi. Maceo Snipes, a veteran, was murdered in Butler, Georgia, Egerton informs us, "soon after he became the first black registered voter in Taylor County." In July, Private Samuel Hicks was beaten to death by whites at a Spokane, Washington, base. In August, J. C. Farmer, another veteran, was shot dead by a posse near Baily, North Carolina; John C. Jones was lynched near Minden, Louisiana. In September, in Atlanta, veteran Walter Lee Johnson was shot by a street car motorman; in December, veteran William Daniels was shot by a guard of the union commissary in Westfield, Alabama (64–66). In Walton County, Georgia, four young tenant farmers were lynched. One of them, Roger Malcom, had fought with and stabbed his landlord's son, Barney Hester, when the latter tried to molest Dorothy Malcom, Roger's pregnant wife. As a consequence, Roger had been jailed, but on July 25 Roger was released on bond put up by Loy Harrison, a local white planter. Roger rode away from the jail with his wife; his in-laws, George (a veteran) and Mae Dorsey; and Harrison. Harrison drove the two couples to Moore's Ford and delivered them to an awaiting lynch mob of some two dozen unmasked white men. After one of the women pleaded with a member of the mob she recognized, "the four young people were lined up and shot." In 1981, after thirty-five years of claiming innocence of any involvement in the killings, Harrison gave a more authentic account to Clinton Adams (who at ten years of age had witnessed the event): "Let me tell you something about them you don't know. Up until George went in the army, he was a good nigger. But when he came out, they thought they were as good as any white people."[22]

Characteristically, Harrison spoke for many white Americans in the postwar era, and even three decades or more after the war he still misunderstood. Men and women like George Dorsey were more complex than Harrison could comprehend, and their experiences in the war and the armed services had been filtered through a historical consciousness and cultural values remote from the world Harrison imagined. Some of that world view was inadvertently recorded by Samuel Stouffer and his colleagues at the Research Branch of the Information and Education Division of the United States Army. In August 1944, Stouffer led a research project surveying the social psychology of U.S. veterans, among them Black veterans. Among the project's data, eventually published in four volumes as *The American Soldier* in 1949, striking differences were apparent between white and Black soldiers. For one, Southern Black soldiers were nearly twice as likely as whites not to return to the South (and by 1950, more than half of those in their twenties during the war had migrated). The longer their army service, the more likely the Black veterans were to plan migration. As well, Black soldiers were considerably more optimistic (41 percent compared to 25 percent) about their postwar chances than white soldiers. Most surprisingly was the variable that most accounted for Black optimism:

> The black southern soldiers who reported that their lives in the World War II army had been the least divergent from what most of them had known before—had been the least engaged in the technical rationality of the modern democratic army—had most resembled the personalistically dependent social relation of production in southern agriculture, were the most optimistic about how things would change after the war. For many soldiers like this, the war seemingly evoked millennial optimism, so characteristic of Afro-American history.[23]

Perhaps for people like George Dorsey, it was not so much that military service had spoiled them, or that the war had changed them, or that they had somehow belatedly arrived at the notion that their lives were as valuable as any other. Indeed, their war experiences, as far as racial oppression goes, were familiar, and the Afro-Christian tradition had for generations assured them that their lives were of the same value as whites. Rather it was that a revolution of consciousness and faith had occurred. War had extinguished their belief in human justice, and in that context the white South was no longer their master or their mistress. For the Black Republican political culture, it was imperative to foster the belief that the war had transformed American "race relations." For the alternative Black political culture, the one largely pinioned by a nonsecular moral tapestry, the advent of such a change was remote and perhaps sacrilegious. The sheer apocalyptic carnage of the war (something like 32 million civilian and military casualties) had thrown into question the superiority of a white-directed social order and any claim that mundane authority could overturn divine will.

The Cold War and the Race War

The Second World War was followed by decades of race war on a global scale. Two of the most intensive sites of the war were the United States and South Africa. While the official world contestation, the Cold War, has been taken to have subsumed all other conflicts, it is now possible to cast the competition between the two imperial hegemons, the United States and the Soviet Union, as a historical sidebar to the struggles to obtain or vanquish racial domination. Contrary to the mammoth cultural, political, technological, military, and propaganda industries manufactured on behalf of the cold war obsession for the past forty years, the transcendent and more enduring dualism has been what Fanon recognized as the racial order of a manichaean colonial domination: "The cause is the consequence: you are rich because you are white, you are white because you are rich."[24] From there he calculated, "It was not the *organization of production* but the persistence and *organization of oppression* which formed the primary social basis for revolutionary activity." (88)

The race war of the postwar era proceeded not merely from the determined attempts to preserve the organization of oppression of the prewar years. The Second World War had loosed resistance from the colored oppressed and a state of revulsion, loathing, and trepidation from among those whites implicated by the race order. In this era, hard on the heels of striking evidence of an alternative reality swept forward by the war, some were propelled into an intervention for a more just order. The decades-long race cataclysms implemented by Nazism in central Europe, fascism in Africa (Ethiopia, Libya, and Somalia), and Imperial Japan in Asia (Mongolia, China, and Korea) were insufficient warnings for the governments of the Atlantic States. The West's political leaders gave secondary signifi-cance to the impulses of racial domination so central to the imperial wars of the nineteenth century and the global wars of the twentieth century, concealed as they were beneath the discursive cloak of internation con-flict. Instead, political and corporate leaders ratcheted up the contest with the Soviet Union and Communist China into a Cold War, providing them-selves with an ideological machine with which to preserve imperial and colonial "adventures" among darker peoples and to suppress democratic movements at home.

One of the principal concerns of large employers and political conser-vatives in the postwar era was the expansion of organized labor during the war and the political coalition between trade unionism and Black civil rights. This threat was confronted with a series of legislative, political, and ideological assaults. American communists were labeled subversives, and federal, state, and local governments set about purging communists from service, instituting loyalty tests, and expanding security surveillance (by 1953, 20 percent of the U.S. work force, some 13.5 million, were subject to these requirements).[25] In 1947, President Truman, facing a re-election challenge, signed Executive Order 9835, establishing the Attorney Gen-eral's List of subversive organizations. He soon enlisted the Justice Depart-ment (the FBI, in particular), the Internal Revenue Service, military intelligence agencies, and other federal bureaucracies to root out dissent. The same year, Congress passed the Labor-Management Relations (Taft-Hartley) Act restricting the power of unions and requiring union officials to deny under oath "any Communist affiliation." Eschewing the separation of powers principle, Congress entered into enforcement. In that same year, the House UnAmerican Activities Committee (HUAC) set up hearings in Hollywood and Winston-Salem (it would reach Detroit in 1952) to purge communists from union offices and the labor force. For their part, corpo-rate management employed instruments as varied as gangsters and automa-tion to break the unions. Establishing "blacklists," the government and private enterprise purged radicals from the union. Thus, such organizations as the UAW, the CIO, and the NAACP were turned over or returned to anti-communist "moderate" leaders and more "practical" reformers.[26]

From the 1930s, the NAACP pursued an agenda that reflected Black middle-class interests, political sensibilities, and cultural values. In its legal activism, for example, the organization concentrated on suits to end the exclusion of Blacks from professional and graduate programs in state uni-versities and to equalize salaries and physical facilities in the all-Black pri-mary and secondary public schools. Although these might have a "trickle-down" and symbolic importance for the mass of Black people, these concerns were directly nurtured by those in the Black middle class most likely to receive relief. In keeping with the middle-class Republican creed, by determining to focus on "cases that had the potential of establishing a new precedent of constitutional significance," the organization sought to validate "the importance of laws and of state as a guarantor of social order."27 Until the NAACP signed on as a supporter of A. Philip Randolph's proposed march on Washington in 1941, the organization took a patrician attitude toward mass mobilizations and even the strike work managed by its erstwhile ally, the CIO. Regarding trade union activity, the NAACP was always wary of too close an association with radicalism in general and communist labor leaders and organizers in particular. By 1946, however, with almost 450,000 members in some 1,073 branches, the organization verged "dangerously" toward becoming a mass movement.

Spurred by the democratic militance of its new members, the NAACP staged its last radical act before the onset of McCarthyism. In October 1947, the organization filed "An Appeal to the World" with the newly established United Nations (founded in 1945), seeking intervention in the domestic affairs of the United States. The appeal had been orchestrated by DuBois, who for a short time had returned to the NAACP (he would resign again the next year), and it contained research by Rayford W. Logan, Earl B. Dickerson, Milton R. Konvitz, William R. Ming, Jr., and Leslie S. Perry.28 Mirroring the heretofore unprecedented and unexpected complaint on behalf of Indian South Africans filed by the government of India against South Africa in 1946,29 the petition was supported by the Soviet Union but scuttled by the U.S. delegation.

Nonetheless, President Truman responded. A year before, appalled by the race violence that had swept the country in 1946, Truman had appointed a Committee on Civil Rights. Upon the October 29, 1947, release of *To Secure These Rights,* the committee's report, Truman endorsed its recommendation for antilynching legislation and its condemnations of the poll tax; quasi-legal impediments to Black suffrage; segregation in the armed forces and the District of Columbia; and segregation in public housing, public accommodations, and the distribution of federal funds. Truman reiterated his civil rights position in his State of the Union address and then placed before Congress a legislative initiative that fully encompassed the proposals from the Committee on Civil Rights, including the establishment of a permanent Fair Employment Practices Commission. In the Senate, James Eastland grumbled about Truman turning over the government "to mongrelized minorities," and Tom Connally (of Texas) announced that Truman's program was "a lynching of the Constitution." In the House, in an almost prophetic political warning, John Rankin of Mississippi cannoned across the liberal front supporting Truman the notion that the president had "tried to ram the platform of the Communist Party down the throats of the people of the United States."[30] The Dixiecrats bolted from the Democratic Party in May 1948, leaving Truman free to issue his armed service desegregation order (Executive Order 9981) in July. In order to forestall the attack from his other right wing, the Republicans, however, he appropriated their most volatile and promising campaign issue: anticommunism.

In keeping with its political agenda, which focused on the courts and Congress, the NAACP national headquarters established a Washington bureau in 1942. In 1946, the organization's bureau successfully participated in Washington intrigues by joining forces with Senate opponents of Theodore Bilbo, the "arch segregationist" senator from Mississippi. The Senate temporarily suspended Bilbo from the chamber for corruption and, before he could be officially reseated, Bilbo became ill, dying in 1947. The NAACP, then, was well placed to register the wave of anticommunism that was building in Washington, and its officers, for their own reasons, enthusiastically plunged into the campaign to punish radicals. Internally, the organization began a purge of leftists (which, of course, included DuBois).[31] Meanwhile in the corridors of power, as August Meier and John Bracey, Jr., conclude, the NAACP "employed the threat posed by the Cold War and the influence of the Soviet Union among nonwhite peoples of the world to press its own agenda. The gist of the argument was that American racial practices played into the Soviet argument about the nature of capitalism, imperialism, and racism."[32]

Locked into what Gerald Horne describes as the postwar Red Scare, the NAACP lost membership and its mass character (in the Los Angeles chapter, for example, membership fell from 14,000 in 1945 to 2,500 in 1950), but regained its middle-class character.[33] Thus, in 1951, when William Patterson and Paul Robeson sought a second appeal to the United Nations, the NAACP opposed them. Patterson and his colleagues (Richard Boyer, Elizabeth Lawson, Yvonne Gregory, Oakley Johnson, and Aubrey Grossman) amassed an impressive indictment of the complicity of the federal and state governments in the murders, rapes, beatings, and intimidations of hundreds of Black men and women between 1946 and 1950. The document, *We Charge Genocide*, bore the names of petitioners ranging from leftists like DuBois, Robeson, Charlotta Bass, Benjamin J. Davis, Jr., James W. Ford, Matthew Crawford, and Pettis Perry, to Black nationalists like Mary Church Terrell, Reverend Charles A. Hill, W. Alphaeus Hunton, and white militants like Jessica Mitford, Winifred Feise, and Reverend Eliot White.[34]

But in Paris in December 1951, Dr. Tobias Channing, the chair of the organization's national board, and a member of the American Delegation, presented Patterson with the NAACP reaction:

> [Dr. Tobias] demanded, "Why did you do this thing, Patterson? . . . Make this attack on your government," he snapped.
>
> "It's your government, Dr. Tobias, and my country," I said quietly. "I am fighting to save my country's democratic principles from destruction by your government."
>
> He kept his temper. "But why," he asked, "didn't you write about genocide in the Soviet Union?"
>
> I had not expected such crude red-baiting. "There are two reasons, Mr. Tobias, the first being that I know nothing about genocide in the Soviet Union. . . . The second is that I am not a national of that country. I think I would look rather foolish coming here with a petition dealing with human relations in any country but my own.". . .
>
> "Where do you expect to get with this?"
>
> "That depends in part upon your courage, Dr. Tobias. How far will you help me get?" I added seriously.
>
> Without another word the reverend gentleman turned away. (189)

Similarly, the NAACP bent its efforts to constructing political coalitions with similarly liberal and anticommunist organizations like the Anti-Defamation League, the American Jewish Committee, the American Jewish Congress, and organized labor's sanitized CIO and the AFL, while wresting control from the now largely symbolic National Negro Council (NNC) and the Leadership Conference on Civil Rights (LCCR) from A. Philip Randolph.[35] Simultaneously, it pursued litigation in the federal courts. Its primary focus was institutions of higher education and building on *Missouri ex rel. Gaines v. Canada* (University of Missouri Law School), its 1938 victory. Slowly, the NAACP constructed the architecture of its ultimate constitutional objective: the overturning of the "separate but equal" doctrine of *Plessy v. Ferguson* (1896). It began by pushing states to budgetary crises by securing decisions that required the states to establish separate professional schools for Blacks: in 1948, *Sipuel v. Board of Regents* (University of Oklahoma Law School). Then it forced the Supreme Court to reject this *Plessy*-like solution: in 1950, *Sweat v. Painter* (University of Texas Law School) and *McLaurin v. Oklahoma State Regents* (George McLaurin, a Black doctoral student in education, was "required to sit in a special designated area in classrooms, in the library, and in the cafeteria"), the Court required integration in public graduate and professional schools.[36] Thus, by

1954–55, the Supreme Court presided over by Chief Justice Earl Warren (the California attorney general who had championed the herding of Japanese-Americans into camps during the Second World War) was ushered by the NAACP into the *Brown v. Board of Education* (Topeka, Kansas) declaration that when education is separate, it is inherently unequal. The *Voice of America* broadcast the decision across the world in thirty-five languages.[37]

Civil Rights and Mass Struggle

The social revolution that shunted the NAACP from the center of Black liberalism to the margins came at the apogee of its legal triumphs and from within its own ranks. Having largely decimated the organizational representation of the Black working class and reduced its loyal members to serving as a complaisant chorus to the social agenda designed at national headquarters, the NAACP did not expect the reappearance of activism from a surprising quarter: the southern Black middle class. Certainly, even in the midst of the class that began the social cataclysm known as the Civil Rights movement, what they precipitated grew far beyond anything envisioned at the start. In the vanguard of this movement were Black women, women like Septima Poinsette Clark.

Hidden away in the Cumberland in the southeast corner of Tennessee was a socialist cooperative experiment in multiracial adult education. Begun in 1932, the Highlander Folk School quickly became a center of union organizing for local workers employed by the New Deal's Works Projects Administration and established a community cannery, a community nursery school, and a quilting cooperative.[38] By the late 1930s, Highlander had become a center for CIO organizing and education, and by the war years, the UAW was enrolled. Septima Clark attended Highlander in the summer of 1954, and later that year she was appointed director of education. The fifty-eight-year-old Charleston native drew on her thirty-eight years in teaching and particularly the experience in citizenship training she had done with Black soldiers at Camp Jackson (in South Carolina) during the 1930s. From her first years as a nineteen-year-old teacher on John's Island, Clark fought for the equalization of salaries for Black teachers and their right to teach in South Carolina's public schools. Clark was vice president of the NAACP branch in Columbia, and following the 1954–55 Supreme Court decision when the South Carolina legislature declared membership in the NAACP a criminal act, she was fired along with ten other Black teachers. She had already begun organizing desegregation and civil disobedience workshops at Highlander in the summer of 1955, and she was now free to join the staff. Together with her cousin, Bernice Robinson, Clark trained nearly 1,300 Black teachers and organizers between 1954 and 1961. In 1961, she resigned from Highlander in order to institute leadership training for the Southern Christian Leadership Conference (SCLC).[39]

One of Clark's first trainees at Highlander was Rosa Parks, a seamstress and NAACP activist in youth programs in Montgomery, Alabama. Parks had written to Clark that "I want to come and see if I can do something for my people." Highlander had sent her money to come and provided Parks with a scholarship for the workshop.

> "At Highlander," Rosa Parks recalled, "I found out for the first time in my adult life that this could be a unified society, that there was such a thing as people of differing races and backgrounds meeting together in workshops and living together in peace and harmony. It was a place I was very reluctant to leave. I gained there strength to persevere in my work for freedom, not just for blacks but all oppressed people."[40]

That summer, in August, Chicagoan Emmett Till, fourteen, was mutilated and shot while visiting relatives in Mississippi. In September, two of his accused killers were acquitted, despite the testimonies of Black eyewitnesses rounded up by NAACP field director Medgar Evers, and the country was repulsed by the spectacle of southern justice. Thus, two months after her training at Highlander, on December 1, 1955, the forty-three-year-old Mrs. Parks sat on a bus in Montgomery and flushed the NAACP from its glory as *the* civil rights organization. She claimed she was tired after a day of shopping, but there was something calculated in her refusal to give up her seat to a white man. The bus driver, James Blake, must have had some sense of it: in 1943, eleven years earlier, he had thrown the same woman off his bus for refusing to use the back door. (The next year, 1944, Parks had attended an NAACP leadership workshop organized by Ella Baker.)

As Robin Kelley has amply shown, working-class Blacks, particularly women, were noncompliant passengers on public transport in the cities of Alabama during the Second World War. In Birmingham, Kelley's search of that city's public library provided him with evidence for his thesis that the most neglected part of Black political history has been the "daily, unorganized, evasive, seemingly spontaneous actions" undertaken by Black working people.[41]

> Although the available records are incomplete, it seems that black women outnumbered black men in incidents of resistance on buses and streetcars. In 1941–1942, nearly twice as many black women were arrested as black men, most of them charged with either sitting in the white section or cursing. . . .

Unlike the popular image of Parks's quiet resistance, most black women's opposition tended to be profane and militant. There were literally dozens of episodes of black women sitting in the white section, arguing with drivers or conductors, and fighting with white passengers. The "drama" usually ended with the woman being ejected, receiving a refund for her fare and leaving on her own accord, moving to the back of the vehicle, or being hauled off to jail. Indeed, through the war, dozens of black women were arrested for merely cursing at the operator or a white passenger. (105)

Parks's own history in Montgomery suggests that Birmingham was not unique. In 1955 alone, Montgomery amassed a record of public transport misadventures. Earlier in the year, Claudette Colvin, fifteen, and an elderly Black woman had refused to surrender their ride worth a dime each. Colvin was arrested, and the Montgomery NAACP came to her rescue until it became known that she was pregnant and unmarried. It then withdrew its involvement. E. D. Nixon (formerly of the NAACP, but now head of the Progressive Democrats in Montgomery) "would reach the same decision twice that year about other women who had refused to be humiliated on the bus and gotten themselves arrested."[42] Nixon was looking for "somebody I could win with," and in Rosa Parks he got the chance. The Rosa Parks case, however, became the *cause celebre* of a Black women's group, the only Black middle-class group among Montgomery's NAACP, the Baptist Ministers' Alliance, the Interdenominational Ministerial Alliance, and the myriad fraternal and sororal organizations, that was not riven by jealousies and rivalries.[43]

The Women's Political Council in Montgomery was formed in 1946 by Mary Fair Burks after "Vernon Johns, pastor of Dexter Avenue Baptist Church, mounted one of his scathing attacks on the complacency of his affluent membership."[44] As a teenager in Montgomery, Burks had conducted her own "guerrilla warfare" by persistently violating "For Whites Only" and "For White Ladies Only" notices on park gates and rest rooms. At nineteen she returned to Montgomery with a master's degree from Ann Arbor, and began teaching at the Alabama State Laboratory High School (Parks's alma mater). Later, with the formation of the Women's Political Council from a meeting of some forty Black women, Burks undertook the lead in political action (including voter registration and screening candidates), opposing segregation on buses and in public parks, and literacy and citizenship training. In 1949, Jo Ann Robinson, a Georgian with a master's degree from Atlanta University, joined Burks on the faculty of the English Department at Alabama State College; in 1950, Robinson succeeded Burks as head of the Women's Political Council.

Even before 1955, Robinson made the segregation of buses the principal concern for the council. Six years earlier, during her first Christmas in
Montgomery, she had been threatened by a driver because she had sat too
far forward on a bus. In March 1955, with Burks and other members
(namely, Irene West and Uretta Adair) of the council, she had met with the
Black male representatives of Montgomery's leadership (Nixon, Martin
Luther King, Jr., and Rufus Lewis of the Citizens Steering Committee) to
discuss a boycott following Colvin's arrest. Robinson had agreed with
Nixon on not supporting Colvin's case, but they both agreed that Parks's
was the case they had been waiting for. By Burks's account, on Friday,
December 2, meeting in the basement of Dexter Avenue Baptist, the now
300-strong council decided to move on its own, organizing a boycott for
Monday, the day of Parks's hearing; leaving Nixon to attempt to bring the
male leadership together. David Garrow tells the story a bit differently: at
Nixon's and Reverend Ralph Abernathy's behest, the ministers met on Friday evening and, after a troubling meeting, agreed to support the boycott
and to meet on Monday evening in a community-wide demonstration of
support. On Saturday, beginning at six in the morning (Burks and Robinson had a bridge party that evening), the council began to distribute the
35,000 mimeographed calls for a boycott. (82) That same Saturday, Nixon
and his rival Rufus Lewis independently concluded that a new organization
was needed and the best candidate to head it would be the twenty-six-
year-old Martin Luther King, Jr., a relative newcomer to Montgomery who
was educated, articulate, and unentangled in Montgomery's rivalries. As Jo
Ann Robinson recalled:

> Monday night, the ministers held their meeting [at Holt Street Church].
> The church itself holds four or five thousand people. But there were thou-
> sands of people outside of the church that night. They had to put up loud-
> speakers so they would know what was happening. When they got through
> reporting that very few people had ridden the bus, that the boycott was
> really a success . . . they voted unanimously to continue the boycott. And
> instead of lasting one day as the Women's Council had planned it, it lasted
> for thirteen months.[45]

The boycott spawned the Montgomery Improvement Association (MIA),
still largely an agency of women. But Robinson, Burks, Johnnie Carr, and
the other women serving on the executive board and providing the staff
muscle (Robinson edited the MIA newsletter) for the association, deliberately left the public posturing to King and the other male ministers, understanding that without their church affiliations, the boycott would be

stymied.[46] Rising from the association, the ministers coalesced into the SCLC, with seasoned organizers and ideologues like Clark and Ella Baker.

One measure of the isolation of the NAACP national headquarters from the grassroots struggle was the long-enduring enmity felt there for Martin Luther King, Jr. Nearly forty years after King's deliberately orchestrated rise to national and international celebrity, Denton Watson, a former public relations staffer (1971–79) for the NAACP would still resort to phrases like "King's Montgomery Improvement Association" and "King's movement," testimony to the careful hagiography constructed by the professional Black women in Montgomery's Women's Council, the MIA, and the SCLC (which disguised their own role).[47] Watson praised King's "powerful gift of oratory" and his ability to craft a movement designed for the media, but he wrote somewhat contemptuously of the Blacks in the MIA and the SCLC: "King knew that style was much more important than substance to poor, southern African Americans as his words probed the innermost recesses of the heart with their striking cadences" (459). Watson made clear his own jaundiced view of King and the mass struggle, a view that emanated from his leaders in the NAACP. Some time in the 1940s, Watson reports, Roy Wilkins complained to Constance Baker Motley "that no matter how hard he tried, he could not get African Americans to join the struggle," a surprising lament in the face of Black activism in trade unionism, politics, and civil rights at the time. In 1956, during the MIA's long boycott, another NAACP official had told the *New York Times*: "We've had to overcome a lot of apathy built among the colored over the years." (455–56) According to Watson, Clarence Mitchell, Jr., director of the NAACP Washington bureau, trivialized the role that nonviolent, direct action protests played in the passage of the Civil Rights Act in 1964: "The votes we got were the votes we would have gotten, demonstrations or no demonstration, because they were the people who wanted to do something." (465) Wilkins, who served as executive director of the NAACP from 1955–76, looked upon King as essentially a distracting opportunist. Under Wilkins,

> the NAACP's early leaders anticipated competition from King and the Southern Christian Leadership Conference (SCLC), which he headed, but NAACP leaders never had an effective public relations strategy to counter the overwhelming emotional appeal of King's oratory and the civil rights demonstrations in the South, which were tailored for the news media, especially television. (453)

The enmity Wilkins held for King was so strong that the FBI listed him as a collaborator in its program to destroy Martin Luther King, Jr. Wilkins termed the agency's affection "a damn lie," but in his frequent meetings (from 1960 to 1964) with FBI agent Cartha DeLoach, Wilkins bitterly assaulted King's reputation (and those of James Forman of CORE and John Lewis of SNCC).[48]

Thus, while the NAACP provided legal services to MIA (it secured the integration of buses through the Supreme Court in 1956), to the SCLC, and later to the Students Nonviolent Coordinating Committee, the Congress of Racial Equality, and others, it never got close enough to the movement to discern its organization or its social base. As we shall see, television journalists got it wrong and screened their misapprehension directly to their audiences. The NAACP got it wrong. The FBI and Army intelligence got it wrong. For the Black women who memorialized the movement purposely misled all comers. Thus most of the historians got it wrong.[49]

King's charismatic authority was a tributary of the Afro-Christian tradition embedded in the consciousness of the now mostly urban Blacks in the South and elsewhere. His leadership was grounded on culturally cemented legitimacy rather than organizational management or skills, on the biblical faith tales retold at thousands of places of worship each Sunday, the militant millenarianism of Afro-Christian hymns, and the messianism of the Gospel. When he spoke, his speech rhythms and language conspired with beliefs, concepts, ideas, and icons insinuated into Black Christian consciousness for generations. He clarioned a call to action that was heard wherever Afro-Christians could be found (and beyond, if one recalls Pentecostalism). In this performance, he was less a person than a signature of a social and historical identity. King articulated the salvationist vision of a future but accessible utopia, a golden place whose every ethical and moral stone was familiar to this widely dispersed congregation. Baker and others, whose genius rested in organization and the analyses of social process, recognized both King's unquestioned authority and his obvious limitations. Baker was appalled by the other SCLC leaders' deference to and dependency on King. But they too were hedged in by the prescripted narrative of Black salvationism. Thus, while a Baker or an Abernathy or a Clark might provide organizational integument—that is, practical planning and realistic goals to King's paradigmatic talk—the power of the movement came from the masses, from a century or two of their ancestors, under acute distress, elaborating a vision of the future and how it might be attained. In King they saw their own reflection, not their master, their own ambitions, not his dictates.[50] Through sacrifice foretold by their legends, they would build an alternative moral order. Thus Wilkins, in the cocoon of what Max Weber termed a bureaucratic institution, was (situationally and by habits of thought) unqualified to imagine or recognize the nature of the movement. The national media, by its nature and professional customs, was too alien.

Civil Rights and the Rituals of Oppression

Television, of course, had little capacity to display the divisional and ideological complexities of organizations, but network news producers enthused over the visual possibilities of stark, racial conflict acted out in well-lit public spaces. Television's dramatic canon of simple binaries, good vs. evil, was even more seductive when Blacks symbolized good and whites, evil. With nearly 35 million television sets to compete for, network crews fought each other for primacy in portraying the morality play that civil rights had become. Suddenly, television began to outdistance radio as a source of social theater and information:

> The mixture of pictures and sound via TV was considerably more impressive. The mental suggestion of radio could never match the dramatic impact possible on television. Images of chanting demonstrators being sprayed by fire hoses and attacked by police dogs, freedom riders being abused, sit-in participants being taunted or beaten, and small black children requiring military escorts to enter public schools—these pictures made TV a powerful propaganda tool for those wanting progressive change.[51]

The attempts by local and national civil rights leaders throughout the country were frequently overshadowed by compelling media dramas enacted by Black children facing Southern white state officials, national guards, police, and White Citizens Council-led mobs in the late 1950s. On the public approach to Little Rock's Central High School in September 1957, Elizabeth Eckford, at fifteen, met the power of Governor Orval Faubus's state in the body of armed National Guardsmen who refused entrance to her. She was alone only because of a mix-up (the other eight Black students were being assembled elsewhere by Daisy Bates), but none of that helped as the crowd erupted in cries of "Lynch her!" She found one friendly face in the crowd, but then it spat on her. She walked away and found a bench to await a bus to take her out of that hell. Then a white man sat down next to her, a reporter. Apparently transgressing journalistic objectivity but preserving televisable images, he put an arm around her and whispered, "Don't let them see you cry." His counsel applied to the television audience as well as to the jeering white mob that had come to frighten the Black children.[52]

Three weeks later, President Eisenhower nationalized the Arkansas National Guard, and under the direction of nearly 1,000 federal marshals, Eckford and her eight companions matriculated at Central High.

For the next three years, bus boycotts, sit-ins (in Oklahoma and Kansas), school desegregation, voter registration drives, civil rights legislation (although largely ineffective, the Civil Rights Act of 1957 increased federal responsibility for the protection of voting rights and established a research group, the Civil Rights Commission; the Civil Rights Act of 1960 gave the Justice Department the right to inspect state voter registration records and sue on behalf of persons denied the right to vote), and a gathering of 25,000 civil rights activists at the Lincoln Memorial, in 1957 became a part of the social and political landscape of the country. So, too, was something that came to be called the "white backlash." While integration of some public schools proceeded slowly, some Southern states disestablished their public school systems, replacing them with "private" white schools; in still other locales, schools were bombed to avoid desegregation. At the grassroots level, white supremacy groups proliferated and grew in response to the 1954–55 Supreme Court decision: in Georgia, Eldon Edwards's U.S. Klans recruited nearly 15,000 new members; in Alabama, Sam Engelhardt's White Citizens Councils (mostly business and professionals) competed for prominence with Asa Carter's Ku Klux Klan of the Confederacy (mostly farmers, mechanics, and storekeepers). By 1959, they and their like were amassing a considerable record of violence: six Blacks killed; twenty-nine civil rights activists (Black and white) shot and wounded; forty-four others beaten; eighty-three homes bombed, burned, or damaged; six schools bombed or burned; eight churches bombed or burned; four Jewish temples or centers bombed; and one YWCA dynamited.[53] A series of international events was not reassuring to either the White House or the White Citizens: Ghana acquired self-governance and then independence in 1957, while in 1960, a host of other African independence movements were realized (in effect, isolating southern Africa and Portuguese Africa as the only "certain" redoubts of European colonialism). In 1957, the Soviet Union launched an artificial satellite into space. In 1959, the Cuban Revolution triumphed, ushering this country into a Cold War in Central and Latin America. Perceiving themselves as provoked by the appearance of a revolutionary society so close at hand, American policymakers resolved to act as a brake on the anticolonial struggles in Africa and Asia. At home, by 1960, under the stimulation of Malcolm X, the Nation of Islam had grown to 100,000 members, each recruit a visible rebuke to American conceits.

The sit-in movement began with Black college students at North Carolina Agricultural and Technical College at a Greensboro F. W. Woolworth lunch counter on February 1, 1960. All of downtown Greensboro was shut down by sit-ins by the end of the week. Within days, similar protests appeared in Durham (quickening Reverend Douglas Moore's plans for nonviolent protests), Winston-Salem, Charlotte, Raleigh, Fayetteville, and Elizabeth City. Then they spread to Nashville (where the Gandhian James Lawson ministered), South Carolina, Tennessee, and Alabama. The scenario of the protests became familiar: sitting quietly at the counters, preserving as much dignity as they could muster, the students were abused, taunted, beaten, and eventually arrested. In jail, most refused to pay bail, filling the municipal and county institutions. By now, King was the shining symbol of the Southern Democratic movement, and the students, through Reverend Douglas Moore, invited King to Durham for advice on coordinating the rapidly expanding protests and a show of unity. By March, the sit-ins had spread to Atlanta, the new base of operations for King and the SCLC. There, Ella Baker, the SCLC chief of staff, proceeded to follow up on the students' interest in forming a separate organization for their movement. At a meeting she called at Shaw College on April 15, two hundred students gathered; the next day, operating within the protective sphere of Baker and Lawson, they secured student control of the movement by calling forth the Student Nonviolent Coordinating Committee (SNCC).[54] The student-led movement was rich in young, bright leaders, and some of them grew impatient with the SCLC within the year. Baker, whose impatience with the NAACP had driven her out of that organization, was growing weary of the SCLC's cautious, plodding, and hierarchically obsessed clergy. So, she elected to become the most senior (she was fifty-seven) and seasoned councilor of SNCC.

Three years before the North Carolina sit-ins appeared, Ella Baker—along with Bayard Rustin and Stanley Levison—drew up the tactical plan that the SNCC undertook. In 1957, Rustin argued in a position paper, "until the Negro votes on a large scale, we shall have to rely more and more on mass direct action as the one realistic political weapon." (85–86) Originally designed for the SCLC, this program of legal and illegal mass direct action to obtain Black voting power went far beyond the resources, ambitions, and talents of the ministerial leadership of SCLC. The program also had an acquired taint: both Rustin and Levison were former communists (after Rustin had been with the SCLC for seven years, Adam Clayton Powell, Jr., extorted King into disassociating from Rustin; the FBI, employing similar tactics, divorced King from Levison).[55] With the SNCC, Baker, Rustin, and Levison found their mass action social base. After their years of disappointment with the "leader-centered" decision making of the SCLC, they were also deeply appreciative of the "group-centered leadership" of SNCC.[56]

In May of 1961, James Farmer, the former NAACP program director and new national director of the Congress of Racial Equality (CORE), launched the Freedom Rides, integrated groups of travelers intended to test the desegregation of interstate transportation. The buses and their occupants were attacked outside Anniston, Alabama, forcing the intervention of the attorney general, Robert Kennedy. The new president, John Kennedy, and his brother were Irish Catholics; that is, they were members of groups which white supremacists abhorred. Neither seemed aware that national office had not immunized them from this enmity. Thus, over the next three years of negotiating with Southern officials, the Kennedys would feel betrayed by local authorities (and, indeed, were being betrayed by the FBI, which shared the Freedom Ride itinerary with the Klan).[57] Three months into their tenure, Birmingham's Police Commissioner "Bull" Connor began the brothers' initiation into brokering civil rights and broken deals. Meanwhile, as the Freedom Riders continued on to Jackson, Mississippi, with federal escorts, CORE and SNCC began to distance themselves from King and the SCLC.[58]

SNCC began its voter registration drive in Mississippi in 1961, working secretly in the state, where only 3 percent of the potential Black voters were registered. Although the NAACP's national headquarters were hostile to SNCC and its direct action tactics, state NAACP leaders like C. C. Bryant, Medgar Evers (another of the war veterans), and Anzie Moore, impatient with their own organization, were enthusiastic. Bob Moses, the SNCC program director, was the advance man in Mississippi in 1961, soon followed by Marion Barry, who began nonviolent training for Black teenagers in McComb. Killings, kidnappings, mass arrests, and beatings convinced some local NAACP officials to request that SNCC abandon the project. The next year, Evers concentrated the state's NAACP on the desegregation of the University of Mississippi (James Meredith began school in the fall of 1962) and voter registration. In early 1963, SNCC returned in force, now combining with CORE, the NAACP, and SCLC to form the Council of Federated Organizations (COFO). In 1963, COFO organized a statewide mock election, Freedom Vote, in which some 80–93,000 Black Mississippians participated.

Late in 1963, also sensing the need for a unified movement, A. Philip Randolph pushed the notion of a monumental gathering at Washington, D.C., in August. This march on Washington would serve as a national spectacle for equality, bringing together the NAACP, SCLC, SNCC, CORE, the National Urban League, labor leaders, Jews, Protestants, Christians, and even radicals. The march brought more than 250,000 to Washington in August and was dramatized by King's "I Have a Dream" speech. King pleaded, "I have a dream that my four little children will one day live in a nation where they will not be judged by the color of their skin but by the content of their character," but it was too late for Medgar Evers, who had been gunned down outside his home in July. Two weeks after King's speech, four other Black children had their dreams ended. On a Sunday morning, September 15, a bomb crumbled the Sixteenth Street Baptist Church in Birmingham, crushing the bodies of Denise McNair, seven, and Cynthia Wesley, Carole Robertson, and Addie Mae Collins, all age fourteen. Like Evers, they were free at last. For fourteen years the FBI kept secret the identities of the Klan bombers.[59] Later that Sunday, as if no horror was sufficient in itself, two other Black Birmingham youths were shot. Bull Connor's forces cleaned the streets by hosing demonstrators protesting the violence. It was fascinating television. In November, President Kennedy was assassinated in Dallas, and his alleged assassin, Lee Harvey Oswald was, in turn, assassinated on live television. Then one more striking video image: the train bearing Kennedy's body back to Washington. The centennial year of Lincoln's Emancipation Proclamation had seemed to erase one hundred years of freedom. In the wings stood Malcolm X, whom television had cast as Faust. Because his charisma flowed from the same source as King's, it was inevitable that despite their ideological and political differences, Malcolm had sought to defend King and protect the students and their supporters from the viciousness of their shared enemies. Failing that, he offered an alternative vision. At a press conference in Selma, Alabama, two weeks before his own death in February 1965, Malcolm's maneuver was clear: "I am 100 percent for any effort put forth by Black people in this country to have access to the ballot. . . . And I think that the people in this part of the world would do well to listen to Dr. Martin Luther King. . . . What he's asking for is right. That's the ballot. And if he can't get it the way he's trying to get it, then it's going to be gotten, one way or the other."[60]

Persuaded that the killings of Black activists and innocents had been met with indifference, in 1964 COFO launched Freedom Summer. Inspired by an idea of Allard Lowenstein, the project brought 600 students from northern elite schools to Mississippi to ostensibly engage in Black voter registration. The students were overwhelmingly white and largely from privileged backgrounds. Perhaps, some cynics in SNCC thought, the spectacle of their own—idealistic young white people—being mowed down by segregationists would alter the national consciousness:

> The success of Freedom Summer was premised on the recognition and conscious exploitation of America's racism. The logic ran as follows: if the mur-

ders, beatings, and jailings SNCC workers had endured in Mississippi had not been enough to stir public attention, perhaps America—and, in turn, the federal government—would take notice if those being beaten and shot were the sons and daughters of privileged white America.[61]

Events substantiated the worst fears and highest hopes of SNCC. In June, even as the recruits were gathering in Mississippi, James Chaney, a CORE worker from Mississippi, and Michael Schwerner and Andrew Goodman, two young Jews from New York, were kidnapped and slaughtered when they sought to investigate the burning of a Black church. The Klan assured the nation that "Schwerner, Chaney and Goodman were not civil rights workers. They were Communist Revolutionaries, actively working to undermine and destroy Christian Civilization."[62] By summer's end, fifteen Blacks had died, thirty-three Black churches had been bombed, and the beatings of white and Black civil rights activists defied enumeration. The new president, Lyndon B. Johnson, made civil rights legislation a first priority, and with the passage of the Civil Rights Act of 1964, segregation in all public accommodations was outlawed, federal funding for school desegregation was established, federal funding of all institutions and programs that employed racial discrimination was prohibited, and civil rights cases involving violations of federal statutes became the exclusive jurisdiction of federal courts. The Mississippi Freedom Democratic Party (MFDP) was formed under the leadership of the former sharecropper, Fannie Lou Hamer.[63]

The momentum of the race dramas enacted all over the nation—including the assassination of Malcolm X in February in New York; the murders in Mississippi of volunteer Viola Liuzzo, a Detroit housewife; and in Selma, of Jimmy Lee Jackson and a white Washington Unitarian minister, Reverend James Reeb; and the beating of Richard Valeriani, an NBC reporter—continued into the next year with the passage of the Civil Rights Act of 1965, subtitled "An Act to Enforce the Fifteenth Amendment to the Constitution of the United States." Freedom Summer was costly to SNCC and the movement as well. The killings, assassinations, Vietnam war, race riots in New York, New Jersey, Chicago, and Philadelphia in 1964 and Watts in 1965; the FBI's hostility to the movement and indifference to official and civilian segregationist violence; the Democratic Party Convention's rejection of the MFDP; and ultimately the choice to employ white student shock troops constituted soul murder: the America that King had dreamed of was impossible. Doug McAdam, summing up the conflictual experiences of Freedom Summer's northern volunteers, suggests that "perhaps the major casualty of this process of disillusionment within SNCC concerned the doctrine of interracialism itself."[64]

The Negations of the Movement

In 1966, Cleveland, Milwaukee, San Francisco, Atlanta, Lansing, Wauke-
gan, and other urban sites erupted. In the movement, Stokeley Carmichael,
a Black nationalist, assumed leadership of SNCC. In Oakland, California,
the Black Panther Party was founded. The next year, Black uprisings
appeared in Newark, Atlanta, Boston, Buffalo, Detroit, Louisville, New
York, New Haven, and elsewhere, and H. Rap Brown, an even more deliberate and radical Black nationalist, succeeded Carmichael as leader of
SNCC. The cry of "Black Power" disrupted "We Shall Overcome." Within
months, Adam Clayton Powell, Jr., once the most powerful Black member
of Congress in America's history, spoke to college audiences and his followers in the Abyssinian Baptist Church in Harlem about the necessity of
a Black Revolution. Meanwhile, the FBI, fully sharing the Klan's view of
the Civil Rights movement and now the Black Power movement, ratcheted
up its already extensive repressive surveillance and harassment program.
Inaugurating COINTELPRO ("counter intelligence program"), J Edgar
Hoover distributed field orders, as described by O'Reilly:

> On August 25, 1967, the FBI launched a formal counterintelligence program
> against what it called "black hate groups.". . .
>
> COINTELPRO grew quickly both in size and sophistication. In March
> 1968 representatives from the forty-one FBI field offices then participating
> decided to expand the original goals—a decision made at a "racial confer-
> ence" held at "the seat of government" (bureau headquarters). When seeking
> "to prevent the . . . *growth* of militant black nationalist organizations,"
> Hoover's men wanted "special tactics to prevent these groups from convert-
> ing young people."[65]

Tactically, this meant activities ranging from encouraging violence
between nationalists to recruiting through the "Ghetto Informant Program." Across the country, local police departments, county sheriffs, state
law enforcement agencies, and their corporate counterparts—all largely
managed by right-wing ideologues—conspired with the FBI and military
intelligence in regional programs modeled on the COINTELPRO anti-Black
militant agenda. The repression targeted SNCC, CORE, SCLC, the Black
Panthers, the Nation of Islam—even the Mississippi Democratic Freedom
Party and the NAACP.[66] When many of these organizations were "paci-
fied," the FBI transferred its attentions smoothly to the antiwar movement,
which was contesting the moral and political legitimacy of U.S. involvement in Vietnam. In a seeming paradox, as the Right vitiated the Left, the
unions, and the militant civil rights activists, it seemed to come to an

accommodation with the Nation of Islam. In Los Angeles, as Gerald Horne points out in his study of the Watts uprising, "the NOI [Nation of Islam] stood for separatism and was ambivalent about dipping into public coffers to fight poverty. Here was a scare that could possibly be accommodated."[67] COINTELPRO was ended in 1971 when its activities were exposed by antiwar burglars of a Pennsylvania field office who confiscated 1,000 pages of FBI documents generated by the program.

COINTELPRO was an impressive display of state power: both for what it had intended to achieve and what it unexpectedly spawned. By 1969, for example, it had orchestrated the assassinations of some twenty-nine Black Panthers (including Fred Hampton in Chicago) and the jailings of hundreds of others. But their repression had also forged revolutionaries of young Black men and women whose original intent, as civil rights activists and nationalists, was essentially reformist. Thus, they steeled the antiwar movement into a historical force that toppled presidents (Johnson and Nixon), ended the war, and for decades traumatized Pentagon officials into resisting military adventures that had little public support. Even the prisons—with their populations distended by the political sweeps of militant organizations by federal and local law enforcement—became sites of revolutionary (and, as before, Black nationalist) conversions. George Jackson, for one, struggled his way to revolutionary consciousness as a prisoner. When he was murdered by San Quentin guards in 1971, his death precipitated one of the largest prison uprisings in U.S. history, despite being a whole nation away from Attica. Jackson's struggle and eventual death provided the nation with another enduring Black symbol of the fight for justice: Angela Davis. The public drama of the official persecution of Davis helped install the most enduring legacy of COINTELPRO: the precipitous decline of the public's trust in American institutions. As Robert McNamara, Kennedy's and Johnson's Secretary of Defense, lamented three decades later, the spectacle of injustice took its toll: "I have grown sick at heart witnessing the cynicism and even contempt with which so many people view our political institutions and leaders" and "we were wrong, terribly wrong."[68]

The official campaign to repress militant civil rights activists and Black nationalists also contributed to and coincided with the maturing of the present division between the liberal and communitarian impulses of Black Americans. In the liberal theater over the next several years, extraordinary achievements were registered in the appearance of Black elected officials, and a substantial but proportionally marginal increase in the representation of the Black middle class was accomplished in corporate management, higher education, public service bureaucracies, and similar entrees to middle-class life styles. Indeed, during the conservative presidencies of Nixon, Reagan, and Bush, a cohort of Black conservatives was spawned, who lended their talents to ideologically sanctioned attempts to eliminate liberal institutions like the Commission on Civil Rights and the Department of Education, and to gut antipoverty programs; the Civil Rights Acts of 1964, 1965, and 1968; and the constitutional protections secured through earlier Supreme Court decisions. Even more far-reaching, these Black conservatives provided some scant legitimacy to the reactionary redefinition of the Black poor and youths as criminal populations.[69] In their cozy political relationships with those elements of the conservative establishment, they have assisted in the marginalization of the traditional Black liberal belief that a virtuous and noble Black elite is the guardian of the Black masses.

While most public attention is drawn to the bourgeois nationalists like the Nation of Islam with its antiwhite cant and to the depravity of Black youth gangs operating from the inner cities, the most significant, numerous, populous, and influential institutions among Blacks remain the churches. The Black denominations of Baptists, Pentecostals, African Methodist Episcopal, and African Methodist Episcopal Zion far eclipse the relatively few numbers of Muslims. In them persists a stronger and more resilient communitarianism, one already aggressively responding to the threats mounted against their youths and their poor. Most Black college students (in both the traditional Black institutions and beyond) come from their church congregations. Many of them, like their predecessors at the launching of SNCC in 1960, are militant communitarians. When the cities erupt, as Los Angeles did in 1992, these churches and their youth brigades respond. On any more ordinary week, throughout the country, these institutions conduct food programs, run educational programs, organize political programs, operate day schools for children, and provide legal and social services for their congregations and the needy throughout their communities. Their presence provides the continuity of Afro-Christian belief and vision. Without them the inevitable urban uprisings are empty, episodic expressions of rage. With them, it is always possible that the next Black social movement will obtain that distant land, perhaps even transporting America with it.

Notes

* * *

Notes to Chapter One

1. Alden T. Vaughan, "The Origins Debate: Slavery and Racism in Seventeenth-Century Virginia," *The Virginia Magazine of History and Biography* 97, no. 3 (July 1989): 332 and n.64.
2. A fourteenth householder, Anthony Johnson, probably a Black freeman as early as 1622, moved his wife Mary and their family to Maryland (Somerset County) in 1662, possibly to escape the threat to his children's inheritance under the 1662 law prohibiting property being transferred to the children of Black women.
3. Population figures cited for the colonial period are from *Historical Statistics of the United States* (Washington, D.C.: Bureau of the Census, 1975). The surveys were by race rather than status. But given the small numbers of free Blacks in most areas in the eighteenth century, the term *negro* has been interpreted as being tantamount to slave.
4. Donnie D. Bellamy, "The Legal Status of Black Georgians During the Colonial and Revolutionary Eras," *Journal of Negro History* 74, no. 1 (1989): 3.
5. I have chosen 1628 rather than 1629 as the year of founding, because 180 indentured servants were shipped to Salem to prepare the settlement for the Puritans in 1628.

6. Lorenzo Johnston Greene, *The Negro in Colonial New England* (New York: Atheneum 1974), chapter 1.

7. Cited in David Kobrin, *The Black Minority in Early New York* (Albany: State University of New York, 1971), 11.

8. Edmund S. Morgan, *American Slavery American Freedom* (New York: W. W. Norton, 1975), 327.

9. Joshua Coffin, "An Account of Some of the Principal Slave Insurrections, and Others, Which Have Occurred, or Been Attempted, in the United States and Elsewhere, During the Last Two Centuries," in *Slave Insurrections,* (Westport: Negro Universities Press, 1970), 11. Wish reported three whites killed, but Coffin listed the victims as "Mr. Benjamin Cattle, a white woman, and a negro boy."

10. Marc Newman, "Slavery and Insurrections in the Colonial Province of New York," *Social Education* (March 1995): 128. Humphreys claimed that the population of the city at the time was "12,000 whites and 2,000 blacks."

11. Coffin, "An Account," 15.

12. Herbert Aptheker, "Maroons within the Present Limits of the United States," in *Maroon Societies: Rebel Slave Communities in the Americas,* ed. Richard Price (Baltimore: Johns Hopkins University, 1979), 151–52. Originally published in *The Journal of Negro History* 24 (1939).

13. See Thomas Cripps, *Slow Fade to Black: The Negro in American Film, 1900–1942* (New York: Oxford University, 1977); and Ed Guerrero, *Framing Blackness: The African American Image in Film* (Philadelphia: Temple University, 1993), 19.

14. Aptheker, "Maroons," 161.

15. Herbert Aptheker, *American Negro Slave Revolts* (New York: International Publishers, 1969) 163.

16. Gerald Mullin, *Flight and Rebellion: Slave Resistance in Eighteenth-Century Virginia* (New York: Oxford University Press, 1972).

17. Hugo Prosper Leaming, *Hidden Americans: Maroons of Virginia and the Carolinas* (New York: Garland, 1993), xv.

18. Aptheker, "Maroons," 152.

19. Leaming, *Hidden Americans,* 230, 227–28.

20. Kathryn Holland Braund, "The Creek Indians, Blacks and Slavery," *The Journal of Southern History* 62, no. 4 (November 1991): 606.

21. Aptheker, "Maroons," 153.

22. Cedric J. Robinson, *Black Marxism, The Making of the Black Radical Tradition* (London: ZED, 1983), 184–85.

23. Jane Landers, "Gracia Real de Santa Teresa de Mose: A Free Black Town in Spanish Colonial Florida," *American Historical Review* 95, no. 1 (February 1990): p. 13.

24. Landers, "Gracia Real," 17–18. The text follows Landers's study.

25. Gwendolyn Midlo Hall, *Africans in Colonial Louisiana* (Baton Rouge: Louisiana State University, 1992), 3–5.

26. For these episodes, see Hall, *Africans*, chapter 3.

Notes to Chapter 2

1. Barbara Chase Smith, "The Adequate Revolution," *William and Mary Quarterly* (1992): 689.

2 Linda Grant DePauw, "Land of the Unfree: Legal Limitations on Liberty in Pre-Revolutionary America," *Maryland Historical Magazine* 68, no. 4 (1973).

3. Howard Zinn, *A People's History of the United States* (New York: Harper Perennial, 1995), 62.

4. Jennifer Roberts, "The Creation of a Legacy: A Manufactured Crisis in Eighteenth-Century Thought," in *Athenian Political Thought and the Reconstruction of American Democracy*, ed. J. Peter Euben, John R. Wallach, and Josiah Ober (Ithaca: Cornell University, 1994), 91.

5. William Loren Katz, *Breaking the Chains* (New York: Atheneum, 1990), 103.

6. James W. St. G. Walker, *The Black Loyalists* (Bristol: Longman & Dalhousie University, 1976), 1–4.

7. Herbert Aptheker, "Maroons," 154.

8. Steven Deyle, "The Irony of Liberty: Origins of the Domestic Slave Trade," *Journal of the Early Republic* 12 (Spring 1992): 37–62.

9. Gordon S. Wood, "Equality and Social Conflict in the American Revolution," *William and Mary Quarterly* (1992): 706–707, 714.

10. Gordon S. Wood, *The Radicalism of the American Revolution* (New York: Alfred Knopf, 1992), 186.

11. Quoted in Elizabeth Donnan, ed., *Documents Illustrative of the History of the Slave Trade to America*, vol. 4 (New York: Octagon Books, 1965), 131–32

12. Samuel Sewall, "The Selling of Joseph," in *The Black American: A Documentary History*, ed. Leslie Fishel, Jr., and Benjamin Quarles (Glenview: Scott, Foresman, 1970), 33–35.

13. Frank Lambert, "'I Saw the Book Talk' Slave Readings of the First Great Awakening," *Journal of Negro History* 77, no. 4 (Fall 1982); 195; and Noel Ignatiev, "The Revolution as an African-American Exuberance," *Eighteenth-Century Studies* 27, no. 4 (Summer 1994); 612–13.

14. See Lerone Bennett, Jr., *Before the Mayflower* (New York: Penguin, 1982), 75–76.

15. Aptheker, *Documentary History*, 8–9.

16. Bennett, *Mayflower*, 166–67.

17. John Lovell, Jr., *Black Song* (New York: Macmillan 1972), 125.

18. Martin Townsend, "Harriet Tubman's Troy, New York Raid," in *Eyewitness*, ed. William Loren Katz (New York: Touchstone, 1995), 195.

19. Bennett, *Mayflower*, 207.

20. Hall, *Africans*, 320ff.

21. Francois-Xavier Martin, *The History of Louisiana* (New Orleans: Pelican, 1963 [1882]), 266.

22. The above summarizes Douglas Egerton's discussion in his *Gabriel's Rebellion* (Chapel Hill: University of North Carolina, 1993), chapter 3.

23. Martin, *The History of Louisiana*, 349.

24. Bennett H. Wall, ed., with Light Townsend Cummins, Joe Gray Taylor, William Ivy Hair, Mark T. Carleton, and Michael L. Kurtz, *Louisiana, A History* (Arlington Heights: Forum, 1990), 100–102.

25. The account of the Denmark conspiracy is taken from the official Charleston record of the trials, "An Account of the Late Intended Insurrection Among a Portion of the Blacks of This City, Charleston, S.C.," in Coffin, *Slave Insurrections*, p. 31.

26. "The Confession of Nat Turner," in *The Southampton Slave Revolt of 1831*, ed. Henry Treagle (Amherst: University of Massachusetts, 1971), 306–19.

27. John Lovell, Jr., *Black Song*, 179.

28. Bennett, *Mayflower*, 124.

29. Aptheker, "Maroons," 157–64.

30. J. Leitch Wright, Jr., *Creeks and Seminoles* (Lincoln: University of Nebraska Press, 1986), 104.

31. Joshua Giddings, *The Exiles of Florida* (Columbus: Follett, Foster and Co., 1858), 37.

32. Kenneth Wiggins Porter, "The Negro Abraham," in *The Negro on the American Frontier*, ed. K.W. Porter (New York: Arno Press and the *New York Times*, 1971), 299–304. Originally published in 1946.

33. Joshua Giddings, *Exiles of Florida*, 94.

34. Wright, *Creeks and Seminoles*, 251.

35. Porter, "The Negro Abraham," 308–309.

36. Wright, *Creeks and Seminoles*, 275.

37. Giddings, *Exiles of Florida*, 99.

38. Kenneth Wiggins Porter, "John Caesar: Seminole Negro Partisan," in *The Negro on the American Frontier*, 339–58.

39. Porter, "The Negro Abraham," 377ff.

40. Rebecca B. Bateman, "Africans and Indians: A Comparative Study of the Black Carib and Black Seminole," *Ethnohistory* 37, no. 1 (Winter 1990): 6–8.

41. Scott Thybony, "Against All Odds, Black Seminole Won Their Freedom," *Smithsonian* 22, no. 5 (August 1991); 90–101.

Notes to Chapter 3

1. An excellent source of slave and free Black opinion in the mid-1850s is the writings of James Redpath. See Redpath, *The Roving Editor; or, Talks with Slaves in the Southern States* (New York: A. B. Burdick, 1859).

2. For Garrison on the Constitution, see Benjamin Quarles, *Black Abolitionists* (New York: Oxford University, 1969), 43.

3. See "Stephen S. Foster Is Sure that Revolution Is the Only Remedy," in *The Anti-Slavery Argument*, ed. William Pease and Jane Pease (New York: Bobbs-Merrill, 1965), 474–79.

4. For Smith, see Robert Cover, *Justice Accused* (New Haven: Yale University, 1975), 149–58.

5. Staughton Lynd, "The Abolitionist Critique of the United States Constitution," in *The AntiSlavery Vanguard* ed. Martin Duberman, (Princeton: Princeton University, 1965), 209–10, 239.

6. See "Frederick Douglass Asserts that the Constitution is AntiSlavery," in *The Anti Slavery Argument*, 348–60.

7. "The Dred Scott Decision," in *The Black American: A Documentary History*, ed. Leslie H. Fishel, Jr., and Benjamin Quarles (Glenview: Scott, Foresman, 1967), 206.

8. Louis Filler, *The Crusade Against Slavery, 1830–1860* (New York: Harper & Brothers, 1960), 18; and Katharine Du Pre Lumpkin, *The Emancipation of Angelina Grimke* (Chapel Hill: University of North Carolina, 1974), ix–xi.

9. For the "slave stealers," see Stanley Harrold, "John Brown's Forerunners: Slave Rescue Attempts and the Abolitionists, 1841–51," *Radical History Review* 55 (1993): 89–110; and Quarles, *Black Abolitionists*, 149ff.

10. Quarles, *Black Abolitionists*, chapter 7.

11. Harrold, "Slave Rescue," 90, 95–96; and Quarles, *Black Abolitionists*, 164.

12. Leon Litwack, "The Emancipation of the Negro Abolitionist," in *The Anti-Slavery Vanguard*, 150.

13. Filler, *Crusade Against Slavery*, 200.

14. Quarles, *Black Abolitionists*, 3–8.

15. See Shane White, "'We Dwell in Safety and Pursue Our Honest Callings': Free Blacks in New York City, 1783–1810," *The Journal of American History* 75, no. 2 (September 1988); 447–70.

16. Quarles, *Black Abolitionists*, 19–20.

17. Litwack, "Emancipation of the Negro Abolitionist," 137.

18. In Newport, the African Union Society "sponsored a unified scheme of emigration" in the late 1780s; in Boston, Prince Hall "and seventy-five other blacks" petitioned for permission to emigrate to Africa in 1787. See Will B. Gravely, "The Rise of African Churches in America (1786–1822)," *Journal of Religious Thought* 41, no. 1 (Spring–Summer 198): 63–64. For

emigration to Haiti, see Christopher Dixon, "Nineteenth Century African American Emigrationism: The Failure of the Haitian Alternative," *The Western Journal of Black Studies* 18, no. 2 (1994): 77–88.

19. Howard H. Bell, "Negro Nationalism: A Factor in Emigration Projects, 1848–1861," *Journal of Negro History* 47 (June 1962): 42–53. For the opposition to emigration of Delany, Douglass, Watkins and Brown, see Floyd J. Miller, *The Search for a Black Nationality* (Urbana: University of Chicago, 1975).

20. Howard H. Bell, "Introduction" to *Search for a Place: Black Separatism and Africa, 1860*, by Martin R. Delany and Robert Campbell (Ann Arbor: University of Michigan, 1969), 5.

21. Howard H. Bell, "The Negro Emigration Movement, 1849–1854: A Phase of Negro Nationalism," *Phylon* 20, no. 2 (Summer 1959): 132–42.

22. Bell, "Introduction," 7.

23. Miller, *Search for a Black Nationality*, 133.

24. "The Pioneer National Negro Convention, 1830," in *A Documentary History of the Negro People*, 99ff.

25. Bell, "Negro Emigration Movement," 134ff.

26. Miller, *Search for a Black Nationality*, 125–26.

27. Bell, "Introduction," 8-9.

28. Bell, "Negro Emigration Movement," 141.

29. Bell, "Introduction," 34–35.

30. Dixon, "Nineteenth Century African American Emigration," 80.

31. Miller, *Search for a Black Nationality*, 244–45.

32. Bell, "Introduction," 69.

33. See James Wesley Smith, *Sojourners in Search of Freedom: The Settlement of Liberia by Black Americans* (Lanham, MD: University Press of America, 1987); and E. Lee Shepard, Frances S. Pollard, and Janet B. Schwarz, "'The Love of Liberty Brought Us Here,' Virginians and the Colonization of Liberia," *The Virginia Magazine of History and Biography* 102, no. 1 (January 1994).

34. Sean Wilentz ed., *David Walkers Appeal to The Coloured Citizens of the World, but in Particular and Very Expressly to Those of the United States of America* (New York: Hill and Wang, 1965).

35. John R. McKivigan, "James Redpath, John Brown, and Abolitionist Advocacy of Slave Insurrection," *Civil War History* 37, no. 4 (1991): 297–98.

36. Harriet Beecher Stowe, *A Key to Uncle Tom's Cabin* (London: Sampson Low, Son, 1853), 181–82.

37. Lisa Whitney, "In the Shadow of Uncle Tom's Cabin: Stowe's Vision of Slavery from the Great Dismal Swamp," *New England Quarterly* 66, no. 4 (December 1993); 562.

38. Stowe, *Key*, 186.

39. Stowe, *Dred* (Boston: Houghton Mifflin, 1988), 482.

40. For the letter and the speeches in this paragraph, see Benjamin Quarles, ed., *Blacks on John Brown* (Urbana: University of Illinois, 1972), 18, 22, 25–26.

41. W.E.B. DuBois, *John Brown* (New York: International Publishers, 1969), 106–107. Originally published in 1902.

42. According to DuBois, there were also among the free Blacks John Anderson and Jeremiah Anderson: "The seventh man of possible Negro blood" (282).

43. Stephen Oates, *To Purge This Land with Blood* (New York: Harper Torchbook, 1972), 242–46.

44. Jeremiah Anderson had accompanied Brown for months; it still is not certain whether John Anderson, a Black, arrived in time.

45. Seymour Drescher, "Servile Insurrection and John Brown's Body in Europe," *The Journal of American History* (September 1993); 499–524.

46. DuBois, *John Brown*, 361–62.

47. Oates, *To Purge This Land with Blood*, 301.

48. DuBois, *John Brown*, 346.

49. Drescher, "Servile Insurrection," 511.

50. Harold Hyman, *A More Perfect Union: The Impact of the Civil War and Reconstruction on the Constitution* (Boston: Houghton Mifflin, 1975), 46–47.

51. DuBois, *John Brown*, 353.

Notes to Chapter 4

1. John Hope Franklin, *The Militant South* (Boston: Beacon Press, 1964).

2. James McPherson, *The Struggle for Equality* (Princeton: Princeton University, 1964), 49.

3. These figures are for Blacks in uniform and do not include civilian labor auxiliaries (for example, in all some 29,000 Blacks served with the Union navy). See Ira Berlin, Barbara Fields, Steven Miller, Joseph Reidy, and Leslie Rowland, eds., *Slaves No More* (New York: Cambridge University, 1993), 52.

4. Robert W. Fogel, *Without Consent or Contract* (New York: W. W. Norton, 1989), 95, 101, 157–62.

5. McPherson, *Struggle for Equality*, 42.

6. For earlier antiabolition mobs, see Leonard L. Richards, *Gentlemen of Property and Standing* (New York: Oxford University, 1970).

7. Iver Bernstein, *The New York City Draft Riots* (New York: Oxford University, 1990), 27.

8. Alexander Saxton, *The Rise and Fall of the White Republic* (London: Verso, 1990), 165.

9. McPherson, *Struggle for Equality*, 24.

10. LaWanda Cox, *Lincoln and Black Freedom* (Columbia: University of South Carolina, 1981), 24.

11. Eric Foner, *Reconstruction* (New York: Harper & Row, 1988), 6.

12. Howard Zinn, *A People's History of the United States* (New York: HarperPerennial, 1995), 185–87.

13. For the Natchez and Second Creek figures, see Winthrop Jordan, *Tumult and Silence* (Baton Rouge: Louisiana State University, 1993), 5; for Culpeper County, see Cornish, 160; for Arkansas and Kentucky, see Zinn, *A People's History*, 189–90; for Missouri and conspiracies, see Herbert Aptheker, "The Negro in the Civil War" in *Essays in the History of the American Negro* (New York: International Publishers, 1969), 171, 178–79.

14. W.E.B. DuBois, *Black Reconstruction* (New York: S. A. Russell, 1935), 62.

15. Cited by Dudley T. Cornish, *The Sable Arm* (Lawrence: University of Kansas, 1987), 11. For Black veteran accounts of Civil War, see William Wells Brown, *The Negro in the American Rebellion* (Boston: Lee and Shepard, 1867); Joseph T. Wilson, *The Black Phalanx* (New York: Da Capo, 1944) originally published in 1887; and George Washington Williams, *A History of the Negro Troops in the War of the Rebellion, 1861–65* (New York: Bergman, 1968), originally published 1888.

16. Cornish, *Sable Arm*, 10–11.

17. DuBois, *Black Reconstruction*, 61.

18. Cornish, *Sable Arm*, 12–15.

19. For Hunter's abolitionism and the Sea Islands Blacks' destruction of cotton gins and looting of Beaufort following the flight of the white planters, see Willie Lee Rose, *Rehearsal for Reconstruction* (New York: Oxford University, 1964), chapters 4 and 5.

20. Cornish, *Sable Arm*, 35.

21. Rose, *Rehearsal for Reconstruction*, 149.

22. Smalls's most recent biographer, with no persuasive evidence, disputes the Hunter connection. See Edward Miller, Jr., *Gullah Statesman: Robert Smalls from Slavery to Congress, 1839–1915* (Columbia: University of South Carolina, 1995), 3–4.

23. Miller, *Gullah Statesman*, chapter 1.

24. Michael Cohn and Michael Platzer, *Black Men of the Sea* (New York: Dodd, Mead, 1978), 118–19. Smalls survived the war, was elected to the South Carolina state house and senate, and in 1875 began five terms in the House of Representatives. He retired as collector for the port of Beaufort and died in 1915.

25. Glenn Carle, "The First Kansas Colored," *American Heritage* (February/March 1992): 79–91.

26. Cornish, *Sable Arm*, chapter 3.

27. Antebellum Louisiana and then South Carolina contained the largest numbers (472 and 162, respectively) of wealthy Black property holders—in each instance over 85 percent of them "mulatto" and nearly a third female. See Loren Schweninger, "Prosperous Blacks in the South, 1790–1880," *American Historical Review* 95, no. 1 (February 1990): 34ff. John Minion observed that the majority of the Native Guard "remained faithful to the Southern cause." See his "Negro Soldiers in the Confederate Army," *Crisis* (June–July 1970): 231.

28. Berlin et al., *Slaves No More*, 42.

29. Zinn, *A People's History*, 187.

30. Black Union troop doggerel during the Civil War. See Wilson, *Black Phalanx*, 100.

31. Berlin et al., *Slaves No More*, 206.

32. Williams, *History of the Negro Troops*, 318–19.

33. Wilson, *Black Phalanx*, 212–19.

34. Ira Berlin, Barbara Fields, Steven Miller, Joseph Reidy, and Leslie Rowland, eds., *Free At Last* (New York: New Press, 1992), 440.

35. Williams, *History of the Negro Troops*, 224–26.

36. Wilson, *Black Phalanx*, 212–19.

37. Berlin et al., *Free At Last*, 445.

38. Wilson, *Black Phalanx*, 222; Berlin et al., *Slaves No More*, 215, 220.

39. Cornish, *Sable Arm*, 195.

40. Wilson, *Black Phalanx*, 330–36.

41. Cornish, *Sable Arm*, 177.

42. Foner, *Reconstruction*, 13.

43. DuBois, *Black Reconstruction*, 81.

44. Cornish, *Sable Arm*, 265, 288.

45. The following remarks are drawn from Cornish, *Sable Arm*, chapters 12 and 13.

46. "Excluded from [Lincoln's Emancipation Proclamation]," Eric Foner recalls, "were the 450,000 slaves in Delaware, Kentucky, Maryland, and Missouri . . . 275,000 in Union-occupied Tennessee, and tens of thousands more in portions of Louisiana and Virginia under the control of federal armies." Foner, *Reconstruction*, part 1.

47. Sefton quoted in William Richter, "'This Blood-Thirsty Hole': The Freedman's Bureau Agency at Clarksville, Texas, 1867–1868," *Civil War History* 38, no. 1 (1992): 77.

48. Foner, *Reconstruction*, 145; and see James D. Anderson, "Philanthropic Control over Private Black Higher Education," in *Philanthropy and Cultural Imperialism* ed. Robert F. Arnove (Bloomington: Indiana University Press), 147–77.

49. Foner, *Reconstruction*, 119
50. Dorothy Sterling, ed., *The Trouble They Seen: The Story of Reconstruction in the Words of African Americans* (New York: Da Capo, 1994), 366.
51. William Peirce Randel, *The Ku Klux Klan: A Century of Infamy* (Philadelphia: Chilton, 1965), 14–16.
52. Woodrow Wilson, *Reunion and Nationalization*, vol. 5 of *A History of the American People* (New York: Harper, 1901), 49–50.
53. Sterling, *The Trouble They Seen*, 383–84.
54. Foner, *Reconstruction*, 435–37.
55. Nell Irvin Painter, *Exodusters* (New York: Knopf, 1977).
56. V.P. Franklin, *Black Self-Determination* (Westport, CT: Lawrence Hill, 1984), 132.
57. "A Leader of the Kansas Exodus: 'We Wanted to Go to a Territory by Ourselves,'" in *Black Nationalism in America* ed. John Bracey, Jr., August Meier, and Elliott Rudwick (Indianapolis: Bobbs-Merrill, 1970), 162.
58. Franklin, *Black Self-Determination*, 133.
59. Painter, *Exodusters*, 147,207.
60. Bracey et al., *Black Nationalism,*164.
61. Painter, *Exodusters*, 14.

Notes to Chapter 5

1. G.E.M. de Ste. Croix, *The Class Struggle in the Ancient Greek World* (Ithaca: Cornell University, 1981).
2. Carter G. Woodson, *The History of the Negro Church* (Washington, D.C.: Associated Publishers, 1921).
3. Gravely, " Rise of African Churches," 60.
4. Delores C. Carpenter, "Black Women in Religious Institutions," *Journal of Religious Thought* 46, no. 2 (Winter–Spring 1989–90): 8–12.
5. William Wells Brown, "Black Religion in the Post-Reconstruction South," in *Afro-American Religious History*, ed. Milton Sernett (Durham, NC: Duke University 1985), 243.
6. Wilson Jeremiah Moses, *Black Messiahs and Uncle Toms* (University Park: Pennsylvania State University, 1993), 79, 96–97.
7. Katherine L. Dvorak, *An African-American Exodus* (Brooklyn: Carlson, 1991), 169.
8. Prathia Hall Wynn, "Called but Not Chosen," *The Women's Review of Books* 11, no. 12/13 (September 1994): 31.
9. Evelyn Brooks Higginbotham, *Righteous Discontent* (Cambridge: Harvard University, 1993), 121–22.
10. Edward L. Ayers, *The Promise of the New South* (New York: Oxford University, 1992), 220.

11. William Edward Spriggs, "The Virginia Colored Farmers' Alliance: A Case Study of Race and Class Identity," *Journal of Negro History* (Summer 1979): 191–204.

12. Ayers, *Promise of the New South*, 234.

13. For the passage from exclusion to segregation, see Howard Rabinowitz, "More than the Woodward Thesis: Assessing *The Strange Career of Jim Crow*," *Journal of American History* 75, no. 3, December 1988: 842–56.

14. Charles Crowe, "Tom Watson, Populists, and Blacks Reconsidered," *Journal of Negro History* (April 1970): 114.

15. Pete Daniel, *The Shadow of Slavery* (New York: Oxford University, 1972), 11.

16. W. Augustus Low and Virgil A. Clift, eds., *Encyclopedia of Black America* (New York: Da Capo, 1981), 541–42. Ida B. Wells believed that between 1878 and 1898 over ten thousand were lynching victims. See Bennett, *Before the Mayflower*, 258.

17. National Association for the Advancement of Colored People, *Thirty Years of Lynching in the United States, 1889–1918* (New York: NAACP, 1919), 29–30.

18. Gail Bederman, "'Civilization,' the Decline of Middle-Class Manliness, and Ida B. Wells's Antilynching Campaign (1892–94)," in *"We Specialize in the Wholly Impossible,"* ed. Darlene Clark Hine, Wilma King, and Linda Reed, " (Brooklyn: Carlson, 1995), 415.

19. Neil R. McMillen, *Dark Journey: Black Mississippians in the Age of Jim Crow* (Urbana: University of Illinois, 1990), 227.

20. Booker T. Washington, "Atlanta Exposition Address," in *Justice Denied*, ed. William Chace and Peter Collier (New York: Harcourt, Brace & World, 1970), 204.

21. Hazel Carby, "'On the Threshold of Woman's Era': Lynching, Empire, and Sexuality in Black Feminist Theory," in *"Race," Writing, and Difference*, ed. Henry Louis Gates, Jr. (Chicago: University of Chicago, 1986), 308–9.

22. Ida B. Wells, *Red Record* (Chicago: Donohue & Henneberry, 1895), 12

23. Bederman, "'Civilization,'" 419.

24. Wilson Jeremiah Moses, *The Golden Age of Black Nationalism, 1850–1925* (Hamden: Archon, 1978), chapter 5; and Stephanie J. Shaw, "Black Club Women and the Creation of the National Association of Colored Women," in *"We Specialize in the Wholly Impossible,"* ed. Hine et al., 433.

25. Dorothy C. Salem, "Black Women and the NAACP, 1909–1922," in *Black Women in America*, ed. Kim Marie Vaz (Thousand Oaks: Sage, 1995), 55ff.

26. Bennett, *Before the Mayflower*, 329.

27. Francis Broderick, *W.E.B. DuBois* (Stanford: Stanford University, 1959), 76.

28. Two years after the foundation of the NAACP, the National Urban League was organized, largely at the behest of Booker T. Washington's supporters (e.g., Ruth Standish Baldwin, wife of W. H. Baldwin).

29. Bennett, *Before the Mayflower*, 338.

30. John Hope Franklin, *From Slavery to Freedom* (New York: Vintage, 1967); for the FBI, see Kenneth O'Reilly, *"Racial Matters," The FBI's Secret File on Black America, 1960–1972* (New York: The Free Press, 1989), 13ff; for films, see Thomas Cripps, *Slow Fade to Black* (New York: Oxford University, 1993), chapter 2.

31. Jacqueline Jones, *Labor of Love, Labor of Sorrow* (New York: Vintage, 1986), 156.

32. Florette Henri, *Black Migration* (Garden City, NY: Anchor, 1970), 51.

33. Bennett, *Before the Mayflower*, 344.

34. William Bittle and Gilbert Geis, *The Longest Way Home* (Detroit: Wayne State University, 1964).

35. Bernard C. Nalty, *Strength for the Fight* (New York: The Free Press, 1986), 75–76.

36. William Loren Katz, *Eyewitness* (New York: Touchstone, 1995), 353.

37. Michael Rogin, "'The Sword Became a Flashing Vision': D. W. Griffith's *The Birth of a Nation*, *Representations* (Winter 1985): 151ff.

38. Franklin, *Slavery to Freedom*, 471ff.

39. W.E.B. DuBois, "The African Roots of the War," *Atlantic Monthly*, (May 1915); reprinted in vol. 1 of *The Seventh Son: The Thought and Writings of W.E.B. DuBois*, ed. Julius Lester (New York: Vintage, 1971), 458–59.

40. Eric Hobsbawm, *The Age of Extremes* (New York: Vintage, 1996), 29–30.

41. Henri, *Black Migration*, 64.

42. Nalty, *Strength for the Fight*, 126.

43. Nancy MacLean, *Behind the Mask of Chivalry: The Making of the Second Ku Klux Klan* (New York: Oxford University, 1994), 29.

44. Katz, *Eyewitness*, 384.

45. Jane Gaines, "Fire and Desire: Race, Melodrama, and Oscar Micheaux," in *Black American Cinema*, ed. Manthia Diawara (New York: Routledge, 1993), 49–70.

46. MacLean, *Behind the Mask*, 29.

47. Leonard J. Moore, "Historical Interpretations of the 1920's Klan," *Journal of Social History* 24, no. 2 (Winter 1990): 341–57.

48. Robert A. Hill, "Introduction," to *Marcus Garvey, Life and Lessons* (Berkeley: University of California, 1987); Robert A. Hill, ed., *Marcus Garvey and the Universal Negro Improvement Association Papers* (Berkeley: University of California, 1983–1995); and Tony Martin, *Race First* (Westport, CT: Greenwood, 1976).

49. Cedric J. Robinson, *Black Marxism: The Making of the Black Radical Tradition* (London: ZED, 1983), 298.

50. Robinson, *Black Marxism*, chapter 9.

51. A. Philip Randolph, "Garveyism," in *Voices from the Harlem Renaissance*, ed.

Nathan Irvin Huggins (New York: Oxford University, 1995), 32.

52. Faith Berry, *Before and Beyond Harlem: A Biography of Langston Hughes* (New York: Wings, 1992), 142.

53. Robin D.G. Kelley, *Hammer and Hoe* (Chapel Hill: University of North Carolina, 1990), 220.

54. Cedric J. Robinson, "The African Diaspora and the Italo-Ethiopian Crisis," *Race & Class* 27, no. 2 (1985); 51–65.

55. *Black Americans in the Spanish People's War Against Fascism, 1936–1939* (Veterans of the Abraham Lincoln Brigade, n.d.). The five activists in the text are Salaria Kee, Oliver Law, Langston Hughes, Paul Robeson, and James Yates.

Notes to Chapter 6

1. Thomas Cripps, *Making Movies Black* (New York: Oxford University, 1993), 31.

2. See James D. Anderson, "Philanthropic Control Over Private Black Higher Education," in *Philanthropy and Cultural Imperialism*, ed. Robert F. Arnove, (Bloomington: Indiana University, 1982), 147–77.

3. Richard W. Hull, *American Enterprise in South Africa* (New York: New York University, 1990), 198.

4. Gunnar Myrdal, *An American Dilemma: The Negro Problem and Modern Democracy*, vol. 1 (New York: Harper & Brothers, 1944), 60.

5. Stephen Graubard, Preface to "An American Dilemma Revisited," *Daedalus* 124, no. 1 (Winter 1995): xvi; and also Walter A. Jackson, *Gunnar Myrdal and America's Conscience* (Chapel Hill: University of North Carolina, 1990), 261–64.

6. Karen Tucker Anderson, "Last Hired, First Fired: Black Women Workers during World War II," *Journal of American History* 69, no. 1 (June 1982): 82–84.

7. Robert Korstad and Nelson Lichtenstein, "Opportunities Found and Lost: Labor, Radicals, and the Early Civil Rights Movement," *Journal of American History* 73, no. 3 (December 1988): 793–94.

8. Bennett, *Before the Mayflower* (367–68; and Walter Morrison, "Black Defenders," *Crisis* 99, no. 4 (April–May 1992): 34.

9. Louis Grundlingh, "'Non-Europeans Should Be Kept Away From the Temptations of Town': Controlling Black South African Soldiers During the Second World War," *International Journal of African Historical Studies* 25, no. 3 (1992): 540. For the U.S. military, see Bernard C. Nalty, *Strength for the Fight*, chapter 11.

10. E. Valerie Smith, "The Black Corps of Engineers and the Construction of the Alaska (ALCAN) Highway," *Negro History Bulletin* 51–57, no. 1–12 (December 1993): 31.

11. Kenneth Coates and William Morrison, "Soldier-Workers: The United

States Army Corps of Engineers and the Northwest Defense Projects, 1942–1946," *Pacific Historical Review* 62, no. 3 (August 1993): 293.

12. Ruth Wilson, *Jim Crow Joins Up: A Story of Negroes in the Armed Forces of the United States* (New York: William J. Clark, 1944).

13. Grundlingh, "Controlling Black South African Soldiers," 541.

14. Coates and Morrison, "Soldier-Workers," 295.

15. Imanuel Geiss, *The Pan-African Movement* (London: Methuen, 1974), chapter 18.

16. Bennett, *Before the Mayflower*, 368.

17. *New York Times*, February 27, August 11, August 20, and September 30, 1946.

18. *New York Times*, December 29, 1946.

19. William Patterson, ed., *We Charge Genocide* (New York: Civil Rights Congress, 1951), 62.

20. John Egerton, *Speak Now Against the Day* (New York: Alfred A. Knopf, 1994), 362–63.

21. Patterson et al., *We Charge Genocide*, 61–63.

22. Egerton, *Speak Now*, 369

23. John Modell, Marc Goulden, and Sigurdur Magnusson, "World War II in the Lives of Black Americans: Some Findings and an Interpretation," *Journal of American History* 76, no. 3 (December 1989): 838–48.

24. Frantz Fanon, *The Wretched of the Earth* (New York: Grove, 1966), 32–33.

25. Frank J. Donner, *The Age of Surveillance* (New York: Vintage, 1981), 27.

26. Michael Honey, "Operation Dixie: Labor and Civil Rights in the Postwar South," *Mississippi Quarterly* 45, no. 4 (Fall 1992): 349ff.

27. August Meier and John H. Bracey, Jr., "The NAACP as a Reform Movement, 1909–1965: 'To Reach the Conscience of America'," *Journal of Southern History* 59, no. 1 (February 1993): 15 and 6.

28. Broderic, *W.E.B. DuBois*, 205–206.

29. Lorna Lloyd, "'A Family Quarrel': The Development of the Dispute over Indians in South Africa," *The Historical Journal* 34, no. 3 (September 1991).

30. Egerton, *Speak Now*, 475–77.

31. Kenneth O'Reilly, *Black Americans: The FBI Files* (New York: Carroll & Graf 1994), 24ff.

32. Meier and Bracey, "NAACP as a Reform Movement," 22.

33. Gerald Horne, *Fire This Time* (Charlottesville: University of Virginia, 1995), 173.

34. William Patterson, *The Man Who Cried Genocide* (New York: International Publishers, 1971), 180–81.

35. Meier and Bracey, "NAACP as a Reform Movement," 23ff.

36. Jacqueline A. Stefkovich, "A Legal History of Desegregation in Higher Education," *Journal of Negro Education* 63, no. 3 (1994); 408ff.

37. Alex DeConde, *Ethnicity, Race and American Foreign Policy* (Boston: Northeastern University, 1992), 144.

38. Donna Langston, "The Women of Highlander," in *Women in the Civil Rights Movement*, ed. Vicki L. Crawford, Jacqueline Anne Rouse, and Barbara Woods (Bloomington: Indiana University, 1993), 146–47.

39. Grace Jordan McFadden, "Septima Clark and Rosa Parks at Highlander Folk School," in Crawford et al., *Women in the Civil Rights Movement*, 89–90.

40. Juan Williams et al., *Eyes on the Prize* (New York: Penguin, 1988), 64–65.

41. Robin D. G. Kelley, "'We Are Not What We Seem': Rethinking Black Working-Class Opposition in the Jim Crow South," *Journal of American History* 80, no. 1 (June 1993): 76.

42. Williams, *Eyes on the Prize*, 63.

43. David J. Garrow, *Bearing the Cross* (New York: Vintage, 1988), 11ff.

44. Mary Fair Burks, "Trailblazers: Women in the Montgomery Bus Boycott," in Crawford et al., *Women in the Civil Rights Movement*, 78.

45. Williams, *Eyes on the Prize*, 71.

46. Anne Standley, "The Role of Black Women in the Civil Rights Movement," in Crawford et al., *Women in the Civil Rights Movement*, 186.

47. Denton L. Watson, "Assessing the Role of the NAACP in the Civil Rights Movement," *The Historian* 55, no. 3 (Spring 1993): 453–68.

48. O'Reilly, *Black Americans*, 25–42.

49. Standley, "Role of Black Women," *passim*.

50. On charisma, see Cedric J. Robinson, *The Terms of Order* (Albany: SUNY Press, 1980), chapter 3.

51. J. Fred MacDonald, *Blacks and White TV* (Chicago: Nelson-Hall, 1992), 81.

52. Daisy Bates, "The Long Shadow of Little Rock," in *The Eyes on the Prize Civil Rights Reader*, ed. Clayborne Carson, David J. Garrow, Gerald Gill, Vincent Harding, and Darlene Clark Hine (New York: Penguin, 1991), 102–3.

53. David Chambers, *Hooded Americanism* (Chicago: Quadrangle, 1965), 343–50.

54. Garrow, *Bearing the Cross*, 132ff.

55. Charles Hamilton, *Adam Clayton Powell, Jr.* (New York: Atheneum, 1991), 336–37; and Garrow, *Bearing the Cross*, 361–62.

56. Ella Baker, "Bigger than a Hamburger," in Carson et al., *Eyes on the Prize Reader*, 121.

57. O'Reilly, *Black Americans*, 26–27.

58. Garrow, *Bearing the Cross*, 150, 159.

59. Katz, *Eyewitness*, 520.

60. Quoted in Steve Clark, ed., *February 1965: The Final Speeches* (New York: Pathfinder, 1992), 24.

61. Doug McAdam, *Freedom Summer* (New York: Oxford University, 1988), 33.

62. Katz, *Eyewitness*, 463.

63. Mamie E. Locke, "Is This America? Fannie Lou Hamer and the Mississippi Freedom Democratic Party," in Crawford et al., *Women in the Civil Rights Movement*, 30, 32.

64. McAdam, *Freedom Summer*, 32.

65. O'Reilly, *Black Americans*, 48–49.

66. Frank Donner, *The Age of Surveillance* (New York: Vintage, 1981), 212ff.

67. Horne, *Fire This Time*, 132.

68. See the *Los Angeles Times* and *New York Times*, April 9, 1995. The McNamara quotes are excerpted from Robert McNamara with Brian VanDeMark, *In Retrospect* (New York: Times Books, 1995).

69. Cornel West, *Race Matters* (Boston: Beacon, 1993), 56ff.

Index

* * *